A
CHRISTIAN GUIDE
to
SEXUAL
Counseling

Other Books by Mary Ann Mayo . . .

Parents' Guide to Sex Education

The Sexual Woman: Understanding the Unique Identity of a Woman

A
CHRISTIAN GUIDE
to
SEXUAL
Counseling

*Recovering the Mystery
and Reality of "One Flesh"*

Mary Ann Mayo

Wipf and Stock Publishers
EUGENE, OREGON

Wipf and Stock Publishers
199 West 8th Avenue, Suite 3
Eugene, Oregon 97401

A Christian Guide to Sexual Counseling
Recovering the Mystery of Reality of "One Flesh"
By Mayo, Mary Ann
Copyright© January, 1987 Mayo, Mary Ann
ISBN: 1-59244-135-1
Publication date: January, 2003
Previously published by Zondervan Publishing House, January, 1987 .

To Joe

CONTENTS

PREFACE

Why a "Christian" guide to sexual counseling? Is this another pretense in making something "Christian" to mask what is simply a secular (nonspiritual) interest? Some detractors of an effort such as this may reason that if a person were walking in the Lord, he wouldn't be having problems in the first place! Others may appreciate the need for sexual counseling but, finding secular therapeutic approaches and techniques to be working fine, question whether Christians have a distinctive approach to sexual counseling that warrants writing a book about it.

Both opinions miss the purpose and the necessity of a distinctively Christian treatment of sexual problems. My experience as a marriage and family therapist and as a teacher/speaker in the church has pressed me to challenge the traditional methods of dealing with sexual problems: on the one hand, by denying and not dealing with them, or on the other hand, by ignoring the need for a uniquely Christian perspective.

Some readers will find a hard edge in some of my words. Because I have seen too many sexually related tragedies, I write with deep concern and strong conviction and, occasionally, intense passion. I have seen how refusal to face reality contributes to the breakdown of the family, illegitimate pregnancy, and immoral behavior—all of which Christians purport to abhor. But abhorrence is not a sufficient response. There must be a Christian way of understanding and giving expression to sexuality that serves as a model for all human beings to follow. Such a perspective is based on the realities of the human situation and the norms and ideals of Christian living.

*   *   *

Even in this day of so-called sexual enlightenment, ambivalence about sex abounds. Part 1, "Recovering the

Mystery," challenges leaders in the church to offer the people of God a sane, reliable, and accurate way of understanding and dealing with their sexual concerns. Chapter 1 reviews the historical and theological influences that have resulted in our ambivalence. Biblical Christianity teaches that the creature of God is a unity of body and spirit. But the mind-body dichotomy in Western thought has contributed heavily to the difficulty of many Christians in seeing themselves as integrated spiritual and sexual creatures.

Chapter 2 provides a brief overview of the way Scripture offers both direct and indirect perspectives on sexuality from Jesus' teaching in the Gospels, from Paul's letters to various churches, and from the love poem, the Song of Songs. The fundamental premise of this chapter is simply that God made sex. It has true meaning only within His guidelines. It was meant to provide pleasure, but equally important, through its expression men and women unlock some of the mystery of who we are: creatures made for relationship, completed and defined through the other.

Chapters 3 and 4 examine the assumptions, fears, and ambivalence of the church, and especially church leaders, as they face the challenge of correcting the distorted Christian teaching about sensuousness and sexuality. Regrettably, the church is no longer viewed as a reliable and credible authority for Christians in learning how to deal with their sexuality. I maintain that the church must become involved in leading Christians toward a positive view of sexuality, and such involvement will focus on clarifying the difference between the Christian and secular viewpoints.

It is not enough for like-minded Christians to admit that something needs to be done and that the church must be at the heart of the doing. We individuals who believe this must be prepared to take action. Accepting the task involves a challenging personal reevaluation. Those who want to lead the church in this matter, and those who want to counsel others who need a Christian perspective on their sexuality, must know themselves as sexual beings. Chapter 4 concludes with self-evaluation.

Part 2, "Discovering the Reality," is, quite simply, an

examination of how God has made us to be sexual beings. There is considerable pressure among some Christians to deny that God Himself is the Creator not only of sexual differentiation, but of sexual feeling and desire. They prefer instead to believe that sexuality is some lapse from God's plan or a demonic intrusion into a nonsexual creation. But the One who designed His creatures as sexual beings has never renounced His original design. Chapter 5 examines male and female sexual responsiveness as it was designed to operate. Chapter 6 surveys a multitude of factors that commonly affect normal sexual functioning.

Part 3, "Becoming One Flesh," is an orientation for pastors and Christian counselors as they approach the task of counseling couples with sexual difficulties. Chapter 7 examines sexual counseling as it is currently understood and practiced. It offers an overview of the task, some goals and intended outcomes of sexual counseling, and general procedures that a counselor should follow. Chapter 8 examines the most common sexual problems that couples experience and suggests responses and treatments. Sexual problems commonly found exclusively among women are discussed in chapter 9, and those found exclusively among men in chapter 10. Each chapter presents ways of diagnosing and treating the problems that are common to that sex.

The concluding chapters gathered into part 4, "Special Concerns in Christian Sexual Counseling," address sexual issues of particular concern to Christian leaders and Christian counselors. While some may consider homosexuality, sexual brutality, or adultery as legitimate choices for sexual life, Christians recognize that sexual choices and behavior are to be experienced within the guidelines God set forth. If church leaders want people to abide by those guidelines, they must be prepared to offer leadership, to teach and counsel, and to give overt encouragement and support to Christian people who desperately need it.

Chapter 11 offers some explanations as to why people misuse and abuse their sexuality. Sexual problems are seldom simply *sexual* problems. People frequently choose or follow immoral paths because of many kinds of tensions, sins, and difficulties in their lives. The church must be able to offer practical and effective assistance to such persons and help disentangle them from nonproductive habits and lifestyles.

The plight of the Christian single is explored in chapter 12. Singles must not deny their sexuality but learn to live comfortably with it as the gift it was meant to be. Often single adults are judged sick if they choose to remain celibate, but celibacy is a choice which God will honor and which the church must help to support. Those who are single-again need help reordering a life that until the recent past, perhaps, included genital sexuality. Few pastors, counselors, or teachers take the initiative to struggle with issues of sexuality with this ever-growing group of people.

It is popular to moan, groan, and agonize over the demise of the family. But little of our energy and concern goes into making sure new families are properly prepared for the stresses, joys, and especially the sexual component of marriage. A conscientious pastor or Christian counselor has an opportunity to influence the direction a new couple will take. Chapter 13 explores some of the important issues that should constitute premarital counseling and education. In chapter 14, I offer some simple guidelines a pastor or counselor can follow in deciding what sorts of problems should be referred and to whom they should be referred.

*   *   *

It is a rare person who is comfortable and gifted in dealing with another person's sexual life. But even those pastors and Christian counselors who use their modest gifts and abilities to teach, counsel, and encourage Christians in their sexual growth and awareness can make a tremendous difference in a believer's ability to express his or her sexuality in a way that glorifies God.

When a pastor or counselor takes the time to learn and then to teach God's design for sex, he or she has taken a first and monumental step toward changing the way things have been. I have written this book to help many readers take the first few steps and to help others continue a course they have already set for themselves. I do not expect this book to be used as the basis for in-depth sexual counseling. But I pray it will be a motivational force for some to seek the additional expertise needed to approach the common sexual problems that bring women and men to seek some kind of intervention.

I intend that this book be more than a handbook, however. Christians often depreciate their bodies and fail to use the opportunity to glorify the Lord through accepting their full sexual inheritance. Granted, the exploration and adoption of a correct biblical view of sex is not easy. But I want this book to be a modest contribution to that task. I want us no longer to ignore the fact that God made us to find completeness through our relationships: man with woman and woman with man. We have overlooked the fact that marriage is to be sealed with a bond of genital intimacy accompanied by joy, enthusiasm, and a unique kind of committed love. Christians have settled for a small, tattered remnant that only hints at what was meant to be!

If we are to recover the mystery and the reality of what it is to be "one flesh," then we must begin by reexamining God's message. In light of His revelation, we can reexamine hearts, assumptions, aspirations, and fears—the very things that make up so much of the confused world of human sexuality. Who will care enough about God's people to take the risk to deal with these matters? My hope in writing this book is that pastors, counselors, teachers, and all sorts of responsible leaders in the church will take the risk. And I offer the book as help to them as they rise to the challenge.

Sincere appreciation and love is expressed to Mike Smith, without whose editorial vision and encouragement there would be no book.

Special thanks to Melanie Schiebout, Dean Kliewer, Fred Chay, Bob Kraning, and Dan Wingerd, who shared their most fleeting commodity, their time.

PART ONE

RECOVERING THE MYSTERY

God, in His sovereignty, could have made mankind any way He wished. Reproduction could have been accomplished by cloning or some other process that left sexual relations out completely. Men and women could have been created without the need for relationship as well. But God chose to do otherwise. He created us to be two distinct sexes and to need and want one another for reproduction, for comfort, and for communion. Sex is, therefore, a God-given mandate.

Because God's purpose has become misunderstood and distorted and is in need of correction, the church must take a fresh look at the original aim of sexuality. This part, "Recovering the Mystery," seeks to do that by pursuing four avenues of inquiry: (1) Why have we Christians been reluctant and ambivalent in reexamining the distortion? (2) Why have we Christians been willing to neglect or ignore what the Bible teaches positively about sexuality? (3) What is the role of the church if we are to be responsibly involved in recovering and teaching the true meaning of sex? and, (4) How do we prepare the pastor and counselor so that he or she can begin to do something positive to rectify the problem?

Christian sexual counseling will not be effective unless the church becomes active in offering positive teaching about the meaning and purpose of human sexuality. These first four chapters attempt to lay a foundation for the church's active participation in reclaiming sexuality and glorifying God through it.

Chapter One

THE PROMISE OF PLEASURE
Christian Ambivalence
Toward Sexuality

Did you ever play the party game "I've got a secret"? The secret originates at one end of a group of people and emerges at the other a mutant of its original self.

We Christians have been playing just such a game for the last nineteen hundred years. We have a secret the whole world is vigorously searching for—the true meaning of sexuality. And like the party game, the original truth has become as distorted, withered, and alien to current thinking as "Jon dares to be different" is to "Tom bares his indifference."

The outcome of playing "I've got a secret" at a party is innocent and immediate amusement. The result of the Christian version has been long-term confusion and ambivalence. The true meaning of sexuality, which was given to God's people to experience and model for the world, has been distorted as much as the silly phrases passed along in the party game. This distortion has had serious consequences for millions down through the ages. Much pain and suffering and sin have accompanied the garbled message.

For example, I remember well the reprimand I received when I was a five-year-old giving my interpretation of Isadora Duncan, a dancer whose reputation was not a model for the morally upright. I heard the murmurs that I would grow up to be a "streetwalker." I was puzzled as the hall mirror was covered with a towel and my scarf confiscated. I had no idea what a streetwalker was and knew nothing about sexual intercourse, but I surmised that using one's body in a sensuous way was somehow a gross violation of some moral law and an evil thing. Consequently, even today, being sensuous and openly sexy within my marriage is something for which I must repeatedly give myself permission.

By adolescence it was clear to me that there were two types of women: the sexy and "naughty" ones, and the modest and "nice" variety. I knew I must conform to the second type, so any tendency I had toward overt expression of my sexuality had to be constrained and made to fit what was socially acceptable. I took great care to ensure, even on my trim young frame, that nothing jiggled, wiggled, or protruded more than it absolutely had to.

My parents were no more repressive of sexuality than most parents in their day. They wanted to raise a "good" girl, and stifling sensuousness was the only method they had ever seen modeled. They were not alone. This generation has seen many women, whose marriages are sanctified by the church and informed by Christian principles, enter into the enjoyment of sexual intercourse but hesitate at the point of accepting themselves as beings who can properly and comfortably express and enjoy the many sensuous aspects of their sexuality.

Despite some positive changes, the ambivalence is still with us. Christians have come to accept the propriety of sexual intercourse in marriage (though some still wonder whether the pleasure of it is wrong). But their acceptance of intercourse has not necessarily brought an acceptance of being sexual and expressing it sensuously in the appropriate context.

Men are as susceptible to the distortion and carry the same ambivalence as women. Men feel guilty asking their wives to be more sensuous. If a husband pushes for more than his wife can comfortably be or give, he may react to her reluctance or ambivalence by wondering whether he is some kind of pervert, or worse, by seeking the sexual relationship somewhere else, thus compounding the guilt. But does he know how to elicit the physical relationship he is seeking? Has he suppressed his own sensuous potential and made it even more difficult for his wife to discover and develop hers? Isn't his own ambivalence as much a cause of the lack of communication and failure of a couple to develop a strong and complete sexual relationship?

For both Christian men and women, sensuousness may be more unnerving and threatening than the act of intercourse. To be sensuous is to allow an aspect of one's being to exist in balance with the other proper and God-given aspects. But many Christians warn, "Sex will control you. If you open a place for sensuousness in your life, it will take over and have you under its spell." From this perspective, occasional release through sexual intercourse is a good thing, a safety valve that releases the sexual demon. But a regular and consistent relationship built on sexual expressiveness could be risky, allowing the sexual drive too much opportunity.

In steering away from such dangers, Christians attempt in vain to deny or avoid impulses that are from God. Assuming that their sexual demon is uncontrollable, they protect themselves or try to protect others by avoiding friendships or close relationships with members of the opposite sex. They fail to learn how to channel and control their sexual drives and unwittingly remain subject to their power.

Others decide there is only one outlet for their sexual nature and one context for sexual expression, and this is in the privacy of their bedroom. They live an asexual life except in the moments of intimate intercourse. If sexual feelings arise in some other context, they produce great anxiety because they are presumed to be totally inappropriate except in intercourse with the spouse.

Those who deny the legitimacy of sexual feelings outside the relationship with the spouse are understandably anxious and fearful when unplanned and unanticipated feelings arise. The very presence of these feelings validates the assumption that sex is an autonomous and overwhelming force that, once released, can never be contained. Isn't this what we teach our teenagers?

There is great concern and anxiety today about the sexual abuse of children. No one can ignore the prevalence of the problem or the devastation wrought by it. It stands as one more example of the ambivalence-inducing factors in a Christian perspective on sexuality. But is it possible that our own tendency to repress rather than develop a healthy way of being sexual may contribute to a problem that we so deeply abhor? It is those men and women who have received limited and distorted sexual information and who do not have positive models of sexual wholeness who seek out children to satisfy their twisted sexual desires. Fearful of and threatened by sex in a mature relationship, they prey upon those whom they think they can master.

This ambivalence about sexuality and sensuousness is well-entrenched in Christianity. We Christians have known and spread the good news about sex. But we have also seen and experienced the bad. The Bible shows us both. But it tells us that what God made to be good must be made good. So we find ourselves at a crucial crossroad. If the good news about sex is going to be made clear, we must understand how the bad news has distorted it and how it can be untangled from the good. And Christians must become both the models and evangelists of this good news.

UNTANGLING THE BAD FROM THE GOOD

The discovery that church precepts of sex did not mesh with personal experience has had the tragic result of the church's no longer having authority as the reliable resource for guiding and correcting a person's sexual life. Its credibility will be restored as the church demonstrates that it can offer clear direction and nurture the true meaning of sexuality among God's people. Christianity and sex need to be reunited. The process of reconciliation must be complete. The operative authorities must no longer be medieval theologians or legalistic "prooftexts."

Throughout the Christian era, with the exception of the first few years of the church, Christianity has been perceived as a sex-negative religion. There is truth in that perception. Perhaps this was due to the distancing that seemed necessary to separate it from pagan and often highly erotic cultures in which it was developing. As Christian thinking about body and soul became more dualistic, and as it strayed more and more from its Hebrew roots, the more difficult it became for Christians to see themselves positively as sensuous and sexual beings.

The alienation of Christians from their bodies had many influences. Some may have drawn false conclusions from Paul's warning that, if possible, marriage and family should wait. Others decided their whole mission in life was saving souls rather than helping people participate in the joy of living and loving in its fullest sense. And it is certain that our sex-negative image came about as a result of church writers like Marcion, Origen, Jerome, Augustine, and Aquinas, all of whom raised questions about the body's role in sin and sanctification. Although many of them contributed positively to Christian thought in other ways, their views of sex were somewhat distorted by the assumptions they held.

Today, even among those who consciously reject the more obvious and flagrant mistruths, there is almost universal embarrassment, discomfort, and avoidance of discussions of sex except when it is approached with humor. The unnaturalness and hiddenness of sexuality is often driven home to me in my teaching experiences. I have yet to teach a class in human sexual development in which more than five students out of forty can imagine their parents making love. Is this because good parents cannot also be conceived of as sensuous parents?

Despite their increased comfort level with genital sexuality, Christians have done little to overcome the fear of sensuousness. Negativism is so ingrained that almost any mention of sexuality causes one to think of it as a problem rather than a gift. One writer has summed it up rather appropriately in admitting that Christians have a "pathological concept of our sexual nature."[1]

Sexuality can be expressed in immoral ways, just as anything good can be misused. People can become gluttons, dishonor friendships, or pervert their artistic talents. Rarely do they automatically think of food, friendship, or talent as an evil, threatening, or dark thing, but they do so with sex. Sex was not given as a curse. Sexual expression is good because God said, "It is good" (Gen. 1:31). It was His idea.

THE BODY IS A DIVINE CREATION

Sexuality has positive links with some very fundamental Christian doctrines. Having been made in the image of God, human beings share in the work of creation through procreation. In the sexual union they partake in the deepest expression of love, not just the esoteric variety, but love incarnate, love expressed by body and soul. They become one in their flesh.

The incarnation of the Lord Jesus Christ confirms the dignity and importance of the embodied human person. His physical death and resurrection confront the temptation some have to disavow the significance of the body. Jesus' miracles also speak to the fact He meant people to be "whole." Our sanctification was never intended to exclude our bodies. Sexuality was always intended to be part of a total package.

Jesus Himself, living among mankind in a human body, revealed the true meaning of love in a form with which people could identify. He ate and drank and wept and loved. He was raised to new life in His body. Francis Schaeffer reminds us, "True spirituality covers all of reality. . . . In this sense there is nothing concerning reality that is not spiritual."[2]

Bodies are inextricably wrapped up with personal identity. If I touch your body, I am also touching the essence that is you. When I love you, I am loving your body; when I love your body, I am loving you. In the same way, God knows and loves us as "body-persons."[3]

The desire of men and women to relate and to love is simply another example of the way God's nature is reflected in mankind. Physical and mental desire is for the other because the innate nature comprehends that wholeness comes when men and women are in communion with each other. Lewis B. Smedes writes, "Personal communion is what the image of God is about."[4] Men and women desire one another and long for relationship, and through it they perceive the relationship God desires with mankind. No other expression celebrates so adequately the "otherness" of the opposite sex in accordance with God's declared order.

For married persons this desire to commune with another is expressed in the most intimate and revealing of all communication—the genital sexual relationship. We rightly desire the completeness of becoming "one flesh." The exact manner in which we become one and yet retain our distinct personhood is the "mystery" spoken of by Paul in Ephesians 5:32.

"One flesh" is more than the uniting of genitalia. It speaks both to the unity of bodies and the interwovenness of the totality of our lives. In the uniting of their bodies a couple become whole. Do not confuse this "wholeness" with the fact of being complete persons before God. Those who choose celibacy, or who find themselves single even if it is not a choice, are not any less persons than those who are married.

Married or not, all God's creatures are sensuous. The need for touch is a sensual need so vital that if deprived of it, an infant may fail to develop properly, both physically and mentally. One might speculate that the incessant search for sexual contact in our society relates in some way to this basic need for touch, for connectedness with other people.

There is meaning and purpose in the fact of two sexes. Man and woman were intentionally different and complementary before the Fall. Their sensing of the differences between them teaches them what it means to be a male or a female. And the fullness experienced in their relationship teaches who they are, reflects God's love for them, and enables them to experience the meaning of their sexuality.

AMBIVALENCE IN THE CHRISTIAN TRADITION

Sexuality in the Old Testament is assumed, prominent, and tied to the vocation of the people of Israel. The Hebrew man carrying a strong sense of duty as a "chosen" person of God felt a powerful drive to procreate. Only in this way could he be sure of perpetuating his name and participating in what he perceived as God's plan to continue to bless the creation through His chosen race. A number of laws supported this. The law of the Levirate stated that if a man died childless, his brother was obliged to impregnate his widow (Deut. 25:5–10; cf. Gen. 38); the edict of Deuteronomy 24:5 enabled a man to stay home during the first year of marriage and enjoy the pleasures of marriage as well as assume its obligations.

These are but two examples of the biblical emphasis given to procreation and sexual relations. Not marrying was simply unheard of. Being a member of God's family put the man under great pressure for the perpetuation of a son whose lineage no one could doubt. Wasting seed by withdrawal or masturbation was unthinkable, not because the acts were despicable but because God's plan, for which circumcision was to be the reminder, would be thwarted. The wife was to be a "pure" seedbed. The gift of children was clearly an indication of the blessing of God on the Jewish male.

The emphasis on procreation did not preclude appreciation for the promise of pleasure itself. There was no division between sexuality and spirituality. Religion and sex were integrated for the sons of Abraham in the same manner that their spirituality and all other facets of their lives were combined.

The God of the Old Testament does not reveal Himself as a remote, unapproachable being. He is a God of blessing, and blessing implies pleasure. He is a God of compassion, a God of feelings, and a God of passion for His people. The Psalms reflect the propriety of talking and relating directly to God. The Book of Hosea is filled with images of a sensuous, caring being who is dependable, sensitive (6:3), tender, loving (11:1), and compassionate (11:3–4), whose relationship with His people is defined in the earthy terms of the love of a husband and wife (2:16, 19–20).

All the Prophets and the Wisdom literature confirm a God who made man in His image—a feeling, relating, sensuous God who promised upon His return to provide food and wine (Isa. 25:6) and dancing (Jer. 31:12–14). To the Hebrews, the references to vineyards (Isa. 5:1–2, 7) and the comparisons to a woman in labor (Isa. 42:14) and to a potter (Isa. 64:8; 45:9, 12) were illustrations of their God's approval of their physical and emotional life.

The most compelling evidence of God's endorsement of the joys and pleasures of physical love is the Song of Songs (the Song of Solomon), a poetic song of love assuring all that sex is good and natural as long as it is not misused. Sexual passion is considered a normal activity that one could and should freely experience with one's spouse. Its expression is to be passionate, highly sensuous, and enjoyed by both sexes.

The dualism between body and soul, a Greek ideology, made devastating inroads in the wholesome and positive concept that characterized the Hebrew understanding of sex. With this Hellenistic influence, Christianity lost its inheritance of a unified sexuality and spirituality. This divorcing of sex from the spiritual continues to affect both the attitudes and the behavior of Christians today.

The body-soul dichotomy began to find its way into Christian thought as early as A.D. 150 in the writings of Marcion. The early church existed in a society that included both licentiousness and Stoic retreat from the passions. It is not surprising that in reacting against one, the church tended to choose the other. Unable to grasp the spiritual good in marriage, but unwilling to deny its approval in passages like 1 Timothy 4:3 and Hebrews 13:4, it concluded that an emphasis on procreation justified marriage and gave credence to the Creation account.

Some representatives of Gnosticism viewed the body as so insignificant that what one did with it was a matter of indifference. Others, like Basilides, saw value in the procreative power of sex as long as it was not contaminated by love. "Sex" was a physical release that satisfied a natural and normal desire. Still other Gnostics denied the body in search of fullness of the spirit. It is possible to recognize certain Gnostic equivalents in the "modern" pages of *Playboy*.

Stoic values appeared to provide a middle road that appealed to the first-century church. Enamored with what was "natural," Stoics defined it as any activity not contaminated by sin or human error. For example, it was natural to plant seeds in a field and to plant seeds in a woman. What animals do is natural; the most obvious function for any body part was the natural one. This placed the emphasis on sex for procreation only and detracted from sex being a vehicle for expressing a sharing, creative, or passionate relationship with another, resulting in restrictions and legalism in defining lovemaking. The idea that the vagina, for instance, is meant for the penis only, the penis for vagina only, as limitations on what parts of the body may come in contact with what other parts of the body, reflect the assumptions of "naturalism."

The morality of marriage came to be based on a love that assumed spiritual love to be a higher, true Christian love opposed to a lower, bodily sexual love that was not natural.[5] Sexual desire was bad, but making love to have children was morally right and fulfilled the purpose of marriage.

Origen, who castrated himself to serve God better, claimed that intercourse occurred only after the Fall and that it had no redeeming characteristics. If a man were engaging in it, he was committing the original sin and uniting, whoever the female, with a daughter of Satan.

The first three centuries of the church found Christian sexual morality developing more in reaction to the common immoral practices of the surrounding culture than in comprehension of a marriage covenant and how that might reflect the covenant relationship mankind was to have with God.

By the fifth century two major themes shaped Christian thought: sex is not love because there is is an element of sin in sex, and celibacy is superior to marriage because there is no sexual relationship in celibacy. The growing appeal of monastic life is evidence of the widespread acceptance of these two assumptions.

The gender that suffered most from the dividing of "flesh" and "spirit" was the female. Although Scripture clearly teaches that the female is to be a helper to make things "good" in partnership and union with the male, many Christians failed to see how that truth was in tension with the cultural bias against women. Consequently, Scripture was largely ignored. The assumption of male superiority fit with the prescientific understanding of the day: namely, men had all that was needed to propagate life. A woman merely provided nourishment and bore fruit of what she had received from a man. With no important role in reproduction, any energy expended by her by means of sexual response was viewed as evil, dangerous, and immoral—especially if her actions resulted in a man's feeling satiated and weak after a sexual encounter.

Two types of women emerged in the sexual typology of the age. One was Eve, the seductress, the temptress who caused men to lose their reason, sense of spirituality, freedom, and authority. The other was Mary, the purveyor of unsexed love. Needless to say, the idea of affection having something to do with sexuality was hard to conceptualize in this dualistic typology of femininity.

It is understandable why women in Western society decided it behooved them to become as "sexless" as possible. If spirituality and morality were in conflict with overt female sexuality, and if it were true that women distracted men from their spiritual quest, then women would be inclined to deny expression of their sexual feelings and even sexual self-perceptions. Even today this ambivalence can be heard in statements like, "No nice girl has those kinds of desires" or "A good woman pleases her husband."

A woman's lot did not improve with the theologizing of other church pastors and scholars. Augustine (b. A.D. 354), the first Christian theologian to study the relationship between sin and sexuality methodically, apparently waged a rather diligent but often losing battle against his sexual desires. His struggles and personal reflections are recorded in his *Confessions*. Struggling with his own attraction to women, and undoubtedly influenced by the thinking that came before, he understood that his Christian faith and his theological understanding would provide him answers and mastery over desire.

For Augustine, the result of the Fall was unrelenting desire; the appropriate response was a celibate life. If the Fall had not occurred, marriage would exist but children would be born through unemotional mating. (Sex therapists would be most interested in seeing how that might have worked!) Losing oneself in the passion of the sexual act is unseemly and not "rational." If one is not capable of the single life, marriage is the next (poor but viable) choice—as long as one remembers that sex is just for procreation.

Augustine, who influenced most subsequent Christian thought, allowed that sex is good but passion and desire are sin. "For he who is intemperate in marriage, what is he but the adulterer of his own wife."[6] The differences between men and women were still seen to be the work of the devil, not a gift from God. There were no dissenting voices to this view, for the

27

only voices heard were men's—often celibate men. The good in marriage was merely the propagation of the race. Not many Christian pastors and church leaders could conceive of it as a relationship for the expression of tenderness, friendship, or mutual goals.

Separation of the truly spiritual people from the ordinary folk developed before Augustine and persisted into the Middle Ages. In true dualistic fashion the "spiritual" ones—priests and nuns—quite naturally became more alienated from the "fleshly" ones—everyone else. This was all well and good, according to Thomas Aquinas (1225–1274). For those unable to accept the requirements of monastic existence, marriage was acceptable as long as one did not enjoy sex.

The contradiction between the low view of marriage and the fact of its divine origin (Christ blessed it and used it to describe His relationship to the church) was not entirely missed. Somehow marriage was to be honored as a sacrament because it is analogous to union between Christ and the church.

By the twelfth century, influences outside the church began to affect religious thinking and pave the way for change. One such movement was that of "courtly love." It raised the feeling of affectionate love toward another person to its highest form while simultaneously excluding genital sexuality. Courtly love made the woman in particular the object of chaste desire. It was a step toward the unification of love and sexuality. Men were allowed to be sensitive; women were appreciated for who they were as individuals. True love was nurtured by recognition of the "otherness" of the lover and of mutual rights and obligations. It was never found within marriage.

BACK TO THE ORIGINAL "SECRET"

It was not until the Reformation that church and state concurred to give spiritual and judicial meaning to marriage. Christian attitudes toward sexuality and marriage had been relatively homogeneous until the development of Protestantism, at which time divergent paths evolved.

Among the many reforms that Martin Luther (1483–1546) called for, of greatest interest to us is the argument for an end to celibacy among the priesthood. He grasped that marriage is honorable because of God's grace and not because it is a sacrament. He also recognized that spiritual good could result from faith translating physical desire into an expression of Christian love.

As positive as this was in undermining a spirit-versus-body religion, neither Luther nor Calvin (1509–1564) nor the reformers who followed them could go as far as to see sexual desire as a positive gift of God. It was a necessary part of life made clean by the grace of God, but not good and healthy in its own right. Mankind's vulnerability to sexual sin was still perceived as a sign that sexual desire is not a good gift from a loving God.

The Catholic response to these Reformation ideas was to maintain the distinction inherited from the Stoics to counter the Gnostic disdain for creation and emphasize natural law. This resulted in the continuation of the split between soul and body, reinforced by a hierarchical perspective that determined that the more spiritual the man, the less sexual. Today the same natural philosophy promotes the view that sexuality is fundamentally a differentiation for the purpose of procreation. As in early church history, this viewpoint resulted in a deemphasis of the possibilities marriage holds for the expression of love, tenderness, and unity through the sexual relationship.

By the sixteenth century, morality for Catholics was imposed from outside and had become associated with fear of sin and error.[7] The double-bind created by a belief system that declared on the one hand that marriage is good but on the other that spiritual fulfillment comes through denial of the body resulted in two pathways: one for the laity, one for the clergy.

By contrast, the Protestant ethic attempted to make grace rather than the fear of sin the basis for the believer's relationship with God. The significance of the Reformation for understanding sexuality lies in its explicit rejection of the dualism that had been a part of Christianity from the first century. Body and soul, having been created by God, are to be acknowledged as a unity—distinguishable but nevertheless an integral creation. Not to acknowledge them thus is to deny God's order revealed in Scripture.

Because the Bible values marriage, the Reformers did also. So they went a few steps beyond the limitations imposed by the dualistic framework of their predecessors. Some began to recognize the link between sexuality and spirituality. "Agape is not simply the fulfillment of eros: it also restores its natural vitality."[8]

Both the Protestant and the older Catholic ethics seek to bring man and woman into a closer relationship with God. The Catholic seeks God by distancing himself or herself from the reality of his or her basic sexual nature. The Protestant seeks God by discovering Him in the midst of a love relationship.[9]

Clearly, there is no compelling reason for us to hang on to views of sexuality that have been forged out of erroneous ideas about God and the meaning of His creation. People hunger for a lucid and meaningful interpretation of their sexual appetites. There is one, and it is consistent with the truth of Scripture. But in order to see it we must be willing to examine the prejudice, cultural bias, and poor exegesis that have been handed down to us by our ancestors.

For those who have held sex-negative convictions for a lifetime, true renewal of the mind is in order. They must be willing to change the ways they think about, feel about, and conceptualize sex. "Do not conform any longer to the pattern of this world, but be transformed by the renewing of your mind. Then you will be able to test and approve what God's will is—his good, pleasing and perfect will" (Rom. 12:2).

Peter also reminds us that believers have been given everything they need that pertains to living life in a godly way (2 Peter 1:3–9). The combination of mindset, Scripture, and reappraisal of our theological inheritance holds out a promise for answers to the important questions of sexuality that previously have been guarded, tentative, and raised all too infrequently.

If Christians continue to ignore the critical problems, distortions, and confusion that plague their existence as sexual beings made in the image of God, they have three choices: (1) they may try to live with the discrepancy between the unexamined "truth" they have been told and the reality they actually experience, (2) they may accept the suggestion that

Christians do not have sexual problems and conclude that something is wrong with their spiritual walk, or (3) they may, out of desperation and defeat, accept the world's understanding of sex since it is the only freely available source of information and learning.

None of the three is healthy, correct, or moral. There should actually be a fourth option, because it is wrong for Christians to ignore their responsibility to develop mature believers by presenting the truth in love. And it is wrong to withhold from a needy world a meaningful and fulfilling message about sexuality. Consequently, the church faces, as one of its most important tasks for the decades ahead, the challenge of teaching with accuracy and compelling clarity the purpose and validity of human sexuality.

Sex was not designed so that its escape would bring us closer to God or so that its expression would be part of the downward spiral toward our death. Sex has meaning beyond the act itself. It is a gift and a reflection in some way of a proper, orderly, and good creation. It is time to face facts. If bodies are blessings and not the curse of the devil, if our senses are blessings and thus our sensuousness also, Christians are rather tardy in becoming thankful for the grace of being able to experience bodily pleasure as well as the gift that allows mortals a glimpse of divine love.

Chapter Two

ACCEPTING THE PROMISE
Christian Ethics and Sexuality

One of the underlying causes of Christian ambivalence toward sexuality is the reality that sex is a fundamental moral and ethical issue. Consequently, there is no better place to start reexamining our sexual ambivalence than with the ethical teachings of Jesus.

"If you hold to my teaching, you are really my disciples. Then you will know the truth, and the truth will set you free" (John 8:31–32).

Elaborate rules and laws were not the center of Jesus' teaching. The claims of God on a person were easily summed up in two great commandments: the first, to love God; the second, "Love your neighbor as yourself" (Matt. 22:39). If our sexual behavior had these commandments at its source, our sexual decisions and actions would result from asking ourselves such questions as "Will my choice of action glorify God? What is in my heart? Will my neighbor (boyfriend, girlfriend, spouse) experience my action as loving? Is this a way God wants me to express my love? What will be the effect?"

The world hungers to know that, as one writer has so aptly stated, "We are not orphans shivering in an absurd world with no other hope for reassurance but the warm flesh of others."[1] Sex is linked with love, emotion, the quality of a relationship, and commitment. It is like a seal on the very values that Jesus teaches us.

Rather than being an alien and contrary force in Christian ethics, sex should be very much at home. Like the approachable God of the Hebrews, Jesus, as His Father's Son, shared our earthy reality. The Eucharist itself is defined in the most carnal of terms: a gift of Jesus' blood and body. The Messiah was not an enemy of parties, feasting, or wine. He attended banquets and defended His disciples for not being ascetics. He had special and meaningful friendships with both men and women. His friends touched Him, leaned against Him, anointed Him, and washed His feet. He found peace in nature, frequently going alone into the serenity of the wilderness, mountaintop, or garden.

Jesus expected His disciples not to remain unmoved, unemotional, and passionless at another's unjust treatment, at appropriate times of sorrow and happiness, or when presented with the truth. The Pharisees were described as callous and "hard-hearted," and such people were likened to an "empty vial." Jesus did not call for His disciples to reject the passion and the feeling of life, but rather to submit it to God and His kingdom.

Love entails being open to passion. Unless we feel, we cannot be moved. Empty vials do not have compassion and do not put another's needs first. Real love is the capacity to care more for the other than oneself. This ability to put someone else ahead of oneself, so alien in the world of "fallen ME-firsts," is possible only as a result of God's grace.

Jesus' expression of love was not distant and restrained, but immediate and gracious. It was not confined to one sex. A kiss, a touch, or a hug honored God because it was disciplined, controlled, and directed by the command of Jesus to love others as we love ourselves.

The physical expression of love honors God if it is not an attempt solely for self-gratification. In other words, the ethical requirements of love give rise to expressions of love, and such expressions are always in a sexual context where two human beings are involved.

Jesus' command to love one another mandated a certain

kind of relationship. The command calls on us to want it, but reminds us that we have been graced with the ability to accomplish it. Romantic love—the pleasurable love of a woman for a man and a man for a woman—is not so much commanded as assumed. But despite the fact that romantic love grows naturally over time, the command of Jesus still applies. Such love is not just the action of glands and genitals. It is a process of discovering, cherishing, and giving to another.

Chastity is not merely refraining from sexual relations, but also a means of honoring the gift of singleness and its calling and, sometimes, waiting on true love. Modesty is not merely observing proprieties, but the affirmation of the person. Virginity is not merely absence of intercourse, but an expression of spiritual integrity.[2] And what about marriage? It is not merely a social commitment, but a true renewal of a covenant relationship with God, shared with our worship-mate.

Jesus' references to marriage always allude to Genesis and God's original intent of a permanent covenant relationship between man and woman and their God (Matt. 19:4–6; Mark 10:1–9). Sexual differences are God's handiwork. The monogamous couple is the goal of sexuality and the basic order and primary desire of God.

Marriage affects society because it is to be the model of the ultimate relationship with God. As the partners interact, disclose themselves, and learn to live with and love one another, they reflect what a covenant life with God means. The Book of Hosea seeks to reveal this deeper meaning of relationship between husband and wife, God and Israel, and mankind and God. It is no surprise that so many of today's couples take their marriage vows lightly, for marriage can find its deepest meaning only in the context of faith. Like all the profound wisdom of God, its significance goes beyond understanding into mystery.

"The image of God is reflected in desire for the other, openness, incompleteness that can be fulfilled only through encounter with the other through love with a particular being."[3] Through marriage, couples begin to perceive what unconditional love means. Desirous to be together forever, they begin to grasp the true implications of eternity. And in the most ecstatic moments of intercourse, when they transcend their ego boundaries and become whole, perhaps they come closer than at any other time to understanding the mystical experience that makes them "one flesh." They experience deeply the intensity and the selflessness that characterizes God's love for us. Somehow being one flesh enables them to glimpse that which unites them with God and gives some understanding to the mystery of the Trinity.

Although quick to condemn sexual sin, Jesus never condemned, shamed, or ostracized the sexual sinner. Clearly He did not indicate that we should hold sexual sins to be the most reprehensible. It helps to keep in mind that the "seven deadly sins" are listed as pride, envy, anger, sloth, avarice, gluttony, and lust.

Jesus' ministry was not one of condemnation, guilt, and punishment but confession, forgiveness, and salvation. He came to seek and save the lost. Those who rejected Him condemned themselves. Those who accepted Him accepted a new way of life and a possibility for being made whole.

THE ETHICS OF PAUL

The apostle Paul's sexual ethics revolved around three points. He recognized the attraction between men and women to be the result of God's grace. He also recognized that God graciously provides His creatures the will and the power to control and direct this attraction so that He will be honored. And he called on the church to be aware that, whether married or single, a person has a responsibility to glorify God in the way he or she uses his or her gift of celibacy or marriage. For Paul, sexual wholeness is an issue of either giving oneself freely and lovingly to the marriage partner or else controlling one's desires for the sake of other concerns in the kingdom of God. In either case, the kingdom of God is a controlling factor.

Paul had a ministry primarily among gentile converts. Unlike the Jews, they lived in a world of sexual immorality. For that reason, much of what he wrote to the gentile churches about sexuality had a negative tone. His letters were full of admonitions. He warned them of the power of physical self-indulgence to keep them apart from their Lord. Indeed, many of the gentile converts were trying to serve two masters. It was not that they merely enjoyed the sensual pleasures life had to offer. Rather, it was their desire to make sensual experience a god and to dedicate their lives to it that Paul attacked.

In writing to the Thessalonians Paul says that believers are to be holy, no longer living in passionate lust like the heathen (1 Thess. 4:3–5). They were to avoid "sexual immorality" (4:3), not sex itself. Lacking the ability to comprehend sensual enjoyment as a gift of God and instead making it into a god, some opted for complete rejection of sexuality and marriage.

These believers' concern to "put on the new self" raised many questions, including whether or not divorcing or remaining single would enable them better to serve the Lord. Paul's reply was for them to "retain the place in life that the Lord assigned to him and to which God has called him" (1 Cor. 7:17). Married or single, the issue was not whether one state was morally superior but that both states could be proper, useful, and conforming to God's will. The state of celibacy allowed one advantages and flexibility in kingdom service; it was not for the purpose of some supposed spiritual superiority, a refuge from relationships with members of the opposite sex, or simply a good excuse for one to be alone. Likewise, marriage was to be "in the Lord" and not simply for one's convenience or to fulfill personal needs. But Paul does recognize that some people are unable to control their desire for sexual union. Those people, he advises, should seek a marriage partner because they will be tempted to sin if they do not (1 Cor. 7:8–9).

A positive view of marriage is forcefully conveyed through Paul's analogy between the relationship of a man and a woman in marriage and of Christ and the church in redemption. Christ brings the church into existence by His personal sacrifice. The husband brings the marriage into existence by the personal sacrifice of giving up his selfish desires, independence, and freedom from responsibility. He gives his name to symbolize his gift of self to his wife. (Today a husband's giving his wife his name is rarely viewed in any other way than as symbolic of his desire to own her.)

Christ is the Savior of the church, the husband the

"savior" of his wife in the sense of one who calms, guards, protects, spares, leads to a goal, and rejoices with.[4] Implicit in the relationship is the expectation of fidelity and loyalty. In the world in which we live this may sound eccentric, if not archaic. But it was intended to be lived out by Christian men and women even in a world that does not understand or accept it.

Some translations say the wife is to "fear" her husband (Eph. 5:33). But the use of *fear* in its feminine form means she is not to act independently of him. The result is that both are to behave in a way that acknowledges God's plan of interdependence. The wife's relationship, like the church's to Christ, gives meaning to her husband. She brings him into focus and defines him, but does not replace him.

From Genesis to Revelation the Scriptures clearly teach the interrelatedness of husband and wife. The first purpose of sex was to end loneliness and isolation. The woman was not made of new and different material, but was taken from the rib of the man. She makes him complete, for Adam's aloneness was declared "not good."

The husband's authority, like Christ's, is never to be expressed by selfish force, but in the manner of a loving Savior (Eph. 5:23), by giving himself (5:25) and by positive leadership (5:27). "We have thus come to the heart of theological reflection on marriage: human love, freed by the gospel from all kinds of conformity and from legalism, can signify the love of Christ for His Church."[5]

THE CHRISTIAN SEX MANUAL

Where else do we look as we continue to probe, shake up, and turn inside out the hodgepodge of half-truths and untruths we have been hanging on to? How we are to practice our genital sexuality is poignantly presented to us in Song of Songs.

Throughout history there has been much speculation as to why the Bible contains so racy a book as the Song of Songs. Out of embarrassment some conclude that it simply means something other than what it says; thus the insistence on an allegorical rendering.[6] But even if it is regarded as an allegory, it is important that we admit God used an erotic poem to represent marital love as it was meant to be. The implication of His approval of an erotic aspect of life cannot honestly be ignored.

Because interpretation of poetry can vary according to the predisposition of the person reading it, the symbolism can be tamed and domesticated for almost any taste. It is not blunt or graphic but subtle, leaving the images to be supplied by the imagination. Yet the undeniable fact remains: the Song of Songs is an erotic love poem.

The poetic form of the Song of Songs catches a truth about sexuality: it is perhaps more lyrical than prosaic. The experience of sex is more than the sum of its parts, more than the mere physical performance of sexual intercourse. The intense and ecstatic experience of intercourse transcends the ordinary experiences of life. Sexual intimacy, at its best, is spontaneous and not self-conscious or timid in asking, seeking, or achieving its objective.

The poem itself captures and conveys to its readers pictures from the lives of the two main characters. Although some interpreters think the poem is an aggregate of individual pieces, there may be more unity than they have thus far perceived. Each segment contains a thread that ties it in with all the others. Joseph C. Dillow describes its consistency as that of a movie with flashbacks.[7] Things may be out of logical time sequence, but they all belong together.

Dillow also sees the chorus as a literary device that provides transitions between scenes or adds emphasis. The story describes King Solomon's love for a country girl, a Shulammite. Throughout the story the theme of love is repeated: love as it is relished in the palace (1:2–4), longed for when the lovers are apart (3:1–5; 5:6–8), enjoyed when they are together (4:1–5:1), and reserved exclusively for the marriage partner (2:16; 6:3; 7:10).

In reading the Song of Songs one reaches only the second verse before the physical dimension of love is mentioned. Shulamith expresses a positive anticipation of being with Solomon. He calls her "my darling," translated from the Hebrew *vaghah*, meaning "to guard, to care for, and to take delight in having intercourse with."

"Little Things Mean a Lot"

The Song of Songs provides many clues as to how a husband and wife are to relate. One of the most obvious is the priority given to verbalizing their feelings and thoughts. The different culture makes one wonder whether a particular statement ("Your hair is like a flock of goats" [4:1; 6:5]) is really a compliment! As strange-sounding as they might be now, in the context of the culture the words were immensely flattering.

Throughout the book the man and the woman freely praise each other. Chapter 1 is full of their mutual admiration. Chapter 4 adds an especially erotic tone as the new groom feasts his eyes on his wife. He begins with her head, makes mention of her teeth and the fact that they are moist (with sexual arousal there is increased salivation). He even dares to appreciate her genitals, "the mountain of myrrh and . . . the hill of incense" (4:6). Their sweet smell and attraction are alluded to in the metaphor, and again through reference to exotic fruit in 4:13–14. Repeatedly the sensuous beauty of husband and wife are lauded. And we readers are told these things so that we can celebrate with them and learn how to praise the gift of our own spouses.

In addition to verbal praise, tangible gifts are meant to be a seal of our commitment (1:10–11; 5:5). In both examples the gifts were not "practical," but tokens of esteem, jewelry, and perfume. Obviously Solomon was a romantic. I doubt whether Shulamith would ever hear him say, "But I told you I loved you when I married you! I turn over my paycheck to you every week, what more do you want?"

Shulamith was quite a beautiful and desirable woman. She availed herself of ways to enhance her beauty and desirability for her husband by wearing lipstick, jewelry, and sensuous bedclothes. Her approach to Solomon took into account the fact that men are aroused by the physical, just as his approach to her recognized the importance of romantic gestures.

Not only were the man and woman conscientious about their appearance out of regard for one another, but they also cared about their physical surroundings. Their bedroom and bed were the finest money could buy (1:16). They acknowledged that a change of scene was a sexual stimulant and spoke of making love in different locations (7:12). Throughout the poem mention is made of all five senses being stimulated.

A warning is given in 2:15-17 to be aware of the "little foxes" that can destroy a vineyard. Couples are wisely told not to ignore the small problems that can eventually cause the downfall of their relationship. A public affirmation of the love and commitment announces to all the intention of leaving, cleaving, and having sexual intercourse (3:6-11) within an exclusive relationship (2:16; 6:3; 7:10; 8:6-7).

"If You Could Read My Mind"

Some people falsely assume that kings don't have problems and thus we ordinary folk cannot relate. The love life of this couple was beset with at least two problems. Apparently King Solomon liked late-night sex and Shulamith preferred her sleep (5:2-6:9). Their approach to the impasse was as fine as any sex therapist might have suggested and can be applied to any kind of sexual problem. They took responsibility for themselves. Solomon did not whine about how hard he worked and how much he deserved his conjugal rights. Shulamith did not tell her best friend what an insensitive cad the king was. Instead, they reevaluated and approached one another in ways that were meaningful and significant to the other person.

Solomon continued to be loving and verbally supportive. At no time did he use guilt or coercion to get what was "rightfully" his. Shulamith began to do something about her low sexual desire; she allowed herself to visualize Solomon in as erotic a way as possible. She became accountable for her sexual response and followed up by seeking him out and vocally expressing her desire.

While we may be taking some liberties with the poem in order to apply it to a more systematic and therapeutic approach to sexual counseling, there are, nevertheless, some truths about sexual relationships to be gleaned and pondered. It is a mistake for anyone to think that sex will be perfect throughout a marriage. As we will see in future chapters, there are too many contingencies affecting sexual intimacy for this to be so.

"That's the Way I Always Heard It Should Be"

It is clear that Solomon and Shulamith were sexual and unashamed. They had an attitude of acceptance and appreciation for God's gift of sex and the body through which it was to be expressed (5:1). Love is compared to wine, which in the culture suggested "a joyful banquet of celebration."[8] They asked for what they wanted and expressed openly their desire for one another: "Strengthen me with raisins, refresh me with apples, for I am faint with love. His left arm is under my head and his right arm embraces me" (2:5–6). The Hebrew for "embrace" means to stimulate or fondle; references to apples and raisins symbolize erotic love; to be "faint with love" means highly aroused. In line with good sexual functioning they did not attempt intercourse until the woman was ready.

There is no evidence of false modesty or passivity on Shulamith's part. There are twice as many erotic references attributed to her than to Solomon. She openly declares her desires and needs. She enhances her appeal to her husband by doing a sensuous dance for him as he looks on approvingly (6:13–7:9). How ironic that in our "liberated" times it is the rare wife who would dare do the same!

Shulamith differs from many modern types, too, as she takes the time to reflect on, appreciate, and contemplate her life. She apparently knew that keeping her priorities and life in balance had much to do with her ability to be the sexual mate God intended her to be.

For the couple in the Song of Songs, the sexual relationship was a way to connect with other aspects of life. They spent much time together, changed locations, stopped, talked, and dreamed together. What better time to discuss goals, hopes, and plans than when you are feeling the most intimate, the most "one."

Of the many marriage manuals on the market, few have more insights to offer than the Song of Songs. The poem assumes that desire, esteem, appreciation, self-sacrifice, and so many other aspects of love come to their proper expression in a physical relationship between the man and the woman. The physical relationship is not merely, or even essentially, intercourse, but a relationship in which all the senses are appreciated and used. Christians should spend more time with it to appreciate its symbolism and its wise counsel.

IS IT WORTH IT?

The goal of this book is to help Christian leaders, especially those who teach and counsel, lead Christian brothers and sisters into appreciating the gift they have received of having love for a spouse. Along with the gift of love, they have the gift of physical expression of love. And because the purpose and meaning of the physical expression of love have been so distorted by the world, we Christians must reconstruct the original vision and help people begin to discover it.

Albert Ellis once argued for sex without love on the grounds that it is much more available. In a similar vein, the television show "Love Boat" counsels us that good sex is the measure of "real" love. People often attempt to use sexual therapists as a last, perfunctory step on the path out of a marriage in which the sex has gone bad. They often assume that the therapist will provide the go-ahead to find solutions in the "if-it-feels-good-do-it" school of therapy. It is no wonder in a world such as this that Christians are confused about the connections between love and sex: so is everyone else.

If someone were to speak of "a Christian concept of sex," chances are that anyone hearing the term would assume that the speaker was, no doubt, talking about the misuse of sexuality by immoral people. A positive and compelling view of Christian sexual ethics has not been prevalent in the church. Only in the last few years have some in the church begun to look at and speak openly and realistically about our being God's sexual people.

The positive, sound, and healthy view of married love that God himself proposed and invented may be making headway among the more discerning clergy and churches. We may be learning to accept ourselves as sensuous and sexual beings who are responsible to use the gift to the glory of God. But there is much ground to be covered before these positive trends are translated into characteristics of the church as a whole.

Chapter Three

LIGHTING THE WAY

The Church's Responsibility
for a Christian Sexuality

It is your birthday. The long-hoped-for golf clubs have mysteriously appeared on your desk. You excitedly open the card only to discover your "gift" is contingent on your never taking them out on a course, practicing with them, or in any way deriving pleasure from them. You begin to wonder, is your benefactor a caring, compassionate soul who has your best interest at heart, or a miserly masochist whose real purpose is to make your life miserable?

God has not given us gifts of bodies that have the capacity for sexual sensation—both to give and to receive pleasure—as some kind of perverse test of our faith. God does not have a problem with our sensuousness, but we do. He knows we have the capability to experience pleasure with our bodies responsibly and morally within His guidelines. We are the ones who doubt it. The church must confront and deal with that doubt.

The church is called not only to maintain moral standards, but also to define goals for God's people based on the Word of God. As we have seen, the church has not been the positive force in the lives of Christians that it is supposed to be. One result of its declining influence has been a selective approach to involvement in the important issues of life. When it comes to sexual concerns, many clergy and churches are more than delighted to remain uninvolved. For them the issue of sex is too explosive and sensitive. They feel uncomfortable, ill-equipped, threatened, or confused. They would prefer not to be made responsible for helping Christians see what God has called them to as sexual beings.

The church is also called to be involved in God's work of redemption. The leadership the church gives her members in understanding sex and living as sexual beings is a part of the redemptive process. It is the ultimate challenge to help God's people take steps through God's power to transcend their fallen nature and reject the call to impersonal sexuality, the temptation of self-indulgence, and the pushing aside of the needs of the soul. Who besides caring Christians will care enough to develop a sane and correct approach to sexuality that reaches those men or women at their point of anguish, despair, or searching?

Though sexuality may be a topic that makes the church uncomfortable, it nevertheless is clearly the church's business. Two of the seven churches addressed by name in Revelation are reprimanded because of their failure to deal with sexual immorality (Rev. 2:14–16, 20–23). In Hebrews we read, "See that no one is sexually immoral" (12:16) and "Let us consider how we may spur one another toward love and good deeds" (10:24).

Because this is not a widely accepted role for the church, I want to examine the arguments given for and against the church's accepting responsibility for modeling, teaching, and counseling a correct, healthy, and biblical understanding of sex.

THE CHURCH SHOULD BE INVOLVED BECAUSE . . .

We offer more than a bandage. "All Scripture is God-breathed and is useful for teaching, rebuking, correcting and training in righteousness, so that the man of God may be thoroughly equipped for every good work" (2 Tim. 3:16–17).

The Bible is concerned with both the history and the destiny of humanity. As it shows us where we have come from and where we are going, it reveals to us the nature of God and His relationship to us. It tells of God's choice to commune, to dwell, and to reestablish fellowship with us. This is astounding, since all other religions reflect mankind's striving to commune with God. This Bible was not intended to address in detail every aspect of our lives. Consequently, we do not always find specific directions (even when in many cases they are there), but we can usually discover the overriding applicable principles. It is these principles of living as male and female as God has created us that both the church and the world must see and hear.

Jesus' teaching about sex and marriage is a message that believers and nonbelievers alike want to hear. Matthew 28:19 calls us to make disciples and spread the Word from one end of the world to the other. The truth about our calling to be male and female image-bearers accepting the gift of sexuality is part of the whole truth and is to be shared as well.

Throughout Scripture we are emphatically warned of false teachers. Most of us are discerning enough to be on the alert when it appears that someone's words or lifestyle is not aligned with the Word of God. We feel we know what is correct doctrine. But despite our good intentions to avoid and not propagate false teaching, we may still manage to mislead or be misled. Instruction by omission, or with a message that distorts the intended joy and wholeness of our marital sexuality and acceptance of ourselves as the sexual beings He made us, is a false doctrine. In the words of an infamous cartoon character, Pogo, "We have seen the enemy, and he is us!"

People will listen to pastors and Christian counselors. Whether they are members of a church or not, people have access to pastors and counselors. People look to them for answers and directions. They often feel more free to seek counsel from a pastor. They often feel safer going to a pastor than to a "shrink." Pastors frequently have the advantage of knowing the person in context. They can use the body of believers as a support system. In fact, they are one of the few kinds of people left who can provide guidance and support in a fashion that has continuity with the rest of a person's life.

The position of authority and power given to the pastor can be used to great advantage. If any men and women are in doubt about the goodness and rightness of their sexuality and someone they respect gives them "permission" to enjoy their sexuality with their spouses, they will listen with far more care than if such counsel comes from their neighbor.

Simple respect for authority is not the only positive factor at work in a counseling relationship. There is also the potentially positive effect of transference. (The multiplicity of factors involved in a counseling relationship is so complex, it is probably beyond the understanding of most of us.) Transference describes the feelings a person may project onto a counselor that have their source in some previous setting or relationship. The feelings can be either positive or negative. How many of us, for instance, have had to work through negative feelings toward someone who unfortunately reminded us of the seventh-grade gym teacher who used to reprimand us in front of all our friends for being so clumsy? Positive transference can be an asset and an aid in communication if it is recognized and not abused.

The Bible encourages people to seek out persons who are wise and have the authority of God to instruct: "Listen to advice and accept instruction, and in the end you will be wise" (Prov. 19:20). Scripture spells out the purpose and methodology of a counselor: "Brothers, if someone is caught in a sin, you who are spiritual should restore him gently. But watch yourself, or you also may be tempted" (Gal. 6:1). "We proclaim him, admonishing and teaching everyone with all wisdom, so that we may present everyone perfect in Christ" (Col. 1:28).

Anyone acting in such a position of authority is to have a character that exhibits the fruit of the Spirit described in Galatians 5: to be a loving and joyful person, not quarrelsome, but patient, kind, faithful, gentle, exhibiting self-control. It is right to expect those in church leadership and other positions of authority to live according to such guidelines. They are called to help others in all areas of life inasmuch as God has given them understanding, gifts, and skills to do so.

There is danger, of course, in a pastor's appearing to be holier, more sanctified, or more righteous than those he is counseling and shepherding. If he is not "real" and does not admit to being subject to the same weaknesses, temptations, and sins as others, he will not be able to bring about the very change he might hope to see. People do not like to share their foibles with someone who is "perfect." They fear being lectured, feeling more guilt, and finding little compassion.

A faithful pastor walks alongside a counselee rather than looks down on him or her. People respect the authority of the empathetic counselor. Therefore pastors must take seriously the opportunity they have to minister where hurts, fears, and confusion over sexual issues place individuals and families at risk. John 10:10 reminds us that Jesus came so that mankind might experience life in the fullest. If pastors, elders, counselors, and teachers claim to be His disciples, they are to be compassionately related to the men and women whom they serve, for those who hurt need help to live life to the full.

Christians need guidance in how to live as sexual beings. There is seldom any Christian presence in discussions of sexuality and sexual ethics. Consequently, secular views of sex dominate. By virtue of our discomfort with sexuality, simple neglect, or our refusal to accept our responsibility to counsel and teach, we Christians have allowed our sexual learning to be controlled, directly or indirectly, by the world. While we may react against a particular distortion or false teaching about sexuality, we remain subject to its influences. Consider some of the major differences of perspective on sexuality as Christian and non-Christian frameworks are placed side by side.

CHRISTIAN SEXUAL ETHICS	SECULAR SEXUAL ETHICS
1. Sex has a purpose beyond that of mere personal pleasure and is enjoyed within a well-defined context. There is a requirement for discipline.	Sex has personal pleasure as its purpose and should be enjoyed in whatever ways give the most pleasure. There is a lack of discipline.
2. Sex is the bond of a covenant relationship that requires enduring faithfulness.	Sex is a separate relationship that may or may not be taken as permanent and faithful.
3. Marriage is a union of a man and a woman that reflects the	Marriage is a social convenience that brings together

CHRISTIAN SEXUAL ETHICS	SECULAR SEXUAL ETHICS
union between Christ and the church.	two persons who happen to be in love.
4. Marriage is defined by personal and communal values that are based on biblical guidelines.	Marriage is defined by personal and communal values that reflect social mores and fashions.
5. The meaning of sex transcends its pleasure and is part of a grand plan that touches the meaning of life.	Sex is either an end in itself or it is part of a vague search for connectedness and some meaning in life.
6. A Christian knows he is alive because he communes with the God who made him.	A nonbeliever tries to feel alive through his experiences, especially sexual ones.
7. Sex in marriage is a way to serve one another.	Sex in marriage is a vehicle for wielding power.
8. The focus is on true intimacy, which enhances the sexual relationship.	The focus is on sexual encounter, which is expected to generate true intimacy.
9. God's power is at work through the Holy Spirit to help maintain a marriage and the commitment to it.	Human power is at work to bring about whatever the individual desires or feels constrained by external forces to make of a marriage.
10. Abstinence for the unmarried is the recommended method of preventing unwanted pregnancies.	Contraception and abortion for the unmarried are the recommended methods for preventing unwanted pregnancies.
11. Celibacy is a healthy choice of lifestyle that helps focus on activities outside oneself.	Celibacy is unnecessary and unhealthy because it does not put personal desires first.
12. Love is unconditional.	Love is conditional.
13. Marriage means I am there for you. Your needs are before my own.	Marriage means you are there for me. My needs come first.

CHRISTIAN SEXUAL ETHICS	SECULAR SEXUAL ETHICS
14. Identity comes from knowing who I am in Christ.	Identity comes from how I perform, especially how I perform sexually.
15. Sex is in proper balance in the totality of life.	Sex is either too important or too threatening.

This comparison does not reflect Christian practice versus secular practice, but rather reflects Christian ideals versus the condition that most of us seem to be in—Christians and non-Christians alike.

THE CHURCH SHOULD NOT BE INVOLVED BECAUSE . . .

Sex is merely an instinct that should be left alone to take care of itself. It is a well-documented fact that humans are sexually responsive from birth. At no time in their lives, barring organic illness, are they without sexual feelings. Through repression or its healthier companion, sublimation, some people may convince themselves they do not have sexual feelings and drives— but they do.

If sex is natural and woven into the fabric of our humanness, why bother teaching or talking about it? The answer is simple: while the abilities and mechanisms for responding sexually are natural, the manners, morals, and means of handling our responsiveness have to be taught. People tend to ignore the very positive effect learning and emotional development play in normal, healthy sexual maturation. Although sexual feelings and drives have a natural dimension, sexuality is learned. It is formed by the many cultural, religious, and family influences that go into making us the complex creatures that we are.

Eating provides a useful analogy here. Infants unceremoniously eat whatever they are fed by those who care for them. They are not expected to use the toilet when their bodies have decided to get rid of the waste that has passed through their digestive system. Eating, urinating, and defecating are, for most infants, essentially uncontrolled, *natural* functions.

But as the children grow they are expected to begin using utensils, to wipe their faces, and to take care of their elimination in the appropriate room. As they grow older, they must no longer put their elbows on the table, talk with their mouths full, or leave the table before others are finished. There is more freedom to choose what they eat, but there are also more social manners to be aware of. Many adults eventually learn that, although certain foods are tasty, they can be fattening, upsetting to their stomachs, or not be good for their health and well-being. So they avoid them. In other words, they learn how to deal with fundamental, natural needs of their body in a way that is healthy and also takes account of others.

There should really be no significant difference in our teaching methods or attitude toward instruction when our subject matter is sex. As children grow they are eventually expected to be able to handle their natural sexual appetite in a way that befits a mature and responsible adult. It is as silly to think that a person who has no instruction can grow to have sexual manners, morals, and the means to handle the social ramifications of sex as it is to think a person could learn to eat properly and tend to grooming efficiently with no instruction.

Any necessary teaching about sex should be undertaken as the need to know arises and only by parents. Researchers recognize that healthy sexuality begins with the way infants are handled. If fathers and mothers convey that the baby's body is precious, touchable, attractive, and delightful, the baby is off to a good start. Babies that receive mixed or negative messages about their bodies are likely to have difficulties understanding and appreciating their sexual selves in later years.

Cultural studies indicate there is substantial variation in how people express their sexuality. Parents and the immediate cultural influences shape specific behavior, expectations, and attitudes. To be sure, the basic biological factors that make one either male or female are real. At eighteen months a child has a sense of his or her gender. By two or three they clearly identify as either a girl or a boy. Much of their interaction, however, is imitating the expression of gender differences picked up through watching mom or dad. Overt and covert sexual communication is continually observed and filed away for future reference through this and every later learning stage.

It is not true that children do not need sex education. Nor is it accurate to describe the school age child's sexuality as "latent," as one major theory does. Children have desires to know about every aspect of life. They watch. They gain an increased social awareness of sexuality which motivates the majority of children to involve themselves in "play" with masked sexual themes. Eventually, a combination of broadened interests, better control of drives (the result of personal maturation), and increased awareness of social pressure results in reduction in frequency of such games, but no reduction in their interest in sex.

The learning process continues into adolescence when the sexual body games are replaced by direct sexual fantasies, often with self-stimulation activities. By middle adolescence 90 percent of all boys and 60 percent of all girls have stimulated themselves to the point of orgasm. Their major motivation is the quest to know, understand, and master the body. The bottom line is assurance of normalcy. "Is everything OK?" "Do I work like everyone else?" "Can I love another in the fullest sense?"

And perhaps he or she "falls in love." The outsider (Mom, Dad, teacher) may see it as a perversion of love that is merely selfish fulfillment of personal needs. It is certainly immature love. But as teens or young adults continue to move through relationships, they learn about tenderness, the meaning of their feelings, caring for others, and finally, true love. At last they become capable of putting another's needs above their own.

Throughout one's development toward adulthood, the individual is learning mastery of sexual thoughts and feelings. Restraint is learned or sought after and critical assumptions are made about one's ability to have a sexual relationship. Unfortunately, many people attempt to develop control and restraint in unhealthy ways or determine that restraints are unnecessary.[1]

Learning continues within marriage. Most couples find that their sexual relationship changes over the years. Some are grateful that sexual intimacy has emerged from the awkward first attempts. Others mourn the passing of their early, more spontaneous sex life. Those who are wise continue to learn about their changing sexual needs and adapt it within a loving and accepting relationship.

Without a doubt, people have a need to learn about their sexuality until their dying day. Sexuality is an ever-present reality in any person's life. Keeping one's sexual relationships enjoyable takes considerable knowledge, the ability to communicate well, and an acceptance of one's self that is based on true personal worth in Christ.

What does this imply for Christians? Should we be content that such an important aspect of life—one with tremendous repercussions for our development as healthy creatures of the good Creator—be dependent on hearsay, distorted cultural images, and a one-shot birds and bees talk at age thirteen? A responsible ethic of sex results from a well developed plan— one that reflects the understanding that learning about sex must grow and mature over a lifetime.

I am afraid, and this is too demanding a task for me or for the church. There is well-founded fear that one's interest and openness in discussing matters of sex will be misconstrued. I remember being asked to give a presentation to the parents of a group of Camp Fire Girls only to have an objection raised from someone simply because I was both qualified and eager to do so. "Surely we don't want her influence; she even teaches a class in Human Sexual Development!"

One must be eager and willing to broach the hard topics head-on. And one must be "credible." I *work* at being credible, not because people perceive me as suspect, but because often it takes "work" and careful planning to put people at ease. People are less likely to attack or discredit me if I offer a clear presentation of how sex fits into God's plan for His creatures and why He calls on us to put it in proper balance with other aspects of life. In this day and age we can consider it a gift if we are able to put forward a lucid, acceptable message of Christian sexuality without also stirring up antagonism and fear.

Some pastors, elders, and counselors hesitate to deal with

the intimate details of a couple's or an individual's sexual concerns out of fear they will later be embarrassed in trying to maintain a casual relationship with the person or persons involved. If one knows, for example, that the most senior elder no longer has a sexual relationship with his wife, perhaps this knowledge will be a barrier in having a comfortable relationship with him. This fear is well-founded only among those who themselves lack a comfort level with sexuality. Besides, in other areas, leaders handle "delicate" situations with people all the time. They may disagree with a lay leader over a financial issue and still provide comfort and support in a personal crisis.

Sex is an emotionally loaded issue. Our own motives and sexuality must be intelligently understood before we dare step into the arena of other people's problems. Few people are comfortable with the self-examination that is required to understand ourselves as the sexual persons we happen to be. This leads us to our next concern.

Sex is too complex an issue for churches and church leaders to be concerned about. There are so many demanding problems for the pastor, lay leader, counselor, and teacher to deal with: poverty, nuclear war, hunger, the church budget, finding a new youth leader, Mrs. Brown's grief. All demand attention. Sexuality is also a problem, but it is more complicated and less subject to being affected by the intervention of Christians in ministry. So why invest so much time and energy in something that will not be changed anyway? Or so people say.

Many leaders are reluctant to deal with sexual issues— even if only to refer someone to an appropriate authority—out of reluctance to face areas of misinformation and confusion in their own lives. The Bible reminds us of our propensity to stay stuck rather than trust our ability to handle new and potentially better ways of coping. It even offers a solution in Romans 12:2: "Do not conform any longer to the pattern of this world, but be transformed by the renewing of your mind." Renewing the mind includes taking a look at our own sexual mindset and deciding to make it conform to God's will.

Christians who hesitate to lead the church into a more active program of learning and teaching about sexuality often fear what they, or someone else, might uncover. Will they be found so perverted and awful the Lord will never allow them to continue in leadership? This fear ignores the truth that the Lord does not expect perfection, simply progress. It is not that they think sexual issues are too complex to understand, but rather the complexity of sexuality in their own lives is a bit unnerving.

I do not advise anyone who has not examined his or her own sexual attitudes to try to help someone else with a sexual problem. This does not mean that a helper must have every aspect of his or her sexual life together to be effective. Many times it is a counselor's personal experience that provides the empathy and insight to deal with a problem effectively. But someone needing help will seldom receive it from a person who is ambivalent about his or her sexual integrity. People who fail to observe this guideline often make a problem worse by failing to separate their personal concerns from their clients'. They enhance the possibility of mistaking feelings of counter-transference for "love" and inflating their sagging ego by involvement with a person seeking help. Such irresponsibility can never be condoned morally or in any way construed as a loving or helpful act. It is always wrong. People set themselves up for such involvements when they ignore their responsibility to act in the best interest of the person they are to be helping.

There is no denying that sexuality is a complex issue, but the complexity is no excuse for abandoning responsibility to understand it and lead others into an understanding as well. Nor is it an excuse to leave those who are hurting unattended.

No one has been trained for this. With few exceptions none of us has had good sex education modeled for us. Few married couples communicate well about sex, so it is not surprising that speaking about it with anyone is difficult. Our formal training has avoided sex and our informal training has left us with questions, distortions, and misinformation. So if you decide to begin providing guidance for Christian people on sexuality, you may well be the first on your block or in your town.

It is true that not many people have been trained for the task of informing and guiding others in their sexual development. Even physicians, to whom many will take their most intimate problems, are severely hampered in their ability to help people by their lack of awareness and knowledge. My husband's medical school was the first to offer a class on sexuality. Unfortunately, it dealt chiefly with baboon masturbation, and, so far, he has been unable to use that particular information with the hundreds of women who pass through his obstetrics-gynecology practice. Many schools, including a few Christian ones, now offer such courses. But the majority of people are still ignorant of the vast amount of factual information learned about sex in the last fifteen years.

Christians are particularly hesitant to pick up information and perspectives on sexuality available in the secular market—and with good reason. With few factually correct books in the religious bookstores, Christians appear even less informed than the general public. (The sex manuals by the Wheats and the Penners, listed in the bibliography, are notable exceptions.)

In God's providence, the picture is beginning to change. While few people have been trained to provide Christians with a perspective on sexuality and to deal with sexual problems, many people are beginning to see the need and to respond. Christian colleges are offering courses on human sexuality and some churches are giving attention to the educational needs of the members of the congregation.

Learning the way people function sexually is easy—it simply requires that a person be willing to accept the fact that sexual functioning is both a natural and a proper aspect of human life. I hope this book will make its readers more comfortable with that truth. It is only natural to feel better about teaching about sex or encouraging others to, when you know you are well-informed as to the way God actually made His creatures and that you accept as valid one of the functions of His having made mankind as both male and female.

WHAT MUST THE CHURCH DO?

There is an urgency to the message that calls the Christian community to take responsibility. Christians look increasingly to TV, peers, and information in our society for clues to living their sexual lives. They are aware of no other choices. The result is increased divorce, infidelity, casual sex, unwed pregnancy, and deviant sexual behavior. Change will not come about by people wishing it were different. For Christians the change will come with a realistic, lucid understanding of the reason they are the sexual beings they are.

In society as a whole, those who have taken the opportunity for free dialogue about sex have less distorted information than those in previous generations. Accurate knowledge is a necessary base for any positive change. If Christians could build on such a base themselves, they could expect to see positive changes in the behavior of Christian people. Knowledge about sexuality is not so likely to contribute to immorality as lack of knowledge.

The arguments against the church providing leadership in the area of sexuality are flimsy when compared with the demands that are placed upon the church for guiding, directing, and caring for the lives of the people of God. Sex is a part of life that can be seriously misused; but it need not be the source of human destruction and pain. So the church is presented with the challenge of risking some discomfort and criticism in order to recover her abandoned responsibility. Yes, it is a great risk. It is complex and most everyone feels inadequate for the task. But there are no viable alternatives.

Chapter Four

LEADING THE WAY
The Leader's Responsibility
for a Christian Sexuality

Demonstrating a comfort level is undoubtedly the most significant thing church leaders can do to set the tone for communication about sex. If those who teach and lead and counsel avoid dealing directly with sexuality, the flock will too. I often hear parents declare how open they will be if their child ever asks about sex. "My Johnny is just not interested in such things!" or "My Mary told me she wasn't into that stuff." Mary and Johnny are quite willing to accommodate their parents' discomfort. And so is a congregation.

If church leaders think my call for them to take leadership in such a controversial area lacks sensitivity, let me reiterate my empathy for the ticklish position shared by people in Christian service. If one takes the risk to confront the ignorance and fear that many people have about sexuality and sexual issues, he or she may experience opposition, ostracism, and, possibly, loss of a job or a position. At best there is tension and awkwardness. An old saying advises those of us facing such challenging tasks, "Even a turtle doesn't move ahead unless he sticks his neck out!"

One year my son went to camp for five weeks. Until then, I had not thought of myself as a protective mother. But having been put to the test, I must admit that I was not ready to release him. The same holds true for our sexual attitudes and value systems. Until they are tested we will not be aware of the areas of comfort and discomfort, of maturity and immaturity, in us.

Obviously, church leaders may be as troubled as any other group of people about sexuality. Few of us have grown up in families, religious communities, or cultural contexts in which a positive approach to sexual formation has taken place. Leaders need to appreciate how well equipped they are to lead others in developing a healthy approach to sexuality.

Dean Kliewer, Ph.D., a practicing psychologist and consultant, has developed a scale by which sexual maturity might be measured, in a paper, "Sexual Growth for the Servant of God."[1] Growth can be said to have occurred by measuring positive changes in three areas: overt behavior, attitude/thinking, and response to feelings. I have adapted his scale for the purposes of this book to allow the reader to evaluate his or her own development toward maturity in sexual matters.

SEXUAL MATURITY SELF-EVALUATION

A = ALWAYS   U = USUALLY   S = SELDOM   N = NEVER
Circle one response per question.

Sexual Maturity and Behavior

A U S N   1. I keep my word by meeting and fulfilling the commitments I have made as a sexual person.

A U S N   2. I recognize my vulnerabilities and put limits on myself.

A U S N   3. I am sensitive and respect what others I love value.

A U S N   4. Others see wisdom in my behavior.

A U S N   5. My sexual behavior is moderate, avoiding extremes, excesses, or obsessions.

Sexual Maturity and Attitudes

A U S N   1. I know myself as a person responsible to God and maintain this awareness as I interact with others.

A U S N   2. I am open to learning from others about sexuality because I realize I have much to learn.

A U S N   3. I know and accept my weaknesses and imperfections.

A U S N   4. I avoid using stereotypes and making quick judgments about other people.

A U S N   5. I anticipate what effect my words will have on others and try to think before I speak.

A U S N   6. I try not to presume that my attitudes, interpretations, and personal values are always right.

A U S N   7. I demonstrate my willingness to serve by not insisting on my way sexually.

Sexual Maturity and Response to Feelings

A U S N   1. I am able to trust those close to me.

A U S N   2. I demonstrate my care and concern for myself and my care and concern for other people.

A U S N   3. I acknowledge and welcome my feelings and consider them an authentic part of me.

A U S N   4. I need not be defensive and invulnerable; I feel especially safe with my sexual partner.

A U S N   5. I maintain the ability to play and be open to pleasure and enjoyment in sex.

A U S N   6. I am open to experiencing a full range of emotions and am willing to express them.

A U S N   7. I do not allow anger and resentment to accumulate and be buried inside.

A U S N   8. I am aware of the unresolved issues of my past and work at using them in a healthy way.

If you responded to any items with "seldom" or "never," these are the issues that need more reflection and work. You probably recognize that most of these measures of maturity apply to many other aspects of life, and well they should. Sex is a part of life and as such falls under the same measures of maturity as the others.

Although we could comment on the significance of each "never," most are self-evident. A few warrant further attention, however. For example, under "Sexual Maturity and Behavior," question 1 speaks of keeping commitments. Maturity is probably judged more accurately from this behavior than anything else on the list. Even though failure to act in a mature way sexually is easily hidden from the view of others, we can never justify breaking a covenant with another person or with God Himself. Regrettably we live in a time when even Christians of great influence justify leaving their spouses on the basis of some of the most trivial excuses. They do this rather than accept responsibility for having broken a covenant.

Question 5 in the same section refers to extremes. We can become so fearful of sexual sin that we turn away from even healthy and normal relationships. Some people become obsessed with a particular aspect of sexual sin and see its manifestation everywhere they turn. Their balance is lost in an effort to "save" the sexual sinner (potentially everyone but themselves). It is interesting to look into the histories of men who crusaded to redeem prostitutes; they often turned out to be the ones who needed saving.[2]

In the second section of the self-evaluation, dealing with attitudes, particular attention should be given to questions 1 and 2. Christians are called to be mature and responsible according to the revealed truth of God. To act responsibly we must have an understanding of the one whom we serve as well as ourselves. If, for example, pastors, lay leaders, or counselors have never examined their feelings of sexual inadequacy, fears of aging, or the misguided belief that they are acceptable only if someone approves of them, then life circumstances can make them vulnerable. If they do not grasp the significance of that, they may take advantage of or mislead another because of their own misdirected needs.

As for question 2, it is a major teaching of sex therapy that people realize and put into practice the idea that they are the world's authority on their own sexual needs and feelings. Sex education cannot be reduced to dictating to others what they are to feel and how they are to experience their individual sexuality. It involves both self-discovery and learning from others. Being open to the reality that God made each of us in beautifully individual ways is a sign of maturity.

Receptivity to learning counters the tendency of people to transfer their experiences with one person to another. The sexual relationship of any couple is unique to the two of them and should never be contaminated by leftovers from previous marriages or experiences.

Sometimes contamination comes not from direct experience, but from romanticized notions of what love should be like. Misinformation and mythical romantic novels, movies, soap operas, and television dramas contribute heavily to unrealistic expectations of marital sexuality. Anyone who has been happily married any length of time would surely emphasize the necessity of keeping a learning attitude throughout marriage, for healthy sex is not static but a continuously revitalizing dynamic.

In the last part of the self-evaluation (regarding feelings), question 3 is by far the most important. In sexuality, denial of feelings can leave us convinced of our "asexuality." Sex for the Christian is never meant to be sex with a body, but sex with *a person* and a body. To perform sex devoid of feeling (which is not even a possibility for many people) is a perversion.

There are two major reasons people block feelings about sex: fear of losing control, and psychological blocks in the relationship. As long as the myth is perpetuated that feelings are inherently evil and should be deemphasized, the ability to choose to act on them in a positive and responsible way is limited. Feelings never go away as a result of refusing to acknowledge them. They simply lie in wait for a crack in the armor. Once loose they spew forth wildly with great potential danger, having been unexpected and unplanned for.

The ability of a person to express sexuality in a mutually satisfying way is dependent on his or her having resolved issues from which emotions have been blocked and/or having released any excess anger. The inability of the body to respond sexually while harboring anger and other tension-producing emotions will be discussed in later chapters.

SEXUAL (RE)EDUCATION OF THE FLOCK

Although many ministers may neglect to offer couples sexual counseling, few fail to give practical guidelines for living out some aspect of sexual ethics. Most preachers preach on marriage and family living and, in the process, attempt to offer some guidelines for sexual behavior.

A formal or informal program of sex education within the church is not simply dependent upon "official" words being spoken from the pulpit so much as the attitudes and actions of church leaders in situations where sexual issues are being modeled or discussed. I know it is trite, but it is also true: actions speak louder than words. Our comfort level and attitudes are reflected in the manner in which we treat our spouses and other members of the opposite sex. The openness and willingness with which a leader provides counseling and teaching on problems of sexuality gives clues to the congregation and other church staff as to whether it is safe to broach sexual issues with that person.

Church leaders typically choose instead to ignore sexual problems and needs until some instance of sexual immorality forces them to deal with them. Picking up the pieces is not an adequate teaching device. It is much more satisfying to help people learn to live victoriously with their sexual nature.

The message that it is valid to talk and learn about sex comes through when church leaders practice an open, nonjudgmental attitude that honestly faces the reality of sexual struggles instead of pretending they do not exist. People then begin to learn that communication about sex between men and women is approved and that much can be learned when they allow themselves to share wisdom, problems, questions, and experiences across sexual and generational boundaries.

Many people assume that sex education is the exclusive responsibility of home and family. Research done in response to conflict over sex education in schools suggests that sex education in the home is simply an ideal that has very few supporters in practice. Parents do not teach their children; they just *think* they do. They often convey misinformation or an unbalanced picture. They simply do not know how to do better. They need help. They need guidance. They need motivation. They need good models. They need reinforcement.

Because sexuality is so deeply bound up in the task of learning to live a godly life, there is no more appropriate institution to help children learn the way of Jesus Christ as it applies to their sexual being. Christians need healthy Christian instruction to direct their growth. The church offers a variety of formats that can be appropriately used. In addition to sermons and classes, speakers can be brought in from outside, videos discussed, or most effectively, a task force of members can work together on a presentation that is unique to the church's needs. Even the most reluctant person has trouble objecting when fellow church members have followed a well-outlined procedure: (1) establishing a need, (2) developing support on many levels, (3) organizing an agenda consisting of well-conceived objectives, and (4) building in an evaluation process. Using such a task force of laypeople is one of the safest ways to present potentially controversial material. It ensures sensitivity to the needs of the unique church situation and to those who need special reassurance. It is accountable to the leaders of the church.

Official programs are not enough. The congregation must catch the spirit of mutual concern for one another, including the concern for growth in understanding and developing as sexually defined creatures of God. Helping each other develop maturity in all aspects of life is a goal of the Christian life that most congregations want to see being practiced by the members. In the matter of sexual self-understanding, people do not always need experts as much as they need willing and sympathetic friends to talk with. By encouraging such an attitude among its members, a church begins to focus on problems not as tragedies, but as opportunities for growth and development of the members as sexual beings who are capable of glorifying God.

Churches can accomplish much merely by approval and recommendation of good books on sex and sexuality.[3] We can be grateful that Christian sex books are appearing on the shelves despite the fact that many are rather simplistic in their approach. Often these books fail to emphasize the importance of discussing sex together or the healing power of prayer and praise. Readers need to appreciate the fact that although the typical book does not suggest it, couples often benefit from talking with others, including professionals.

Books help us to begin the thinking, understanding, and

attitude-changing process. But a point comes in that process when talking with others is necessary. Although sex is not the end-all of a relationship, problems with it often reflect our basic feelings of masculinity or femininity. Such feelings cloud the question and make it difficult for the partners involved to resolve troublesome issues alone.[4]

TO DO OR NOT TO DO:
SEXUAL COUNSELING IN THE CHURCH

There is nothing in the Bible that prescribes a psychologist's office, once-a-week therapy, or a lifetime of analysis. But there is plenty that affirms our obligation to come to the aid of one another.

"Love one another. As I have loved you, so you must love one another" (John 13:34).

Praise be to the God and Father of our Lord Jesus Christ, the Father of compassion and the God of all comfort, who comforts us in all our troubles, so that we can comfort those in any trouble with the comfort we ourselves have received from God (2 Cor. 1:3–4).

Get rid of all bitterness, rage and anger, brawling and slander, along with every form of malice. Be kind and compassionate to one another, forgiving each other, just as in Christ God forgave you (Eph. 4:31–32).

We proclaim him, admonishing and teaching everyone with all wisdom, so that we may present everyone perfect in Christ (Col. 1:28).

Let the word of Christ dwell in you richly as you teach and admonish one another with all wisdom (Col. 3:16).

The purpose of counseling is revealed in the words "that we may present everyone perfect in Christ." Being perfect in Christ is not only placing God first, but accepting the fullness of the life He offers. The "how" is implied through these and other Scriptures.

Unlike secular counseling, Christian counseling must proclaim and reveal Christ if it is to live up to the claim of being "Christian." Those who are looking for answers or for help should expect to find help for problems among God's servants, the leaders of the church. Their job is to ensure that growth and change are pleasing to God and that God's people are taught, admonished, counseled, and guided with compassion and care.

The ultimate responsibility for guidance may lie with the appointed leaders of the church, but that does not preclude their judicious use of others in the church—especially lay counselors. Paul assures us in Romans 15:14, "I myself am convinced, my brothers, that you yourselves are full of goodness, complete in knowledge and competent to instruct one another." He echoes this belief in Colossians 3:16.

One of the challenges that church leaders face in introducing the church to the correct message of sexuality is dealing with their own areas of blindness or short-sightedness. It is easy to see why and how others have problems, but far more difficult for individuals to deal head-on with their own. A leader's emotional maturity concerning sex is on exhibit as he or she interacts with family members, church members, and others in the community. Once the leaders have made peace with themselves as sexual persons, they are better able to intervene in people's lives as no other person or institution can. The respect that most people have for pastors, elders, and counselors provides a basis for them to offer tremendous leadership to God's people in sexual matters if they are open to modeling, teaching, and counseling an unambivalent message.

PART TWO

DISCOVERING THE REALITY

One often hears complaints that sexologists have reduced the mystery of sex to mere mechanical stimulation of the genitals. Indeed, the mystery of sex cannot be discovered merely by understanding the techniques of human sexual functioning. The mystery is to be found behind, above, and beyond the reality of the mechanisms of sexual response.

The truth about sex is that it has the potential for unlocking and revealing great mysteries of life even as it comes to expression in hesitancy, anxiety, sweat, odor, embrace, movement, and so many other "earthy" and "bodily" realities. The man and the woman were made to be naked and unashamed. In actuality, because men and women have misunderstood both the mystery and the reality of sex, they often find their sexual lives falling far short of the promise. One reason is that they either do not understand nor easily accept sex to be an earthy, bodily function governed by natural bodily processes. This part, "Discovering the Reality," deals with the manner in which God made men and women to respond to one another as sexual creatures, and the most common factors that interfere with that response.

Chapter Five

THE GLORY OF GOD'S DESIGN
Normal Patterns of Sexual Functioning

"For everything God created is good, and nothing is to be rejected if it is received with thanksgiving, because it is consecrated by the word of God and prayer" (1 Tim. 4:4–5).

This chapter and the next will provide new information for some readers and review for many others. Before we can properly understand the problems couples may have in their sexual relationship, we must be certain that we have a working model of normal sexual functioning and the common factors that affect one's ability to respond sexually as intended.

SEEKING THE NORM

In Bali, women take the initiative in sex while men are passive. Among the Hopi, masturbating a child to soothe and relax it is an accepted practice. Some African tribes encourage women to manipulate themselves from childhood to ensure pendulous and, from their point of view, especially lovely genitalia. Asking what is "normal" sexual practice makes for a complicated discussion.

Obviously many sexual patterns are culturally influenced. A particular practice will gain acceptability on the basis of what an individual has grown up with. Consequently most discussions center not on what is universally "normal," but on what is the norm of one's particular culture and community. Those who risk stepping outside the cultural norm may indeed feel "abnormal." Even so, in a given population there is as great a variation among people and their individual sexual expressions as there is among people and their various abilities in math. Too narrow a concept of normality causes unnecessary pain and unrealistic expectations.

In the minds of most people, "normal" equals moral and "abnormal" equals immoral. This is not necessarily valid, and one must be careful not to confuse the categories. It is true that morality is always tied up with sexuality; no culture is devoid of moral standards in sexual relations. Even among the most liberal, such as the Turu of Tanzania where extramarital sex is built into the economic system, there are rules as to how the adultery "game" is to be played. Discovery by the husband is essential so that he may grant permission and collect his financial compensation.[1] Moreover, no known society is without regulations that govern incest of one form or another. The most nearly universal prohibition is mother-son.

Variations in assumptions and expectations about sexuality help to create variations in sexual behavior. The Chinese and Indians have always viewed the female as highly sexed and have trained them to be responsive and assertive partners. Western culture has portrayed the female as the passive sex. It is not surprising that American women believe and act as if they are not as captivated by sex as their men. The frequency of sexual relations varies from expectations of several times a night among certain Polynesian tribes to total shutdown of female feeling, communication, and information about sex among those in an isolated Irish community.[2]

Despite cultural variations in sexual practices, there are many commonalities. Restrictions are more severe for the female than the male. All societies acknowledge a sexual drive that becomes more active as puberty is reached. No matter what the philosophy for the young, eventually heterosexual coitus becomes the most common sexual expression. And everyone, regardless of race, culture, or socioeconomic standing, functions the same physiologically.

THE SEXUAL RESPONSE CYCLE

Until Masters and Johnson there was considerable guessing and very little fact as to how male and female bodies actually respond to sexual stimulation. A major contribution of their work was the discovery that the mechanism of response is the same for all people and that the means of stimulation does not change the way the body reacts. There are four common phases of sexual response for men and women: excitement, plateau, orgasm, and resolution. Men have an additional stage experienced between orgasm and resolution known as the refractory period.

The Excitement Phase

The excitement phase often begins for men and women without their being aware they are receiving sexually arousing stimuli. The male may then become conscious of a swelling penis; the female less obviously detects a moist vagina. At this point what has been an involuntary response to something they have learned to connect with sexuality becomes voluntary as they sort out the circumstances and determine whether they will allow the body to continue to respond or squelch any further reaction.

The first response is a reflex mechanism (independent of the brain) that links genital organs and adjoining areas. What is experienced subjectively as so pleasurable is merely the result of vasocongestion and myotonia. The swelling of tissues by blood (vasocongestion) and muscle contraction (myotonia) sound anything but sexy or dangerous! But that's how it all begins.

Nerve fibers connected to the walls of arteries cause them to relax or contract. The parasympathetic system sends that unsolicited message to the blood vessels to expand and allow blood into the area and, in the case of the female, to release serous fluid (the lubricating fluid) through the walls of the vagina. The same system sends a chemical to the brain that registers a sensation of pleasure.

As the possibility of privacy and opportunity presents

itself, the changes of the excitement stage intensify. There is a general rise in body tension, the heartbeat quickens, blood pressure goes up, and vasocongestion results in increased swelling of genital tissues. Pressure in the swollen areas sends off pleasurable impulses to the brain. Externally there may be a sex flush on the abdomen or shoulders and definite breast swelling in premenopausal females who have not nursed extensively. Nipple erection can occur both in males and females, and sweating—particularly on the hands and feet— can also be observed.

The Plateau

As excitement reaches a peak, the second phase of sexual response is reached: the plateau. Both male and female desire intromission as they individually reach this stage. The majority of coital time is spent in the plateau phase. Despite the term *plateau*, it is anything but, for excitement levels peak and ebb, maintaining the delicate balance between high arousal levels and the release of orgasm. Fluctuations of sensation are normal and, unless one worries about them, they cause no problem. A self-fulfilling prophecy of failure can be set up when there is fear whether one can again achieve a high level of response.

The vagina, which opened up in the excitement phase, contracts in the plateau, causing the gripping feeling felt by the penis. This clamping and resultant expansion of the penis followed by increased friction stimulates more gripping, which sets in motion a reciprocal heightening of pleasure. Although the vagina does not have the mobility of the penis, it does have the vitality.

All kinds of internal changes begin to occur as the excitement phase moves toward the plateau. Within the female these changes often increase the possibility of pregnancy. The uterus rises, pulling the upper portion of the vagina in such a way that it becomes open, or "tents." The vagina itself, normally a collapsed tube, increases about an inch in length and expands two to three times its normal width.

The male testes enlarge with increasing vasocongestion. The tightening muscles around the vas deferens draw the testicles upward. The urethra is prepared for the passage of seminal fluid by the Cowper's gland's release of a secretion that modifies the pH. Sometimes called the "distillate of love," this pre-ejaculate fluid often contains sperm, rendering withdrawal a poor method of birth control.

The penis, perfectly designed for expansion from increased blood flow, does not depend on bone, cartilage, or any other rigid material to become firm. Erection is due solely to blood flowing into three spongy cavities, each surrounded by a fascial capsule and collectively enclosed in a fibrous coat. The muscular attachment at the pubis and ischium enable a man to move his penis to a limited degree. With no muscle or bone to depend on, a firm erection depends on a physical and mental mindset that allows the parasympathetic nervous system to do its job. This is why a man may lose his erection amid mental or physical distractions.

The Orgasm Stage

The closer the male gets to ejaculation, the higher the elevation of the testes. (Since the left testicle is lower on 85 percent of all men, it is frequently pulled up last.) Sure signs of impending orgasm are testicular elevation, the expansion of the penis in diameter—especially the glans—and often a color change around the coronal ring.

Ejaculatory inevitability is present as seminal fluid is collecting in the prostatic urethra, after which ejaculation occurs through the urethra and urethra meatus. Once the level of excitement has reached this point, even a major interruption will not keep the man from orgasm.

The internal sphincter to the bladder closes as the ejaculate passes. Although in some cultures men are trained to allow retrograde ejaculation to occur as a means of birth control, most of the time it is not desirous, since much of the subjective feeling of orgasm for a man is related to the sensation of the ejaculate going through the urethra. It is generally true that second ejaculations are not as satisfying as the first, for they lack the volume of seminal fluid. Prostate infections, certain illnesses, and the side effects of drugs such as tranquilizers are all known to result in semen flowing into the bladder.

For the female, orgasm is heralded by a change in color of the minor lips. She has no warning of orgasm as her male partner does, and she can have her orgasmic response interrupted at any point. As with the male penis, the size of the clitoris has no bearing on ability to respond. Since male sensuality is so heavily focused on the shaft of the penis and the glans, it is hard for men to conceptualize that the same is not true for the woman's clitoris.

It is rare for a woman to masturbate by touching the clitoris glans directly; she may stimulate the shaft, but more commonly will use a circular motion over the mons. As excitement increases and the orgasmic stage is reached, the clitoris protectively retreats under its hood. No position of intercourse directly stimulates the clitoris, although clitoral response may occur most rapidly and with greater intensity with the female astride the male.

As important as the clitoris is to female satisfaction, the orgasmic platform (the lower third of the vagina) is as sensitive as the penis shaft and is responsible for much of what is experienced as orgasm. The clitoris, labia minora, and orgasmic platform all respond simultaneously. Swelling and contractions in these areas give the sensation of pleasure. The norm is five to eight contractions; a very intense orgasm might be eight to twelve. Childbearing enhances the possibility of pleasure by increasing the venous capacity of the pelvic area.

The grabbing and contracting of the vagina can hardly be considered "passive." It is accompanied by a feeling of warmth spreading from the pelvic area that is usually coupled with intense clitoral-pelvis awareness. The uterus increases in size and contracts, as do the anal sphincter muscles. A subsequent orgasm, unlike that of the male, may be more intense. A woman can continue to increase her satisfaction.

Although the majority of women have a clitoral focus of sensation, there are some who subjectively or physiologically experience most of their sensations in the uterus or, more frequently, within the vagina. Most often this feeling is in an area about two inches up in the anterior wall that is called the

"Grafenberg" or "G" spot. Women who are aware of this or other sensitive areas vary in their opinions of the part it plays in their overall pleasure. The lack of uniform opinion warns us not to assume that all women must or will experience similar sensations in similar locations. Quite simply, there are variations among female sensation patterns.

There are also great variations in orgasmic patterns among females, and even within the individual. This is frequently a source of frustration for men, whose patterns of response are much more predictable and physically based. A cookbook approach might work for them, but never for a woman. She discovers to her husband's dismay that what was sensational the previous night is a turnoff the next.

Judith Bardwick describes the patterns of female orgasm that I have seen most frequently in my own practice. She emphasizes that "the combination of infrequent masturbation, an unerotic vagina, the absence of significant genital stimulation until middle or late adolescence, and the inhibitions resulting from the 'good-girl' syndrome combine to make arousability slower and customary levels of arousal lower."[3]

The result is that young and relatively inexperienced girls frequently describe their orgasms as "tingly." They have reached the plateau stage and have some minor surges toward the orgasmic level. They might be said to be having a "minor" orgasm characterized by a nice feeling and no frustration of having been left unfulfilled. Gratification results equally from having been loved as much as from the physical sensations.

As experience increases and the woman finds herself in a trusting, loving relationship, an intermediate level of orgasm occurs wherein more intense bodily responses are achieved. There may be several orgasms. A majority of women learn to respond at this level. Affiliative and affectional considerations are still important in evaluating the experience.

Lastly, there are women whose response most closely parallels what we find in men. They reach a high plateau stage, achieve a maximum type of orgasm, and experience a rapid resolution that returns them to a level below the excitement phase. Such women may be skilled at controlling their arousal level, enabling them to have several minor orgasms before the final one. Their climax results in being lost to anything but their physical response. They are able to focus intently on pure sensation. Failure to experience release of sexual tension leaves them feeling frustrated and uncomfortable. Women who conform to this pattern are few and far between. Yet this pattern is frequently the one modeled in the media, books, and sex clinics as characteristic of the responsive female.

For men and women, the culmination of the plateau phase and orgasm results in muscles becoming taut from head to toe. Pelvic thrusts are characteristic of us as mammals. Our perception of pain is reduced because the more powerful the orgasm, the greater the loss of sensual acuity. The heart rate elevates from between 60 and 80 beats per minute to between 100 and 160.

The panting, contortions, and grunts that oddly accompany what is perceived as pleasure are due to involuntary contraction of muscles, including respiratory muscles. There is an increase of saliva, so that the man and woman literally drool over one another.

As Masters and Johnson have demonstrated, whatever the source of stimulation, the bodily responses we have been describing are, with consideration of individual differences, predictable. The most intense sensations occur with self-stimulation, then partner stimulation, and lastly through intercourse. The rhythmic contractions and sensations of release last no more than three to ten seconds, occurring about eight-tenths of a second apart. Rectal contractions are weaker but coordinated.

Both men and women are able to reach orgasm within two to four minutes. But it is a well-established fact that two to four minutes of intercourse will result in the majority of women failing to reach orgasm. The delay is not the fault of physiology, but is due to psychological, social, and mechanical differences found within the act of intercourse.

The Refractory Stage

Although some women are capable of multiple orgasms (it is not known if all women are), few men have the ability and the potential of increased enjoyment to have one orgasm immediately followed by another. Although we commonly use the term *orgasm* to refer to ejaculation, each has a distinct reference: ejaculation is release of semen, and orgasm is a feeling. As we have already seen, some men are able to control their ejaculate, and others are able to reach notable highs of response that one may or may not call an orgasm, especially with prostate manipulation.

Most men must allow their bodies to rest and return to the excitement level before they will again respond to sexual stimulation. The time elapsed may vary from a few minutes in a young boy to many hours in an older man. Health, level of excitement, and many other factors play a part in the time involved. There is no equivalent period for the female, for she is still physically able to respond. With an explosive type of orgasm she may feel satiated and will choose to wait before resumption of sexual stimulation.

The Resolution Stage

The time needed for the body to return to a state of nonarousal varies. If excitement has been very high and there has been no release through orgasm, resolution can take a long time. It seems to occur more quickly in men than women. Desire for stimulation may continue or may be irritating, depending on the individual and the circumstances.

AGING AND SEXUAL RESPONSE

There is no question that bodies become less efficient as wear and tear take their toll. People must be realistic about this fact and learn to focus on the positive opportunities that such changes may bring. There is no reason for healthy older folks to give up the intimacy, pleasure, and release of sexual energy. Sexual fulfillment is not only a possibility, but also a healthy practice among many older people today.

The one criterion that determines whether people will be sexually active in the later years is the consistency of sexual activity throughout their lives. Body responses are less intense and consistent with age, but the same mechanisms are at work that have always been at work. Physical limitations are less a factor in slowing down sexually than are monotony, preoccupation with something else, and the acceptance of what has been an unsatisfactory sex life.

Women find the thickness and elasticity of the vagina is reduced. Lubrication is lessened. The potential pain that might result from such changes is eliminated when extra lubrication is used or vaginal creams containing estrogen are applied. Older women with painful uterine contractions can be helped with a combination of estrogen and progesterone taken orally. Although the major lips lose fat and no longer respond to vasocongestion and the minor lips continue to change color until the eighties, clitoral response remains the same.

With aging, the male desires sex less often (though we are still talking about one to two times a week typically). He takes longer to become erect, but may be able to remain erect longer than in his youth. He will never have as firm an erection as he did at seventeen; in fact, he will not become fully erect until right before ejaculation. He requires direct stimulation for a longer period before ejaculation simply because his body needs it and not necessarily because he has lost interest in sex.

Orgasms with the male, as with the female, are experienced with slightly less intensity and fewer contractions. Men may be less aware of ejaculatory inevitability or experience it as prolonged. Sometimes there is seepage instead of an ejaculatory force. Male scrotal changes may not occur, testicles do not increase in size, and testicular elevation is reduced.

Rather than these changes inevitably resulting in less satisfaction, many couples find that the release from fear of pregnancy and the extra time and flexibility of schedules make for increased pleasure. Happy, well-adjusted couples make the adaptations with little or no interruption of their sex life.

THE AMERICAN WAY OF LOVE

Cross-cultural and other anthropological studies have been conducted for many years, but sexual research per se was unheard of until well into the twentieth century. Despite contributions from Richard von Krafft-Ebing (*Psychopathia Sex-*

ualis, 1886), Sigmund Freud (*Three Essays on the Theory of Female Sexuality*, 1905), Havelock Ellis (*Studies in the Psychology of Sex*, 1936), and others, our primary sources of information regarding the sexual practices of Americans are Alfred C. Kinsey's work in the late 1940s (*Sexual Behavior in the Human Male*, 1948, and *Sexual Behavior in the Human Female*, 1953), and the Playboy Foundation Study (M. Hunt, *Sexual Behavior in the 1970's*, 1974).

The Kinsey Report had a large scale: 16,000 people interviewed in person, 7,000 by Kinsey himself. It is criticized as not offering a random sample, though it sought to include a great variety of people from all over the United States. Another weakness was its dependence on volunteers as subjects. Although dated, the study is about the best we have.

The Playboy survey is claimed to be more representative of the U.S. population, but is much smaller than Kinsey's, with 982 males and 1,044 females responding to a written questionnaire. It raises the usual questions of sample bias and the value of a written questionnaire being able to touch on the complexities of sexuality.

Others making contributions in the field, but not strictly limited to statistics of sexual practices are Margaret Mead and her work on other cultures; Shere Hite, who interviewed 3,000 women on their subjective views of sex and their bodies; and Masters and Johnson, whose emphasis is the physiology of sex. Although many disregard Freud's work on sexuality, he and the psychoanalytically oriented therapists who followed him did bring sex into the open as a topic of discussion.

In comparing the two chief surveys, it appears that over the years there have been some major shifts in marital sexual behavior. The variations reflect different attitudes about women than were prevalent in Kinsey's day. In particular, Americans have decided women not only are capable of enjoying sex but would like to! We are one of the few cultures ever to conceive of women as not being highly sexed.

Frequency

In all age groups today, coitus occurs with greater frequency, and there is more time spent in intercourse and foreplay. In Kinsey's sample, three-fourths of the men ejaculated within two minutes of intromission. Ten minutes is more the average now, with at least fifteen minutes devoted to foreplay. With there being freedom from the concept of sex being for the male's release only, there is also a greater tendency to experiment with different positions and other methods of sexual release such as oral sex.

Positions

There is no one position that is right for every couple or every experience. There are some positions in which the possibility for pregnancy is increased. Some positions, like the female on top, enable greater freedom of movement and are used, at least occasionally, by three-quarters of married couples as compared with one-third in Kinsey's day. Rear-entry positions are used by two out of five couples, but of these the vast majority are practiced in the younger age groups.

After some experimentation partners will generally settle on a favorite position and will tend to use it frequently. Often this is the face-to-face, or "missionary," position. It permits interaction to take place such as kissing, watching the expression of the other partner, and talking, all of which add greatly to the experience. Deeper penetration occurs when the woman's legs are flexed. It is a good position for the female if the male has a weak erection, and it provides the greatest chance of pregnancy. The primary disadvantage is the restricted movement of the female.

The female-on-top position offers the woman the greatest control of movement and consequently the best position for her to achieve orgasm. Some men may find this position threatening, but its use has increased greatly in the last thirty years.

There are many other variations: kneeling, seated, or in the "Roman" tradition, squatting. Side positions eliminate weight problems and allow for shallow penetration, which is sometimes desirable when the woman is pregnant; they also can sustain a very leisurely type of lovemaking and have the advantage of face-to-face interaction.

Rear-entry positions, with few exceptions, have not been

THE GLORY OF GOD'S DESIGN

the standard practice of any culture.⁴ Perhaps the isolation the couple feels is the reason. It is not true that the clitoris would not be stimulated, for just as in other positions, stimulation occurs indirectly through the movement of the mons. The female may find that lying down in a rear-entry position can be restful if she is ill or pregnant. The male may use his hands for backrubs and stimulation of his partner's body.

Intromission

Whatever the position a couple may assume, penetration is sometimes difficult even in a well-lubricated vagina. Any tension or fear may result in an unconscious clamping down of the pubococcygeus muscles, which can render penetration quite painful. The male may have a partial erection, or the position may complicate matters. Any insecurity that manifests itself as lack of cooperation between the partners may preclude the assistance and guidance that makes intromission easy.

External Conditions

Most people prefer privacy and a certain amount of attention given to the environment in order to gain the most from their lovemaking. In this respect humans are not unlike some animals, as many a perplexed zookeeper has discovered when two prized and healthy specimens refuse to cooperate because some nebulous factor found in the wild is missing in the confines of the zoo. Should we be less choosy about our external conditions for sex?

The amount of time spent is not a major consideration for successful lovemaking, nor is the time of day. Most people choose to make love at night, because this is often the most convenient time for getting together. But it may not be the best for being rested and being able to give one's full energy and concentration to the partner.

Surveys tell us that far from being related to genetics, race, physical prowess, or religion, sexual habits are more often affected by our social class and education. In one study, for example, men in a lower socioeconomic setting, as a result of limited education, experienced less masturbation, were more dependent on prostitutes, and had more extramarital affairs and homosexual encounters early in marriage. Higher socioeconomic males masturbated more, had less contact with prostitutes, and were more involved in extramarital affairs or homosexual encounters in their later years.[5]

Women who are educated are more orgasmic and more open to variations of sexual expression than those who are not. What they are exposed to in their social milieu and the learning they derive from it play a vital part in the way they choose to express their sexuality. That is one of the fundamental assumptions of this book.

Men and women, strangely enough, have very different patterns of sexual interest as reflected by sexual outlets. By adolescence men have developed a sexual drive that is almost at its peak, elevating slightly around thirty and declining rather steadily with age. Women, by contrast, experience increasing interest and outlets from fifteen, peak at thirty, and remain there for approximately ten years. Declining interest after forty follows a path similar to that of men. It is curious that the greatest number of extramarital sexual encounters for women occur, not during the ten-year peak, but from forty-one to fifty.[6]

WHAT IS A SUCCESSFUL EXPERIENCE?

Our earlier definitions of successful sex came from old wive's—or possibly, husband's—tales and other hearsay. More recently science has supplied surveys and statistics that suggest what is "normal" and thus "successful" sex. It is worth examining these and the impact of the cultural and social milieu on sexual practices, as well as the commonalities shared, so that we can define for ourselves what constitutes a successful sexual experience. Without question, it is more accurate to speak of "successful" sexual experiences than "normal" ones.

Performance has little to do with being successful. One wonders, then, why there are so many authors, experts, and personalities all extolling the virtues of multi-orgasmic marathons that leave lovers satiated and limp? Frequency, endurance, comfort, time spent, or relief are no sure measures either.

High performance may be a virtue for race cars, but it is not the essential ingredient in a successful sexual relationship.

Successful sex occurs when, in the words of Eric Fuchs, "it is free, mature, creative and integrated."[7] In other words, successful sex occurs when both partners participate because they want to, when their maturity enables them to break down their ego boundaries and allow another in, when they are free to relate in a way that takes sex beyond the mere physical relationship, and finally, when the act does not conflict with the rest of their existence. For Christians this includes lovemaking that takes place within the framework God intended. A successful experience is measured subjectively and emotionally.

On some occasions, hugging one another is a successful sexual experience. At other times, coitus with mutual orgasm is the measure of success. On still other occasions, success may mean the sexual release of one partner with the help but passive sexual involvement of the other. "Successful" sex cannot be reduced to a simple formula that works every time or for everyone. Each encounter has its unique criterion. Success is what meets the physical and emotional needs of the husband and wife at any given time; maximum, mutual gratification is the goal. For the single it is honest acknowledgment of sexual feelings and managing them successfully. Such a definition gives a successful experience a very personal and variable flavor—quite in keeping with the creative and physical differences and needs of each individual.

Chapter Six

UNDERMINING GOD'S DESIGN
Factors That Affect Sexual Functioning

I once asked my husband, a physician, how he narrowed in on a diagnosis. He replied, "When I hear hoofbeats in Redlands (California) I look first for horses. Then, if I find none, I look for zebras." In other words, look for the more obvious causes before you begin looking for the esoteric.

There are many quite common factors that affect normal sexual functioning. Whenever there is a problem, the obvious factors should be considered first. We have a tendency to assume that any hang-up or difficulty with sex is inevitably deeply rooted—probably requiring years of psychotherapy to uncover. This is not true for most people. Granted, there are some serious disorders that cause difficulty in sexual functioning. But often the problems presented to counselors are common and relatively easy to solve.

COMMON PSYCHOLOGICAL AND SOCIAL FACTORS
AFFECTING SEXUAL FUNCTIONING

Many of the following factors may be found in both simple and serious disturbances. The degree determines whether the factor creates a serious dysfunction or a temporary one that requires only minimal intervention.

Communication

Encouraging open discussion and teaching more successful ways of communication should be a high priority for the astute pastor and counselor. If nothing else is accomplished in the counseling, improvement in this regard will be far-reaching. Everyone recognizes the importance of clear communication in all areas of life, but putting it to practice in sexual relations seems impossible for some. Whether they are married or single, sharing needs, feelings, or information enables people to correct misunderstanding and handle sexual desires better.

Sexual needs are so personal and variable that it is impossible for anyone to know what someone else needs unless the person is willing to share. But most people have great difficulty speaking about sex at all, let alone sharing what their personal sexual needs might be. Consider the difficulty many couples have in communicating something as simple as what they want to eat. Reflect on a typical scenario of a wife who wants to go out for a steak dinner, but doesn't want to *say* so:

> SHE: What do you want to do for dinner, Dear? *(The Bible says put his needs first.)*
>
> HE: I don't care. *(I don't know what you want, so I'll play it safe.)*
>
> SHE: *(I wonder if dog food would do?)* Let's go out. *(I'm still okay if I don't tell him it's what I really want.)*
>
> HE: Where would you like to go? *(Ahh, a clue!)*
>
> SHE: I don't care. *(Be submissive. Be submissive. Be submissive.)*
>
> HE: *(I wonder if Bernie's Gym and Eats would really do?)* How about Chinese? *(I'd rather have a steak, but she loves that international stuff.)*
>
> SHE: Oh, great idea! *(Yuck! I had Chinese food for lunch.)*
>
> HE and SHE: *(I wonder why he/she doesn't seem to be enjoying this dinner and night out? He suggested it? She wanted to come? Oh, for a big, juicy steak!)*

The result of this couple's unwillingness to verbalize will be a meal neither one wanted. Sexual scenarios reveal similar disappointment for the same reason: lack of honesty. People think that by withholding the truth they are being respectful and putting the other's needs first. They may also fail to be honest for fear of being shamed for expressing their particular desires. Lastly, they believe that people who "really" love one another always want the same thing and they dare not risk discovering they have differences.

Consider, instead, this version, in which both partners dare to share the truth:

SHE: Hi, Honey, I'm really hungry for a steak tonight and would love to go out.

HE: I'm a little tired, but eating out does sound nice. Any chance I could interest you in seafood?

SHE: I'm really craving a steak, but I do have some nice ones in the freezer. I'll fix them tomorrow, and we could go to "The Beach" tonight.

HE: Great idea!

Did the couple end up this time with something they did not want? In the first incident both sacrificed their desires for the other; in the second, a comfortable compromise was reached. In the first, both lost; in the second, both won.

It is sad that couples have to be reassured that they can risk being honest. Taking responsibility for their feelings and appetites and communicating them to a person who values them should present only minimal risk. Most important, it should increase the chances that they will both get what they want.

Owning and sharing sexual needs is no riskier than sharing anything else. Most people love to cooperate if they know how much something means to a partner, are clear about what is being asked of them, and trust that their personal values and comfort will be considered.

As a counselor I am forever being pleasantly surprised at the compromises and cooperation that eventually come from a seemingly deadlocked position of two people who are at odds but who love one another. Certainly it reflects the power of love and the creativity of the Maker when couples finally share, hear, and accept the reality of their feelings and needs.

Finally, healthy and honest communication releases the husband, in particular, from the impossible expectation of knowing what, when, and how his wife cares to be sexual. When the popular myths are relinquished ("As a man I'm supposed to know everything my woman needs," "If he really loved me, he would know what I need"), the wife is freed to share and the husband is freed to listen.

Imagine the anger people would feel if, upon entering a restaurant, they were told what they were hungry for, how to season their food, and when they were satisfied! Even if the restaurateur had their best interests at heart and was partially right, they would be resentful that he had not acknowledged that they are the only authorities on their appetites.

Refusal to communicate ensures frustration. It is as absurd to let someone else take charge of you sexually as it is to let another tell you what you want to eat. Married people who maintain a conspiracy of silence find behavior they dislike reinforced and repeated because the partners have no way of knowing it is repulsive to them. Single people find themselves in difficulty when they abdicate their power and refuse to acknowledge and communicate their particular needs to be touched or not to be touched. In all such situations, the miscues and resulting misery may build up, leading to expressions of anger, adoption of avoidance techniques, or assumptions that the partner is uncaring or unable ever to meet one's needs.

Low Self-esteem

Low self-esteem affects sexual functioning in two major ways. First, if people feel unworthy, there is a good chance they will deny or fail to acknowledge love and sexual pleasure that do come. A person either discounts the reasons someone professes for caring, or sets up a self-fulfilling prophecy and alienates the other person so that fears of being unlovable are realized. Second, if a person's view of self is low, he or she dare not risk asking for pleasure. To have the request rejected would be too much for an already hurting ego to handle. Again, caught in the vicious circle, such people experience "proof" of their unworthiness as their sex life proves unfulfilling for them and their partners.

Depression

Like stress, the specific effects of depression cannot always be predicted. But there will inevitably be a response. Depression can leave people totally apathetic to sex or can motivate them to seek the comfort they need by increased sexual demands. It is noteworthy that depression is found to accompany most sexual problems. Desire is particularly vulnerable to depression. Lack of desire is found in 61 percent of depressed persons versus 27 percent of nondepressed.[1]

Guilt

Christian therapists are different from most secular counterparts in their willingness to acknowledge that sometimes people deserve to feel guilty. If people have sinned, they must face the immediate and long-term consequences of their acts. It is not their lot, however, to carry the burden of guilt forever, for they have the only sure-fire method of release: confession and God's gracious forgiveness.

Legitimate guilt over sexual matters is obviously associated with adultery, fornication, lustful and obsessive behaviors, refusal to accept the mutuality of marriage, and failure to give one's partner the sexual expression of love that he or she needs.

As if there were not enough real guilt, false guilt over sexual matters abounds. People agonize over whether they should or should not enjoy sex, over being oversexed or undersexed, over a high degree of sensuousness or almost none at all. They worry about their particular idiosyncrasies and personal preferences. The list can go on and on.

It has been stated that people cannot say yes until they can say no. Some parents (and Christians are more susceptible than others) do such a fine job of teaching their children that life is filled with duties and responsibilities that pleasure is precluded. Who has time for such a luxury? Or it may be that sex in marriage is seen as simply another duty, eliminating the possibility of saying no without guilt. Nothing extinguishes the possibility of pleasure faster than not being able to say no when mind, body, or mood has eliminated the appetite. (Remember the definition of successful sex from chapter 5.)

Upbringing

Much of the way individuals relate to one another is dependent on the way in which they were raised. In my previous book, *Parents' Guide to Sex Education*, my goal was to help parents realize that their influence begins from the moment of birth and has as much to do with their overt attitudes and behavior as with their words.

What is not said often speaks as loudly as what is spelled out. It is likely that each reader carries a statement imprinted from youth. There are countless examples:

"All that men ever want is . . . "

"A woman just has to endure."

"Only a prostitute would do that."

"Keep it up and you'll be a slut just like Aunt Lucille."

"Nice girls don't do that."

"Sex is dirty—save it for someone you love." (The irony of this statement never ceases to amuse me!)

"A girl never really means no."

"All women are teases."

"I'd love to come and see you, but your dad just can't bear to see you pregnant."

"You'll never make it to the altar as a virgin."

"You're as cold as your father."

And you can add to this list statements of your own that had great significance in forming your attitudes.

Despite the apparent demise of the family in American society, it is still the place from which the majority of our values come, especially if our parents have made any effort at all to verbalize them.[2] There is no point spending time deriding parents for their poor job, because in most cases they did the best they could with the knowledge they had. The reality is this: people who have been victims of poor sex education must reeducate themselves. Accessible, clear, factual information about sex is a blessing (mixed, perhaps) for this generation of young parents. Having more accurate information, they may, if they recognize God to be the author of sex, be able to bring about responsible changes that we wish had come many generations before.

Education

When people first began seeking help from sex therapists, their presenting problem was often a lack of knowledge. That is not a frequent problem any longer. But how I love it when a client comes in who simply needs some education! It makes for quick and fruitful therapy! Unfortunately most people have secondary problems as a result of their misinformation. The simplicity of an educational solution belies the great amount of pain that a mistaken idea can cause.

My heart breaks for the individual or couple who have suffered long and needlessly because they lacked the courage or opportunity to bring their concerns to someone who could correct them. It is here that the pastor and the Christian counselor can do much good work. No heavy-insight therapy or long-term work is involved, just an open attitude, a little knowledge, and a willingness to intervene.

Fear

Like most fears, sexual fears have as their root cause a lack of information or misinformation. Fear of any sort—of pain, of losing one's separateness, of being deserted, of performance—contributes to the common inability most people have to receive and be naturally aroused by sexual stimuli. Our bodies cannot be relaxed and tense simultaneously. A tense body blocks the natural response cycle from being set in motion or developing fully.

A person—especially a single person—may fear the consequences of any sexual expression and literally become insensitive to the natural feelings of arousal within the body. This fear can carry over to nongenital relationships and can be perceived by another as coldness and aloofness. Later, in the context of marriage, the habit pattern of nonrecognition of feelings results in poor sexual functioning. The ability to feel has simply been blocked.

Sometimes sex is perceived by a person to have tremendous symbolic meaning—so significant that it paralyzes sexual expression. A person will worry that he or she will not measure up, will not perform according to expectations. This anxiety is the primary cause of sexual problems in men:

"Am I the best lover she's had?"

"Will I be better than last time?"

"Can I get (sustain) an erection?"

Painful intercourse can be the result of a tense body, which then adds fear of the pain itself to a never-ending cycle. Pain can be very real when based on past traumas that range from an insensitive doctor's exam, to rape, to unsuccessful or callous coital attempts. (Major physical causes of pain will be discussed in other sections.)

Male-Female Differences

It is unfortunate that people who appreciate their own masculinity or femininity risk being considered sexist. There *are* differences between men and women, and members of both sexes should be able to experience the privilege of being one or the other. It is common for scientists who acknowledge innate differences between the sexes to find their work either ridiculed or ignored—if they have the courage to publicize it. For instance, W. J. Gadpaille, M.D., notes that in the great majority of societies, the female is in charge of child care while raids and aggressive behavior are almost entirely male.[3] Intercourse, even in cultures where women are seen as highly sexed, is typically viewed as a favor that women grant or withhold and that men attempt to gain. Differences such as these may reflect something more than mere cultural conditioning.

Universally men are seen to display more sexual jealousy and possessiveness of their mates than women. They also have a greater need for variety in sexual encounters and for coitus as the culmination of intimacy. Clifford and Joyce Penner point out the tendency of a man who does not have his desire filled to want sex more often. By contrast, when a women is unsatisfied, she tends to lose interest.[4]

Despite the popular speculation that the liberation of women is having an emasculating effect, studies do not bear this out.[5] Female assertiveness does not necessarily result in male impotence, but often fills the man with joy and surprise along with a healthy byproduct of decreased fear and anger. Solomon and Shulamith had the right idea! There is usually more strain with the traditional roles (man active, woman passive), in which expectations to perform according to the stereotypes are high.

Women in counseling more often have subjective complaints about their sexual functioning, whereas men will present physiological concerns. Consequently the typical treatment of a male is usually different in form from that of a woman. Men are usually challenged to develop better control over their sexual response in order to increase confidence, but women are usually encouraged to "let go" and enter more freely into the sexual encounter. Further discussion of how male-female differences cause difficulties in understanding and affect sexual functioning is provided in chapter 8.

Body Rhythms

Unlike most mammals, which mate only in keeping with a limited estrus cycle, humans can mate anytime. One easily concludes that human mating habits have a broader purpose than that of the other animals; otherwise, humans would desire one another only at times when pregnancy could result.

We are all aware of the rhythms of the body when it comes to sleeping and eating. Some people are aware as well of creative times, poor health times, or seasons in which they tend to be depressed. But sexual cycles are noticed only by a few people. There is debate as to the actual existence of sexual cycles. The best evidence of a human sexual cycle is related to the menstrual cycle of the female. Some women find themselves more aroused and desirous of intercourse in mid-cycle. This coincides with hormonal changes that result in ovulation.

First Intercourse

It is a common myth that a couple's first coital experience should feel wonderful and leave them with an ecstatic feeling of elation at being a man or a woman. The truth is, up to one-half of all females and one-quarter of all males find the first experience unpleasant. Of the rest, very few experience the mythical ecstasy.[6]

One's first experience with sexual intercourse has major personal and social ramifications.[7] Because most people sense the life-changing significance of the occasion, they are frequently disappointed when they find the whole experience trivialized by the setting. Many people are simply not prepared for intercourse. They may assume that because they are *capable* of sexual intercourse, they should find an opportunity. Such a decision to engage in intercourse will usually be regretted later in life, even if it is not on the basis of a moral system or value system that requires intercourse to be an aspect of the marriage covenant. Clearly, the individual must have reached a certain stage in psychosocial readiness for intercourse to be the positive experience it is intended to be.

The majority of people choose to have intercourse because they care for another person. A study of college students reported 85 percent of them became involved sexually as a means of giving love, 19 percent were seeking self-esteem, and 5 percent were responding to pressure and role obligations.[8] Another study confirms the high percentage of affectional reasons for engaging in coitus.[9] In this study, three-fourths of the females, but only one-half of the males expected the relationship to be one of commitment.[10]

Setting

We have already observed that certain factors must be present before some animals will mate. People likewise require certain conditions to be present if they are to enjoy the experience of sex. Although most people are not totally aware of what they are, many cite environmental conditions that are important to them. A sliver of light through a window, music, serenity, a pleasing scent, clothing, lights on or off, candles— any of these can affect the ability to respond by enabling a person either to relax or to be distracted. Maximizing the environment for sexual success makes good sense and is a nonthreatening place to begin intervention.

The most commonly shared environmental preference is a desire for privacy. Even in villages where communal houses establish the domestic pattern, sexual intercourse will usually take place indoors, away from prying eyes. Most animals share no such inhibitions. This lends credence again to our unique nature and the richly laden meaning sex holds for humans.

I have counseled people who have had a multitude of sexual problems vanish as a result of something as simple as putting a lock on the bedroom door. Some people mistakenly believe they are not just physically, but also psychologically locking their children out by doing so. Yet it is a greater disservice to children not to be taught that parents require private time together to keep their marriages strong.

Creativity and variety enrich one's sex life. You may have heard the expression, "You get tired of ice cream all the time." As good as your sex life is, a change of place and pace serves as an aphrodisiac. Solomon and Shulamith varied the location of their lovemaking. They also spent considerable time and money making their bedroom a place of beauty and relaxation.

The Big Three: Preoccupation, Boredom, and Fatigue

When Masters and Johnson reported their original research, they listed religion, upbringing, lack of knowledge, illness, stress, and psychological problems as the major factors in sexual dysfunction. Later they added what has become the most prevalent complex of causes: preoccupation, boredom, and fatigue. These are the horses, not zebras, in the world of sex counseling.

Everyone is susceptible. Young mothers find themselves

especially vulnerable to all three. Hard-driving career people and those who in "Superman" or "Wonder Woman" fashion find themselves with jobs, volunteer work, carpools, and dogs to take to the vet become so caught up in the things that must be done that no time is set aside to contemplate the desirability of the spouse or to arrange the special time and surroundings in which love can flourish. They settle for same time, same place, same thing—and reduce lovemaking to a physical mating. Quite naturally it loses its appeal.

If couples do not make the sexual relationship some kind of priority, problems of response may easily develop and secondary dysfunctions may naturally emerge. Fatigue and boredom with sex are the chief complaints the doctors hear in my husband's OB-GYN office. Most of those who register such complaints are not aware of the relationship of their patterns and priorities of life to their sexual dissatisfaction.

Ann Landers's recent survey, in which 90,000 married women reported they preferred a sincere hug to intercourse, makes sense in light of such findings.[11] Bodies are most responsive when they are rested and in good physical condition. Good sexual functioning requires that bodies be relaxed and that lifestyles permit the time and energy to make healthy sexual relationships a priority. Many people need to be taught this even though it appears to be mere common sense.

COMMON PHYSICAL FACTORS
AFFECTING NORMAL SEXUAL FUNCTIONING

Physical Pain

With increasing age, the female can face a variety of problems. She may experience pain and irritation as a result of the thinning of the vaginal lining. Occasionally uterine cramps, which in her youth disturbed her only a little, now have become unbearable in connection with her orgasm. Both conditions may be relieved through hormone therapy.

A woman may experience pelvic relaxation, the anatomical weakening of the pelvic floor, causing sexual discomfort by allowing the internal organs to be subject to trauma with penile thrusting. Bleeding may occur as a result.

At any age a woman might be subject to adhesions from previous pelvic surgery or infections. Intercourse becomes painful due to immobilization of the internal structures. Unfortunately, once they have formed, surgery is the only remedy for adhesions.

Infections of the upper or lower genital tract can result in acute or chronic pain, depending on the infecting organism. Herpes is a painful, recurring problem that can infect newborns and have potentially disastrous results. Treatment can accelerate temporary remission, but cannot cure. There are also various bacterial infections, trichomoniasis, and moniliasis. These infections are easily treated with pills or vaginal creams. With trichomoniasis, both partners must be treated even though the male is asymptomatic.

More serious problems involve the uterus, tubes, and the abdominal cavity. The most common include chlamydia, gonorrhea, E. coli, and anaerobic bacteria. These may require hospitalization if oral therapy fails. The pain results from the swelling, inflammatory irritation, and in some cases, actual pelvic abscesses. Chlamydia is of particular concern because of its insidious nature and the difficulty of diagnosis. Its symptoms may be very vague and involve upset stomach, low-grade fever, mild abdominal pain, and painful intercourse. If suspected, tetracycline is an effective cure.

Endometriosis, the backward flow through the tubes of the products of menstruation resulting in its growth on or in the pelvic organs, is not only painful, but can result in infertility. Endometrial tissue can implant throughout the abdominal cavity. Besides pain, the first symptoms may be blood in the urine or stool. There is medical and/or surgical treatment available depending on the age of the woman and the severity of the disease.

A woman who has been pregnant may experience severe pain with deep thrusting due to adenomyosis. The implantation site of the placenta may have resulted in the development of a pocket of chronic infection. Problems of adenomyosis will cease with menopause, hormonal treatment, or a hysterectomy.

Occasionally there can be anatomical variations that cause pain. Diagnosis must be done by a physician and treatment determined for individual needs. The most common anatomical problem would be the presence of a rigid hymenal ring. A variation is a hymenal remnant, which may only appear as the vagina opens during arousal. (Many young women today inadvertently tear their hymen as a result of physical activity or stretching it through the use of tampons. Therefore its use— common in times past—as proof of virginity is not always justified.) Episiotomy scar tissue can be very sensitive. Some women are prone to irritation and cuts from hair getting caught in the vagina.

Men may suffer from painful coitus as a result of chronic prostatitis, epididymitis, or urethritis. The inflammation and swelling cause the discomfort. They are treated with drug therapy.

Males are subject to other problems also. External infections that cause pain are moniliasis, which is more common in uncircumcised males, and herpes. Priapism is a disease that can make intercourse impossible; the spongiosm of the penile shaft is diseased by the formation of fibrous tissue, which may cause bending. There is no cure beyond a certain time limit and no real understanding of the cause.

Birth-Control Pills

With the new, lower doses of birth-control pills, there are fewer reports of changes in sexual functioning. It has always been difficult to separate the psychological and pharmacological effects of the pills. One would assume that with less fear of pregnancy there is more sexual freedom.

Pregnancy and Postpartum

The effect of pregnancy on sexuality varies with each trimester. In the beginning, fear of losing the baby, fatigue, breast tenderness, and nausea may preclude desire. During the second trimester the vascular buildup of the genital area results in heightened interest in sex and performance. Desire wanes in the third trimester as discomfort and fear of harming the child become paramount.

There is some evidence that the mechanism of orgasm can trigger labor. Habitual aborters and women who risk premature labor are advised to refrain from orgasm. But there is no medical reason in a normal pregnancy to abstain from sexual activity.

There is a variety of factors related to the resumption of sex after birth. Some studies reveal women who nurse are more eager to return to sexual relations with their husbands, while others maintain the increased prolactin reduces drive. Breast-feeding women may experience discomfort from vaginal dryness, but a lubricant should provide the necessary relief. Depending on pain threshold and the amount of trauma from delivery, there can be great variation in how quickly one can return to sex without pain or discomfort.

Menstruation

Folk tales the world over refer to the mysteries surrounding a woman's monthly cycle. Often rituals and purification rites are prescribed to ensure that the male is not contaminated. In the King James Version of the Bible it is called "the way of women" and "the time of her impurity." Most references to it are found in Leviticus and involve purification rituals.

Despite the warning of Leviticus 20:18 that couples who risk sexual relations during menstruation are "impure," there is no physiological reason to abstain from making love. Nevertheless, the woman's distress and the couple's aesthetic concerns are major considerations.

Most women are aware that the buildup of discomfort they feel is relieved with the onset of the flow. The same mechanism that is at work in sexual excitement is at work here. Orgasm relieves menstrual cramping and the feeling of fullness by reducing the vasocongestion in the genital area. Since vasocongestion is already half the process of sexual responsiveness, menstruation is a time when some women can experience orgasm very easily.

Diabetes

The effects of diabetes on sexual activity are often attributable directly to the degeneration of the pelvic nerves. The penile arteries can become occluded. By the time diabetes has progressed to the point where the eyes are affected, 85 percent of the men will have erectile problems. Eventually the result in the male is erectile difficulty; in the female, less sensation and more difficulty with orgasm. The general deterioration of the state of health affects indirectly the stamina for sex.

Vascular Diseases

Vascular diseases such as high blood pressure and stroke do not preclude sex, but the medications taken to control them may inhibit sexual functioning. It is important to request adjustment of medication if a person is affected.

Most physicians encourage resumption of sexual activity after a person's recovery from a heart attack. A review of sexual activity after a heart attack revealed that 75 percent of previously sexually active couples still had not resumed coitus after six months. Sexual activity is no more exhaustive than other ordinary activities in everyday life.[12] Incidents of heart attacks occurring while making love have been linked most frequently to illicit situations rather than within marriage.

Prostatic Surgery

Prostatic surgery can result in impotence. In the past, believing older people to be nonsexual, surgeons were remiss in bringing this up as a possibility. Anyone facing this type of surgery should make it clear he is sexually active so that if possible an alternate technique with less chance of damage may be considered.

Overeating

A large meal does nothing to enhance one's sexual desires. It is one of the most obvious and prevalent but overlooked causes of difficulties in sexual performance, especially as one ages. Obesity limits the variety of physical movements one might ordinarily experience, as it does with any activity.

Pubococcygeus Muscles

Therapists disagree on the extent to which strengthening the muscles around the pelvic area contributes to increased sexual satisfaction. Some base their whole therapeutic concept on it, while others mention it only in passing. It does not take scientific research to grasp the obvious: the better shape our body is in, the greater our flexibility and body awareness.

Using Kegel exercises (described in note 17 for chapter 9) to strengthen pubococcygeus muscles enhances sexual feelings in both men and women. The difference strong muscle control makes has much to do with how out of shape the muscles were to begin with. The exercises were discovered originally to help women with the problem of leaking urine, but they can be used by both sexes. To get in touch with the correct muscles the person is asked to stop the flow of urine midstream. Rhythmic contractions done two to three times a day over a four-to-six-week period produce maximum results. It is convenient that once the muscles have been isolated, they can be exercised unobtrusively while the person participates in everyday concerns like driving a car or washing dishes.

Illness

All illnesses affect sexual functioning, even a cold. In this sense everyone has been dysfunctional at some time in life. The manifestations of the problem may vary, but the ability to respond sexually is a natural body function. The sexual system, like the digestive, respiratory, and other body systems, is affected by poor health and will not function as it could if the whole body were in good health.

Disabilities

Most disabilities do not affect one's desire to be loved, touched, and cared for and to reach out in return. Far from living a life devoid of sexual expression, many disabled people and their spouses modify and adjust sexual behavior and find their emotional and physical sexual needs met. Acknowledging desires and receiving practical teaching, which can include some outstanding films, can free couples to add the sexual dimension creatively to their lives.

Abstinence

Contrary to many old wives' tales, abstinence has no permanently harmful effects. Sperm are reabsorbed or released in nocturnal emissions in males, and females basically have no physical adjustments to make. Becoming sexually active after a period of celibacy presents psychological concerns that must be handled with good communication and plenty of time. Many people find abstinence a useful time for self-evaluation, intense concentration, or commitment to a project.

Drugs[13]

In addition to medication given for hypertension, it is always wise to check contraindications of any prescription drug. The following is a list of some common drugs and their sexual side effects.

Alcohol. Alcohol has a decided sequence of effects. In the beginning, in its role as a depressant it lets down inhibitions that enable people more easily to involve themselves in sexual expression. There is no evidence that liquor facilitates sexual pleasure, however. As the effects intensify, alcohol further depresses the body to the point of shutting down sexual functioning. The usual sequence for a male is problems with ejaculation followed by erectile difficulties. Masters and Johnson illustrate the major role alcohol plays in secondary impotence with the scenario of a man who finds himself unable to sustain an erection for whatever reason. He becomes fearful of being able to perform again and relies on alcohol to enhance his nerve. The alcohol precludes his ability to perform, and an insidious cycle is set up. Chronic alcoholics may become permanently impotent.

Amphetamines. Some users claim amphetamines enhance their sexual performance and sensations. Chronic users discover that the original high is followed by a low that leaves them disinterested in sex. Often the effects are extreme, and one becomes too high and jittery to be sexual. Injection of the drug produces the same effects as oral use, but with greater intensity.

Amyl Nitrite. This drug is now illegal, but has been replaced by butyl nitrite. Users "pop" the pill just at orgasm in order to experience what they perceive as an increased vasocongestive response to the genitals. It can cause headaches and heart attacks.

Antibiotics. Antibiotics affect sexual functioning by changing the flora and pH of the vagina, setting up ideal conditions for bacterial and yeast infections. An allergic reaction can cause the vagina to itch. Some women can get an allergic reaction to antibiotics or other drugs taken by a male partner and transmitted in the semen.

Antihistamines. Since the vaginal mucosa is much like the lining of the nose, antihistamines can result in drying of the vagina.

Barbiturates. A depressant like alcohol, barbiturates under chronic use diminish the libido.

Caffeine. Found in chocolate, coffee, tea, and soft drinks, caffeine provides a "lift." The sense of well-being it gives can quickly turn to jitters. One could speculate that a premature ejaculator might have more trouble than usual in maintaining control with a "hyped" nervous system. Although the evidence is unclear, addiction to twenty or more cups of coffee a day has a definite effect on sexual performance.

Cocaine. A sense of well-being probably adds to the reports of sex being enhanced under the influence of cocaine. Some people may last longer with short-term use of cocaine, but ejaculation problems are common after long-term use.

Codeine. Codeine is another nervous system depressant that reduces interest in sex.

Demerol. Demerol is a mood depressant that, like morphine, causes people to be uninterested in sexual performance.

Heroin. Heroin is a depressant that seems especially to

affect the sex drive. Heroin addicts, like alcoholics, lose their drive or have erectile problems.

Inderol. Inderol is a beta-blocker and affects the blood vessels. It interferes with ejaculation and erection.

Marijuana. With low doses of marijuana, many report increases in desire and/or enjoyment. Such a report is very subjective, however, since marijuana causes a dissociation of conscience and morality and alters the perception of time by making it seem to pass more slowly. This allows for what seems to be an increased span of sexual fulfillment. Client reports after several months off the drug tend to discount much of its perceived special effect.

Some people become psychologically addicted to marijuana and feel they can perform only under its influence. High doses and chronic use tend to reduce the sex drive. Young males who are heavy users have a reduction in their testosterone level.

Quaaludes. There is much subjective reporting on quaaludes. Most people find the drugs put them to sleep.

Spanish fly. Large doses of Spanish fly may cause priapism, which is perhaps how this irritant of the urogenital tract got its reputation as an aphrodisiac.

Tobacco. Cigarette smoking can inhibit the production of testosterone, but the major effect of smoking is probably more general. People who refrain from smoking have a higher blood-oxygen level and presumably more energy. Cigarette smokers have an increase in vascular diseases, thus penile vascularity can be affected. People who smoke one pack a day will experience some pharmacological effect; two-or-three-pack smokers will probably not see improvement with sexual problems unless they quit.

Tranquilizers. Regular use of tranquilizers inhibits the sexual drive. A new drug, Desyrel, promises less disturbance of sexual functioning.

Conclusion

Frequently it is the combination of events in a person's life that determines whether a particular drug or any other internal or external pressure results in sexual problems. Intervention always requires that a combination of causes be considered. Remember, some people have idiosyncratic responses to particular medications. Maximum functioning requires maximum health. Before long-term therapy, surgery, or other drastic measures are undertaken, look to the obvious. Horses are often the source of the sound of hoofbeats.

PART THREE

BECOMING ONE FLESH

In this fallen world mankind lives with sexual relationships that do not always function as they should. Anyone is capable of experiencing at least a temporary dysfunction when ill, highly stressed, or confused about some sexual matter. Because this is the case, sexual therapy has become a thriving business. This part deals with some of the problems that send people looking for help and some of the solutions that even nonprofessionals are able to offer. It provides an overview of sexual counseling techniques, perspectives, and theories in order to clarify for the reader the most commonly practiced approaches used in the field. Many of them are reliable techniques that take account of both the physical and the psychic dimensions of a sexual relationship.

Chapter Seven

REGAINING THE PROMISE OF PLEASURE

The Role of Sexual Counseling

When I was new in my practice, I made a number of mistakes. One of them was assuming that certain "educated" people did not need to review the basics of sexual functioning. Although people came to me primarily for sexual counseling, the majority had more general marital problems and concerns as well. Consequently I was not always aware of their needs for very basic sexual information.

Experience soon taught me that my time was always well spent when, at some time in the therapeutic process, I devoted a session to basic sex education. I would often preface the presentation with the statement, "I'm sure you are knowledgeable of many of the things I'm going to share, but review is helpful for all of us. Besides, I want to be sure we are all speaking the same language when we talk about sex." I would then proceed to teach what was probably the first lucid, accurate, and logically presented lesson on sex they had ever heard.

I accomplished several things by doing this. For many people I provided an opportunity to see an adult speak openly, without embarrassment, about sex. For some this was the first time they had talked about sex in mixed company. I offered factual information about the way God intentionally made us. I created an opportunity and atmosphere for clarifying problems and misinterpretations or satisfying curiosity. It is likely that these opportunities stimulated further discussion among couples and created a climate in which problems or concerns could be brought up naturally and comfortably in a current or subsequent session.

HOW DO PEOPLE SEEK HELP?

When people seek help for sexual problems, they often mask their real concerns by a series of statements that can be quite misleading. My husband frequently suspects marital or sexual problems when a patient appears with a thick chart that documents nebulous medical complaints and has a history of "doctor shopping." In my practice the people who presented with sexual problems either were referred to me from other sources because of my reputation for dealing with sexual matters or came as a result of sexual pressures that had become so great that they had abandoned all caution about sharing them.

Unless the pastor or counselor has a reputation of ease in dealing with sexual issues, chances are slim that many people will declare problems outright. Thus he or she may have to provide the opening for the counselee to get at the real issues. Whether or not he or she asks a direct question depends on individual style, comfort level, and rapport with the couple or individual being counseled. Timing is a sensitive issue. A direct question asked too soon will probably be answered with the statement, "Everything is fine." Careful questioning with cross checks gives a clue as to the answer's validity. Here are some examples of permission-giving questions and statements.

Possible responses to a denial of sexual problems:

- "Your sexual relationship couldn't stand improvement?"
- "What is the most special thing about your lovemaking?" . . . "Is there anything that interferes with making that happen?"
- "I'm sure you already know almost everyone has sexual problems at some time or other. I'm wondering how the two of you handle such occasions."

- "Most people develop ways of handling times when things don't go well sexually. Are you happy with the way in which you deal with those occasions?"

  Possible responses to hesitation to share sexual information:

- "You know most people . . . "
- "I've found . . ."
- "I'm wondering how you feel about . . ."

With this indirect and, I hope, nonthreatening approach, I provide a little educational input, offer some information about sexual functioning, and ask for feedback from people concerning how they feel about what I have shared.

People will often be put at ease by gentle questions and freely offered information. The counselor must also be at ease if people are going to feel free to let a conversation drift toward the sexual difficulties that they are experiencing. If the counselor does not want to broach a discussion of sexual issues, he or she can be assured that the people they are counseling will not force the discussion. Most people will back off if they have any indication the counselor is uneasy discussing sexual issues. This means it takes considerable finesse for a pastor or counselor to create an accepting atmosphere.

WHEN DO YOU DO SEXUAL COUNSELING?

In reality the line between sexual counseling and marital counseling is very fine. Therapists like Masters and Johnson and others who confine their work to sexual dysfunctions prefer that all other forms of therapy be done first, leaving the sexual issue as the sole problem. This would be ideal and would certainly increase the likelihood of success. But some couples insist that sex is their problem when it is clear other factors are at work. Others refuse to acknowledge that a sexual dysfunction exists. To be realistic, most people will not commit the time and money involved in a plan that requires several therapists.

Pastors and counselors should incorporate sexual counseling and education into any marital therapy they offer. It is an opportunity not only to make up the deficit in learning that clients most probably have, but also to disclose God's plan for the couple's sexuality. Counselors who are able will do even more. They can develop a formal sequence of events that enables a couple to overcome a sexual problem. There are basic and simple procedures that can be used to handle a variety of complaints or to enrich a couple's sexual functioning.

The first part of this book dealt with the personal and spiritual mindset and perspective of the pastor, counselor, or church leader. The second part concerned itself with how the body is meant to work sexually. This part will deal with the problems of sexuality and ways that one can intervene when sexuality does not function as it should. The chapters following this one will deal with the specifics of how to evaluate and respond to dysfunctions.

If we are to embark on a plan that includes sexual counseling, it must be informed by the following questions:

1. Are there physical problems?
   a. Infections
   b. Drugs
2. Is there another primary problem?
   a. Depression
   b. Substance abuse
3. Is there a real sex problem?
4. Are there positive factors?
   a. Commitment
   b. Hope
   c. Time and money commitment
5. Are there any interfering situational factors?
   a. A family crisis
   b. Recent death
   c. Loss of job
6. Are basic relationship requirements present?
   a. No individual pathology
   b. Clear commitment
   c. Basic communication skills
   d. Relationship-relevant material not withheld
   e. Compatible life and relationship goals[1]

The more carefully these criteria are considered, the greater the likelihood of a successful outcome.

A checklist is helpful, but it is merely a guide. Flesh out the picture by discovering the motivation of a couple for seeking help. Ask them to explain how things got to be as they are. Find out what they think will happen if the therapy works. How will their lives be different? When a couple seems totally dissatisfied and disillusioned with each other, ask why they are still together. Determine carefully their expectations for treatment. Do they see sexual problems to be like an illness, something one can cure completely with the correct medicine?

THE SEXUAL HISTORY

There are many published formats for sexual history. Some are very general and nonthreatening; others elicit the most graphic and personal details possible. Whatever history-taking method used, it must be thorough enough to give the counselor an accurate picture of the actual dynamics of a relationship and the important issues. Self-diagnosis is not reliable and is usually highly speculative.

Take a sexual history from each partner privately. Assure each one of confidentiality and ask permission to use material that might be shared in a joint session. If a client insists on withholding information that is essential to understanding the problem, therapy may have to be terminated.

In sexual therapy the "patient" is not one spouse or the other, but rather it is the relationship. Therefore cooperation and commitment to the relationship are essential requirements for success. For example, a person who has been raped or is the victim of incest needs to be able to deal with that issue openly. If either partner is involved with another person, therapy cannot proceed until all ties with the lover are severed.

A good sexual history[2] will move from general to specific concerns and include information in the following areas:

1. General background information (the families of origin, birth order, relationship to parents, job, education, religious upbringing and current practices, leisure activities)

2. Medical history (surgeries, chronic and acute illnesses, medication, psychiatric history, sexually transmitted diseases)
3. Psychological data (greatest and worst moments, personal self-esteem)
4. Emotional data (feelings about the marriage, children, and job; resentments)
5. Developmental data (reaction to body changes as a teen, problems with aging, hymen, or childbirth)
6. Contraception (attitude and use)
7. Sex education ("How did you learn?" "What was said?"; major influences, attitudes toward nudity, sexual feelings)
8. First sexual feelings, early experiences (situations and reactions)
9. History of sexual encounters (age, type)
10. Marital history (age, number, courtship and wedding, communication, separations, intimacy)
11. Sexual adjustment in marriage (frequency of coitus, changes, awareness of problem, other means of deriving sexual pleasure, ideal)
12. Spousal history (time together, perception of his or her sexual attitudes, disagreements, sense of humor, sexual experiences)
13. Personal sexual image (attractiveness, past and present, changes if you could make them, sexual rating)
14. Erotic data (feelings about touch, music, sexual variety)
15. Presenting symptoms (problem, effect, what has been done)
16. Expectations (of spouse, realistic, of yourself)

OTHER INFORMATION-GATHERING TECHNIQUES

Many counselors are familiar with marriage evaluation tests such as the Taylor Johnson Criss-Cross. Currently there are no accurate measures that give a valid picture of marital and sexual functioning. Those that measure sexual functioning fail to measure satisfaction. "The Sexual Interaction Inventory" devised by Joseph LoPiccolo and Jeffrey Steger[3] seems to be an effort to correct this oversight.

The sexological exam recommended by Hartman and Fithian[4] and practiced by a number of therapists is highly controversial. Its validity is questionable, and it appears to violate Christian sensibilities and the standards of good taste. It includes a teaching session in which the therapist physically demonstrates to each of the partners, among other things, their areas of genital sensitivity.

There are many testing materials that can be adapted for use in sexual counseling. Some psychologists use old standards like the MMPI or innovative testing involving pictures or stories done by the clients. There are questionnaires available throughout the scientific and professional literature.[5] All these gather usable information. Whether they warrant the expense and time is a matter for the individual therapist to decide.

OTHER PRELIMINARY CONSIDERATIONS

Serious Psychological Disturbance

Most of us would readily agree with one writer's assessment that "sex in the real world is a mixture of tenderness and halitosis, love and fatigue, ecstasy and disappointment."[6]

The majority of people who have sexual problems are otherwise pretty normal. But that should not obscure the fact that connections often exist between sexual problems and other kinds of problems. It may seem impossible to ferret out which comes first, the sexual problem or the anxiety, the depression or the marital discord associated with it. As we saw in chapter 6, a great variety of things can and do affect healthy sexual functioning, and most people are affected by some of them sometime in their lives. The more serious problems often have the same origins as the more moderate ones, but differ in intensity, duration, and scope.

One area in which a clear correlation between sexual problems and psychological conditions has been established is in cases of a sexual dysfunction and anxiety. One can, therefore, anticipate certain kinds of problems among anxious people. For example, in dealing with a man known to be a tense person, often frustrated, hostile, and overwrought, one should expect that his poor control of excitement and tension leaves him at high risk for sexual problems. Accordingly, a disorganized, emotional, and hostile female is more prone to sexual dysfunctions as well as neuroses, alcoholism, phobias, hysteria, or obsessive behavior.[7] The more severely she is affected sexually, the more apt she is to share also the characteristics of the tense male described above.

Because of the prevalence of anxiety, hostility, and the resultant tension associated with sex disorders, it is easy to see why sex therapy often involves anxiety reduction and assertiveness training.[8] The greater the dysfunction, the more likely personality and sex problems are both at work.

People who suffer from neurosis or psychosis such as manic-depression, obsessive-compulsion, or antisocial behavior require psychotherapy, not sex therapy. Classic personality disorders often do as well. The narcissistic person wants all aspects of the world to revolve around him or her. The competitive person deals in performance, not love. People with a problem of being withdrawn cannot be dependent for fear of losing themselves or risk being assertive. The sadist or the masochist manifests deep personal problems. All these can be deeply enough ingrained to require the extensive treatment and skills of specialists.

Even the seductive client must be evaluated carefully to determine whether sex therapy is the wisest course. Sometimes a very sexually provocative woman is actually seeking to live out a fantasy—attracting a "daddy" for whom she can remain a little girl. Outwardly seductive, she usually has problems with genital sexuality.[9] She often appears in therapy with a most frustrated spouse. He is blamed if he does not respond to her, but considered a sexual monster if he does. She is a master at what is sometimes called "crazymaking," placing him in a double bind so that anything he does is the wrong thing. Little progress will be made in improving the sexual relationship until her personality problems are resolved.

Incest is another serious problem probably best left to the specialist. A severe trauma such as incest is extremely difficult for people to bring up. Frequently sufferers of incest will block out the experiences and fail to remember. They may complain of an inability to relax, vaginismus, inhibited orgasm, sexual masochism, promiscuity, or aversion to male sexual advances. In some cases sexual identity is confused or distorted, and experimentation with homosexual lifestyles results.[10]

The magnitude of residual problems that can and do affect incest victims is just now coming to light. In the majority of cases of multiple personality disorders, there is a history of violent incestuous experiences along with other dissociative techniques such as self-hypnotic anesthesia and confusion. All women who have been involved in incest suffer at least occasionally from depression and depressive symptoms such as feelings of guilt, low self-esteem, self-blame, a sense of powerlessness, thoughts of suicide, fears, and phobias.[11]

In a society that expects men not to be victims, sufferers of male incest respond with "acting out" behavior. They become overly aggressive in an effort to defeat their feelings of vulnerability and helplessness. Carried to extremes, they may become rapists or, in some rare cases, homosexuals, although there is no clearly established link between male molestation and homosexual behavior.

People who are able to overcome such problems and establish healthy sexual relationships are incest survivors rather than victims. Healing comes when they are able to take control of their lives and place themselves in a position to be nurtured and valued through the mourning and recovery process.

Clinical depression, which can accompany many other psychological problems, must always be treated before sex therapy is initiated. The sexual problem may be the only manifest symptom before a diagnostic test is made. Mild depression, as I have pointed out, is commonly found in sexually dysfunctional people.

Men whose histories include a lack of positive, pleasurable experiences with the opposite sex may tend toward sexual aggressiveness. The overt or hidden hostility toward the female causes both a less pleasurable experience and an increased arousal to scenes suggestive of rape.[12] A major difference between a rapist and a nonrapist appears to be the rapist's propensity to violence.

One should be aware of what is called the Madonna-

Prostitution Complex. In the past, therapists attributed its cause to incestuous wishes and conflicts. That simplistic view is challenged by researchers today. Whatever the cause, it is always complex, sometimes involving a fear of intimacy, a learned distrust of close relationships, a fear of abandonment, or a loss through death.

A man or woman who is unable to have a satisfying sexual relationship with an appropriate partner such as a spouse, but who can function with an inappropriate one could be said to suffer from the Madonna-Prostitution Complex. In its most common form, a man determines that there are two kinds of women: good and bad. The good ones include wives and mothers. One criterion for "goodness" is being asexual or not overtly sexual. Sex is appropriate only with bad or inferior women. Consequently if the only person a man can perform with sexually is an "inferior" person, his state of mind and attitude may lead him to an illicit relationship.

TRANSFERENCE

One criticism of short-term therapy—which characterizes most sexual counseling—is that it does not always account for transference. Brief therapy often results in problems resurfacing after a temporary reprieve. The resistance of the client to therapy may indicate that transference issues are at work.

Transference refers to feelings that well up when one is interacting with a person—feelings related more to significant people from the past than to the person who is now the object of the feelings. Feelings toward parents, relatives, teachers, and authority figures are transferred to the counselor in an attempt to relive the past and perhaps change its outcome.

Although transference is often considered to be a negative or detrimental factor in counseling, it should not always be viewed that way. If the counselor is aware of its capacity to distort and maintains a grasp on the reality of the situation, it can usually be kept under control.[13] The interplay of factors from one's past that spill over into new relationships can be used positively to reveal unresolved and perhaps immature ways of functioning. They can shed light on current behavior.

For some people, positive past interactions encourage acceptance of the authority of the pastor or counselor.

In the same way, counter-transference can disclose the therapist's personal needs and problems. The desire to have a perceived inadequacy met is indeed strong. A therapist's hurt, poor self-esteem, or doubts can be triggered by the personality and presence of the counselee. A therapist whose own marriage is in trouble, whose spouse seems cold and indifferent, is warmed by the client who hangs on every word and who seems oblivious to the new gray hairs and extra five pounds that have recently appeared.

Only Jesus was perfect in this world. The rest of us must be constantly vigilant that our personal agendas do not complicate and confuse interactions with others. The possibility for intimacy in the counseling relationship provides a temptation for counselors to let down their guard and misuse their calling as helpers of others. Counselors must have a clear vision and an honest awareness of their areas of vulnerability.

For years I refused to see children as clients. My own mixed feelings about my parental inconsistencies toward my hyperactive son counseled me to stay clear of therapeutic settings with children. Anyone going through severe marital problems should be especially careful when doing marriage counseling. I know of an outstanding family therapist, author, and seminary professor who nearly destroyed a marriage he was entrusted with because of his inability to separate his midlife dissatisfaction from the therapeutic process. Pastors or counselors who are depressed must be aware that anyone entering their world will seem to be colored by the same shades of gray that constitute their personal world.

As feelings of anger, frustration, love, and guilt well up within the therapist, careful evaluation and emotional maturity determine whether growth occurs or injury results for both counselor and counselee. It is possible to use such revelation positively by seeing it for what it is and knowing that one does not have to be controlled by it. Such interaction can shed light on problems that can then be dealt with in healthy ways.

The most common type of transference and counter-transference in sexual counseling is falling in love. If a person is working with a member of the opposite sex in a friendly setting where one's emotional needs are attended to, that person is vulnerable. This may be the only place where he or she feels respected and heard, so it is easy to mistake the intimacy in a counseling relationship for love.

Fortunately many people who come to ministers for help have clarified some transference issues of who they are and why they are seeking help from a spiritual source. This is advantageous, for if both the client and the helper recognize and accept their defined roles, there is greater likelihood of their continuing to act within the parameters of those roles.

RESISTANCE

There is no "right way" to handle the resistance of a particular client in sexual counseling. Sometimes it is best ignored. Consequently a person sees no effect from it and ceases to resist. Occasionally it can be faced directly with a simple question: "Why are you here when it appears you really don't have a commitment to allow therapy to work?" The method of choice, like many other things in this type of work, depends on the needs and coping mechanisms of the individuals and the counselor's rapport with them.

A counselor is wise to prepare a client for the possibility that a point of resistance may come. I always warn a counselee that things may go exceptionally well only to come to a screeching halt sometime later during therapy. This anticipation of possible delays or setbacks prepares the person for potential hitches and provides the assurance that occasional setbacks are normal.

Therapy proceeds rapidly when expectations are clearly understood and defined. If we use progressive steps with intermediate goals within a clear and realistic time frame, we can help avoid reactions and diversionary games that some people use to sabotage therapy. If all the cards are on the table, the client will be less inclined to second-guess or "play games" with the counselor.

In sexual counseling, homework is the primary sphere in which counselors face resistance. But assignments can be structured to discover possible signs of resistance. For example, a therapist has assigned a footwash, explained carefully how the couple is to proceed, and worked out an agreeable time schedule, but the couple returns with the assignment undone. The therapist can conclude that a misunderstanding of the assignment or time conflicts are probably not their reasons for noncompliance. This may be a sign of resistance that requires further analysis.

Resistance to some plans of treatment is quite natural. The counselor faces a tremendous challenge in requiring a client to suspend intercourse for a time to follow through with assigned sensate focus exercises. My husband and I have heard the following dialogue more times than we can remember:

> SHE: Doctor, I told him you said no intercourse, but he insisted.
>
> HE: Oh, I misunderstood. I thought you said no inter- course next week!
> ... I didn't hear that part.
> ... You didn't say intercourse only?
> ... I understood we were supposed to try it out so we could report in.
> ... I thought you meant we weren't supposed to talk!

When we suspect that couples will resist the directive to suspend intercourse, it is our practice to relieve tension and work through their possible resistance. So we suggest all the possible responses they might come up with and announce, with a touch of humor, that we will not buy any of them!

Resistance to sensate focus exercises (discussed in detail later) is more difficult to handle:

> "I'm ticklish."
>
> "I didn't feel anything."
>
> "This is stupid! What does it have to do with her problem?"
>
> "We have been so busy."
>
> "Well, we started right, but somehow intercourse just happened."

The counselor need not panic or give up when facing resistance. Be sure that you are not dealing with misunderstanding, deficient skills, or too rapid a program. Be aware that progress is seldom a straight line. Encouragement, acceptance, understanding, and reassurance all help work through most situations. Be patient and wait a reasonable length of time. Do not hesitate to ask what the clients think might help!

Resistance can sometimes be prevented. It is helpful to use visualization of a homework assignment to pinpoint potential problem areas. It is also profitable to work on increasing loving feelings by improving communication and problem-solving techniques, by objectifying the situation, and by encouraging "dates" and "caring" days.

VARIATIONS IN SEXUAL THERAPY

Much sex therapy technique has been derived from Masters and Johnson's original format. They were the first to develop a widely accepted systematic approach for the treatment of sexual dysfunctions. Believing sexual responsiveness to be a natural ability, they concentrated on removing the sources of anxiety that affected performance. The crux of the therapy was "sensate focus." Sensate focus exercises were designed to alleviate tension, increase pleasure and communication, and point out problems.

Masters and Johnson considered fear of inadequacy the primary block to healthy functioning. They discouraged the tendency for people to lay blame on their partners and concentrated instead on behavioral changes. Women were given active and significant roles in the treatment process. Their program involved considerable reeducation, a two-week commitment to intensive therapy at Masters and Johnson's headquarters in St. Louis, and a great deal of expense.

Behavioral approaches, which emphasize the learning and conditioning aspects of sexual problems, have been around for a number of years. Indeed, much of Masters and Johnson's approach is behavioral in origin. Systematic desensitization requiring training in relaxation procedures has been widely adopted from the behaviorist tradition.

Albert Ellis in his book, *Human Sexual Inadequa* sized the role a person's attitude and belief system pl her sexual expression. His work provided motivat behaviorists to continue exploring techniques of wor sexual dysfunctions. Their emphasis has been on ...xiety-reduction techniques such as progressive relaxation, directed masturbation, and erectile reconditioning. The use of directed fantasy to reassociate sex stimuli with more appropriate arousal stimuli was also developed in this school.

Arnold Lazarus, a professor at the Graduate School of Applied and Professional Psychology of Rutgers University, is a pioneer in the development of behavioral therapy and, most recently, in Multimodal therapy. Much of his focus has been on the use of imagery techniques. Such methods require a rehearsal of the desired sexual response in the mind before it is attempted in real life.

Helen Singer Kaplan has provided a synthesis of psychoanalytic and behavioral models. She sees sexual problems resulting from many causes, rejecting the psychoanalytic theory of incestuous experiences or desires as being the sole overt or unconscious etiology. A major contribution of Kaplan is her expansion of the understanding of sexual response from a two-stage approach (excitement and orgasm) to one involving three stages (desire, excitement, and orgasm). If the three stages correspond to reality, and if the dysfunction is accurately understood in the context of the stage of sexual response in which it occurs, then diagnosis and treatment are likely to be more effective.

Kaplan, like most sexual therapists today, uses an eclectic blend of sensate focus, marital therapy, and behavioral exercises. There is no question that this combination has the greatest chance for success. It is also the least time-consuming and most cost-effective approach.

In most therapies, individuals or couples are seen weekly. Other formats and schedules have also been effective. For instance, groups can provide a less expensive, time-efficient alternative that is particularly effective with premature ejaculation and anorgasmic women. They can help to weaken resistance to change. Their encouragement, support, and suggestions help reduce performance anxieties and fear of failure. Motivation is improved, resulting in more compliance with homework. Even weekend couple seminars have been found to have a positive effect on sexual functioning.[14]

A therapist's intervention is not always necessary. Reading about a problem has often been effective in improving sexual functioning.[15] Even the most timid would-be helper can muster the courage to suggest a good book or article! More esoteric efforts have questionable results. Mandrake roots, mentioned in the Bible, are perhaps one of the first "cures" for sexual problems. To this day, however, there is no known aphrodisiac (except being in love, as some wise soul has said!).

There are therapies that suggest using surrogate partners. This practice is defended by those who point out that, for a variety of reasons, some people do not have partners they can involve in therapy. This has proved to be such a controversial method of treatment that few reputable therapists involve themselves with it. Besides the moral issues it raises, one has to question the efficacy of teaching someone to perform with a surrogate if the goal is to enhance functioning and pleasure within a specific relationship. For Christians the use of surrogates is clearly not an option.

DIFFERENCES BETWEEN SEXUAL THERAPY AND REGULAR PSYCHOTHERAPY

Sexual therapy differs from many other therapies in that it relies on homework and exercises to be completed at home. These may involve reading, specific communication between partners, or sex exercises. Prescribed exercises often develop in steps to relieve anxiety. If the couple agrees to do them and follows through, the exercises can bring about changes and new patterns that will help solve specific problems.

Much can be learned about a couple's level of resistance, ambivalent feelings, and commitment to the relationship when they do not do their homework. This avoidance of specific activities pinpoints areas that are difficult or frightening or in which the couple feel insecure. Homework may also involve the freedom not to participate in some activity that is threatening or results in failure-producing behavior.

Sex therapy is unlicensed in many states. The American Association of Sex Educators, Counselors, and Therapists (AASECT) is the only organization that licenses the field. In California and a few other states, therapists must have completed a number of hours in formal study of sexual therapy and sexual abuse before licensure.

On the one hand, sex therapy is not as simple a program as people once thought. Successful therapy involves more than applying a formula solution to a routine diagnosis. The failure of the "cookbook approach" has contributed to the development of clinics, usually in university settings, that specialize in the treatment of sexual problems.

On the other hand, sex therapy is often not so complicated and nebulous as regular therapy. A 1984 paper by Norton and Jehu explored the literature for evidence of pathology among people diagnosed with sexual dysfunctions.[16] Although, as one might expect, people with sexual difficulties experience higher anxiety and some psychopathology surrounding the difficulty, analysis of the studies does not suggest that people who have sexual problems suffer from more pathology and anxiety to begin with. The causes can vary from ". . . simple negative conditioning problems to profound characterological disturbances."[17] The relevance of this for the pastor or counselor is recognition that in most cases, a psychiatrist or counseling specialist is not necessary for successful intervention.

No other kind of therapy requires greater use of innovation and creativity. A sexual therapist takes a much more active role with his or her client. In the capacity of teacher, the counselor can decide how realistic a client's goals for therapy are. It is common for some men to believe that the wife's enhanced capacity for orgasm as a result of therapy will solve all the communication and lack of intimacy complaints they experience. Sexual counselors, rather than depending on a simple one-two-three procedure, must have a great deal of sensitivity to discern the direction of therapy, timing of homework, technique, and manner of encouragement.

Bernie Zilbergeld, author of *Male Sexuality*, recalls a case of low sexual desire that he treated by encouraging the wife to use a tennis racket and go through the motions of her warm-up in her bedroom. The object was to help her understand that the bodily excitement and alertness that came so easily with the thought of playing tennis were what was needed for sexual arousal. After their successful treatment, the couple hung a tennis racquet over their bed.

The therapist's questions and decisions should deal primarily with the immediate situation, the here and now. Past history is explored chiefly for its sexual significance and helps to determine the goals of therapy. For example, a sexual counselor would want to to analyze a father-son relationship only from the perspective of its effect on sexual functioning in the present situation. The larger concerns of the relationship and the problems it generates should not be a focus of sexual counseling.

A large part of sexual counseling is the teaching and reinforcement of new behaviors. The goals are much more easily specified and far less vague than in most other therapies. Because they are measurable, there can be a clearer target date for termination. Change is usually rapid. The therapist acts as a catalyst, bringing out diagnostic information and rewarding positive changes and constructive attitudes. He or she models good communication and problem-solving techniques.

Many of these truths suggest that sexual therapy is within the grasp of nonprofessional but competent, insightful helpers. The pastor or counselor can be used to provide support more than insight, teaching, and reevaluation of values and direction. There is no legitimate reason why he or she cannot be a most appropriate healer for the majority of everyday sexual concerns within the body of Christ.

HOW EFFECTIVE IS SEX THERAPY?

Who decides whether sex therapy has been successful? If the goals are clearly laid out, realistic, and agreed to by both client and helper, one can perhaps come as close as possible to a measurable outcome. Usually matters will not be quite so clear-cut.

Bernie Zilbergeld brings up an important point: success is also dependent on the subjective evaluation of the client. For example, a couple comes in for sex therapy with complaints of little response on the woman's part and premature ejaculation on the man's. Therapy "succeeds" so that she becomes orgasmic at least half the time and he gains a measure of control. Are they more satisfied? Does better physical functioning ensure more enjoyment?

People often feel better if someone has attended to them in a way that implies they are understood, have value, and are cared for, even if their situation does not change. There are some who suggest this might be the primary effect of therapy. It is a sad reflection on our society when the only way some people can be heard is to pay for a hearing.

In most cases, with the exception of phobias, sexual problems, and compulsions, no single type of therapy is better than another.[18] The most successful results come with work on phobias, raising self-esteem, and difficulty with orgasm. The least success is found with desire disorders and serious, criminal sexual deviations.[19]

A three-year follow-up of sexual problems not treated revealed female sexual functioning improved with time, but men presented a mixed picture. Men with erectile difficulties and ejaculatory inability improved, but interest and arousal dysfunctions were the same or worse.[20] A 100 percent improvement is not a realistic goal. Sexuality is affected by too many factors for one to expect never to have a problem again.

WHY DO FAILURES OCCUR?

A major problem with some sexual "cures" is the rapid rate at which they come undone. Some see this resulting from a temporary borrowing of the therapist's healthy and open attitude about sex, transference cures, flights into health, or symptom substitution. It may simply be the unwillingness of some couples to continue working on the gains they have made or on the new intimacy they have established. They begin to attempt intercourse when they are too tired, angry, or not "hungry," and their old patterns get a foothold again. Failures also occur frequently among couples who refuse to take their homework seriously or who are in relationships they really want to abandon. The better their mental health or previous history of sexual adjustment, the greater the possibility for success.

THE POSSIBILITIES FOR SUCCESS

An analysis of 140 studies disclosed the following conclusions in the success or failure of sexual counseling:[21]

- Premature ejaculation success rates ranged from 50 to 100 percent after ten to twenty sessions. Success was defined as a sense of voluntary control or lasting longer.
- In erection problems, from 0 to 75 percent improved after ten to twenty sessions, with secondary problems (erectile problems that develop after a period of normal functioning) being more amenable to treatment than primary (lifelong erectile problems).
- Ejaculatory inhibitions were often reported in very small studies, rendering the results fairly nonapplicable; studies of larger populations indicate a 40 to 50 percent improvement.
- In female orgasmic problems, 70 to 100 percent reported success with prescribed masturbation exercises after eight to fifteen sessions. Most successes continued in intercourse with the partner. Secondary orgasmic problems (orgasmic difficulties developing after a period of normal functioning) showed less success.
- With vaginismus, after seven to fourteen sessions, 66 to 100 percent were able to have intercourse. (There is little mention of the incidence of orgasm, since it was not the goal.)
- Sexual desire and arousal problems are rarely reported on. There is some indication that counseling helps some individuals increase initiation of intercourse, assuming that to be a measure of desire.
- Personal interaction and relationship functioning generally improved with decreased sexual anxiety and better communication skills. There is some proof of greater satisfaction even if sexual functioning did not improve.

• Group therapy appears to be as effective as individual therapy for most people.
• It is not known whether there is an advantage to daily versus weekly treatment.

THE SUCCESSFUL OUTCOME

This chapter has helped clarify goals for sexual counseling. First and foremost is the need to educate. Pastors and counselors often have an interest in addressing the whole life of the person in need and thus can provide a view of sexuality that is integrated with Christian truth. The second goal is a careful diagnosis to determine a plan of action that speaks to the actual problem. Third is to set realistic but encouraging and hopeful expectations.

In the real world it is sometimes difficult to assess with complete assurance the true nature of a problem. It is tempting to take a sexual complaint at face value, but often it is only a portion of a complex web of inter- and intrapsychic material. Couples with severe maladjustment to one another will probably benefit little from sexual counseling, even if they insist, "If sex was okay, the marriage would be, too."

But one should not minimize the potential. Sex therapy, especially when done with conscientious diagnosis, can be extremely effective. It can help many people improve communication and develop realistic expectations. For the great majority of people, if sexual counseling is not successful, little has been lost or risked. People who do come out worse are those who lose hope or have lowered self-esteem, seeing themselves as unsalvageable after having "tried everything."

All age groups show improvement, but the longer and more entrenched the problem, the more difficult a cure may be. Unquestionably people who have a basically good relationship in which there is mutual respect, trust, a sense of intimacy, and a balance between control and dependency have a chance for a good outcome.[22]

Individuals with immature ways of coping or character disorders of varying degrees may need personal therapy before serious work on their sexual problems can begin. That still leaves a great number of ordinary people who, by their cooperation with the helper through disclosure, verbalization of concerns and feelings, regular attendance, and doing their homework, maximize the possibility of improvement. Their lives can be enriched by the intervention of a caring helper who has a comfort level, some expertise, and the knowledge of the dynamics of sexual functioning.

Chapter Eight

THE TWO BECOME ONE
The Couple and Their
Sexual Relationship

A survey that I consulted as I began working on this book requested information on the types of problems and situations pastors and counselors see most frequently. The item mentioned most was the lack of understanding between men and women. The inability of each sex to comprehend the other has serious ramifications; unmet expectations, misunderstanding, bickering, sexual difficulties, and divorce are but a few.

The biblical admonition directed to husbands to show their wives consideration and respect (1 Peter 3:7) is ignored by many men, including many Christians, who apparently accept Freud's dictum that women are beyond comprehension. Although humans live in a fallen world that no longer reflects the original, perfect balance of interdependence, grace enables us to work toward achieving it again. The lack of understanding, the competition, and the lack of empathy for the opposite sex that so characterizes twentieth-century living should not be reflected in our Christian walk.

I was saddened to read recently of a study that discovered pastors' marriages and family lives to be considerably less rewarding than those of the flock. It is disconcerting to learn that this is true, because marriage between redeemed individuals who are committed to being active servants of God has the potential for great fulfillment. Tim Timmons states in his book, *Maximum Marriage,* "If God designed it, He should be able to make it work."

Few Christians are able to conceptualize what biblical marriage is to be. Most operate with the limited expectations of the world. The world suggests that men and women are at war and yet, ironically, that true love and fulfillment can be found only in the person of the opposite sex who must be able to meet all their needs. No such person exists, so the man or woman will focus on what is lacking within the marriage and constantly see the weakness or lack in the other. By contrast, a Christian marriage begins with the willingness of each partner to give and not demand, to complement and thereby become oneself in interdependence.

The biblical concept of *agape* love affirms each marriage partner in his or her uniqueness and integrity.[1] It is realistic, allowing for weakness as well as strength; there is no insistence on perfection. Popular cultural images seldom suggest that real married love involves pain and suffering or, even more rarely, fidelity and loyalty. Alvin C. Porteous writes, "When love is thus seen as a bearing with and an affirmation of other persons in spite of their idiosyncracies and inadequacies, it should be obvious that it cannot be separated from suffering."[2]

No one said marriage would be easy. A recent study confirms the importance of acceptance and genuine positive regard for the spouse as a prerequisite for marital satisfaction. Acceptance of the spouse was rated even higher than communication skills.[3] Given today's rates of longevity, consider that for the first time in history many couples can expect to spend an average of forty-five years together, much of that time without children. If their relationship is not based on a complementary relationship and individual dignity of each sex, then the life of the couple will be a long and frustrating exercise in misunderstanding.

THERE IS A DIFFERENCE

God could have made a clone of Adam had He wanted to. He chose, instead, to fashion a new being, related to but different from the first. The biological differences are obvious, but there are others. It is currently very unpopular to point them out, because some people unfortunately insist that "different," especially when it distinguishes women from men, means "less than."

I always find it interesting to read a book or article in which the author expends countless words analyzing or discounting role differences between the sexes. The suggestion that people were made that way by an intentional God is never considered to be a legitimate explanation. Because of the failure to understand Scripture and the vicissitudes of a fallen world, the relationship between men and women has grown more complicated. That they are different is good—not an embarrassment, an inequity, or an excuse for exploitation.

An imperfect world can observe those differences and, by a subtle shift of emphasis, make them irreconcilable barriers between the sexes. For example, females tend to become sexually aroused when certain positive emotional factors are present in a relationship. But males depend on an erotic stimulus to spark their emotional response. The way this simple truth gets packaged, in its exaggerated form, goes, "Women are too emotional; men are unable to be intimate."

Let us examine how such a basic difference as that affects the sexual relationship of men and women. From her earliest days, a female learns to solicit and receive affection. Her expression of emotion, except in unusual and unhealthy situations, is encouraged or at least not discouraged. Identification with and attachment to the mother remain strong, for she and Mom are alike.

The male has to work to separate from Mother, to be his own person. Independence is nurtured and along with it a stoical philosophy about feelings. Emotions are to be hidden behind an exterior of calm, strength, and rationality.

After his years of practice in withholding and denying feelings, it should come as no surprise that a man is unable or unwilling to share them when his wife demands that he do so. He probably no longer knows what they are, is unable to identify emotions, or has no verbal skill to express them.

Intimacy for him is demonstrated through loyalty and his presence—but she wants words!

The man finds himself caught in a double bind. "Macho" is supposed to be out, but he knows it still thrives in the private company of men. He recognizes that other men approve of him because he is powerful at work and a good provider. But at home it is his tenderness and openness that are prized.

The man faces another double bind. He needs to dissociate himself from women to achieve his identity as a man. Yet he experiences the conflicting longing to lose himself in a woman's arms. Confusion and ambivalence result; he alternates between being close and keeping his distance.

The woman, whose ego boundaries are never as impenetrably formed, may sometimes be in turmoil in entering fully into a relationship. She fears her identity as an individual will be lost as she commits herself to the needs, expectations, and demands of another. All her life she has been open to people, but currently our society suggests that to do so is dangerous and sacrificial in nature.

Such confusion gives credence to the myth of polarity. Differences between men and women appear to produce an unbridgeable gap with no common ground and no winners. To love and commit requires being vulnerable and dependent in a world that warns against it. The schizophrenia that results is reflected in erratic behavior that finds both men and women first exploring the possibility of intimacy, then retreating from it. "I can't live with him (her); I can't live without him (her)." Intimacy, the behavior for which they are created, becomes frightening, incomprehensible, and seemingly impossible.

INTIMACY

To further complicate things, marriage has been saddled in recent times with more expectations than it can ever hope to meet. In the past there were people in addition to one's spouse who could be expected to offer some expression of an intimate relationship. Today the spouse has come to be one who is expected to meet *all* the needs of the person for intimacy— sexual partner, parent, friend.

The expectation that the woman is to be sexually satisfied is new as well. Previously men had been under no obligation to prolong intercourse or be skillful and perceptive lovers. Now they are expected to satisfy a woman's appetite without having been taught how.

In the eighties, sex has been burdened with a demand for success. It has become a way of discovering individual identity and worth. The pressure for success has become so overwhelming that couples unconsciously decide to focus on some less threatening facet of their marriage they view as manageable and ignore the apparent mandate for sexual intimacy. To ignore the need for sexual intimacy reduces the meaning marriage is to have for us. It produces boredom and results in sex being no more than genital massage. Physical surrender is easy; it is surrendering psychologically that is difficult.

Conflicts between desire for unity and fear of it, longings to trust and concomitant anxiety over betrayal, and willingness to be vulnerable and alarm over it—these tensions cannot be resolved in a world perceived as erratic and nonsensical. But a world that has order—one in which there is meaning and purpose—enables a person to take the risks necessary for a more complete union. Such is a world in which sex makes sense. A world that has God in and over it is one in which a person can trust.

Intimacy is not nurturance, although many people assume it is. If the motivation for the nurturant behavior is a need to be in control, to ensure another person's dependency, or to keep away loneliness, true intimacy cannot exist. A person can keep so busy nurturing that he or she never reveals a true identity or authentic needs. True intimacy involves both a revelation of the self and an expression of personal need.

That kind of sharing can be so frightening that many adopt a Ping Pong style of relating guaranteed to move them out of danger when things get too close. When their "comfort zone" is encroached upon, they habitually retreat by focusing on the negative attributes of their partner or themselves.

Each couple tends to develop a coping style that is characteristic of them. One partner feels rejected and may give up, become depressed, or opt for an affair. The other feels pushed, invaded, upset, or angry. The Joneses may pick a fight when they get too close; Mr. Smith may absorb himself in a hobby; Mrs. Beatty becomes the pride of the PTA, Girl Scouts, Sunday school, and Mothers Against Drunk Drivers.

DEPENDENCY

Our society formerly accepted the need for men to be independent and women to be dependent. Now women are encouraged not to depend on anyone! But the fact is that men and women were made to need each other. Much of the misunderstanding between the sexes stems from our inability to admit that wholeness and holiness come from mutual dependence.

A man may separate from his mother, but the need for mothering remains. I rarely find myself in a group of women who do not refer to the "need" their men have for them.

"He is helpless when I'm gone!"

"When he is sick, he is a total baby."

"All men are just little boys!"

Men want to be cared for, to be encouraged, to know they are wanted and found desirable. A wife's love and interaction must convey her belief and hope in him. Home may be the only safe place he can express himself emotionally.

It has been my experience that most women seriously underestimate how important confidence building and their loyal support is to a man. The "liberated" thinking of the day fuels a woman's resentment of anyone or anything that depends on her. It demands that men be more open and vulnerable, but maligns them when they are. There are two proverbs that speak to this:

> The wise woman builds her house, but with her own hands the foolish one tears hers down (Prov. 14:1 NIV).

> A worthy wife is her husband's joy and crown; the other kind corrodes his strength and tears down everything he does (Prov. 12:4 LIVING BIBLE).

Women also need to depend on others. Everyone accepts that. The well-kept secret is that women have the capacity of independence and emotional strength. From childhood, interaction with others and what others thought of her have been important. Most significantly women have the strength to be vulnerable and express their emotional needs—unless it has to do with sex. To be open about sex still carries the stigma of being inappropriate for a "good" woman. Boys are "bad" because they rob or destroy property. What do you think of when you hear of a "bad" girl?

PROBLEMS OF INITIATION

Few women have grown up with the belief that sex is something they may initiate. This is unfortunate, because the initiator has a head start. Having the head start offers a distinct advantage to a women. Furthermore, if only men are initiators, then the concept of mutuality in marriage is obscured and men complain, justifiably, that initiating sex is almost always up to them. Judging by the phone calls that come in for my teenaged son, the world may be changing. Women are taking initiative in interacting with men. But for many women, their training in passivity remains a problem that can take many years and much reinforcement to break.

Couples often miss opportunities because the initiator does not send a clear or strong message. It may be that a husband or wife misses the coded message for sex that each gives. When she said she was tired and going to bed, he believed her! When he said he had been "thinking" of her all day, she simply thought that was nice. Sometimes communication techniques need improvement or deciphering. Couples need to be taught the importance of clear communication when one desires an opportunity for making love.

Partners need to talk about the matter of initiating, especially if there is resentment on the part of one spouse because the other either "never" initiates or "always initiates at the wrong time." In the pattern of initiation may lie some attitudes of one spouse toward sex and the sexual relationship. If one spouse lovingly expresses the need for things to change and there is no movement, the meaning sex holds for the reluctant spouse should be explored. A habit pattern can be broken, given time and encouragement. Lack of desire, fear of intimacy, fear of performance, low priority given to sex, anger, and lack of trust can all contribute to the problem.

RELUCTANCE TO BE SEXY

By now we should be well aware of the many factors that cause people ambivalence over expressing their sensuousness. God made humans so that they could be sexy creatures, but Christians have a hard time accepting and acting on that. Because counselors and pastors usually deal with those who misuse their sexuality, sexual counseling is commonly thought to exist because people get out of control sexually and need to be brought into line.

The reality is that *more people suffer from the effects of shame and the resultant inhibitions than from a problem of sexual control.* From 25 to 50 percent of all people must deal with a sexual dysfunction at some time in their lives. The majority suffer from inhibitions and not lack of control.

It is hard for many people to create and maintain an atmosphere of eroticism, but good sex and excellent marriages require it. Most people do not understand the need to work at creating an environment that is conducive to romance and sex. Solomon understood it: his bedroom was a sensual delight. Shulamith knew it: her nightclothes hinted at the promise that was underneath.

If sex were simply a matter of genital coupling, the atmosphere would not make a difference. But atmosphere contributes much to the sexual encounter. A woman who is comfortable with lingerie and other accouterments to attract, stimulate, and "seduce" her spouse adds a dimension to the sex act it was clearly meant to have. Her positive attitude affirms that the body and its mechanisms for sexual response are accepted and that expression of them will provide a bond that affirms the lovers and their relationship.

"To be sexy, then, is to be aware of one's body as an instrument of playfulness and delight, to be able to communicate this awareness to others, and then to commit oneself to a gift of the body in a mutual search for pleasure, delight, variety, and playfulness."[4] Sensuousness blossoms when nurtured with leisure and relaxation. Too many constraints eliminate the playful aspect. Real joy can result from the unity experienced as a result of the combination of play and passion.

A major excuse frequently given for not fostering an erotic atmosphere is the time young couples must spend nurturing children. But parents must be reminded that the best thing they can do for the security of their offspring is to maintain a solid husband-wife relationship. Healthy marriages have enriching and renewing sex lives, a fact the children know intuitively. Like anything of importance, sexual satisfaction depends on the time, energy, and thoughtful planning devoted to it.

AGING AND SEX

The factor that determines whether or not a couple will continue to function sexually as they become older is the frequency and consistency of their sexual expression. Aging should not seriously hinder a healthy sexual relationship, but it is not uncommon for an older couple to reduce or discontinue intercourse. Such couples have very likely become bored with one another; they long ago gave up trying to maintain an erotic relationship (if they ever did). Taking one another for granted is hard on the ego. If sex has never been particularly satisfying, its demise is seen as a welcome relief.

The greatest difference between the sexual functioning of an older and a younger man is the increased susceptibility of the aging man to mental stress. A hard day at the office for a thirty-year-old can be forgotten as he approaches his wife at night. A bad or stressful day more significantly reduces the interest and affects the performance of the fifty-year-old. While mental fatigue is his greatest sexual stressor, overindulgence, particularly of alcohol, is second in importance. The cure that is sought by a number of middle-aged men is a new partner.

Physical and mental infirmities, especially chronic illness in either spouse, reduce functioning. As with all ages, fear of poor performance causes avoidance of sex even though it is rarely acknowledged by the couple as the reason for difficulties.

SEX THERAPY IN MALADAPTIVE MARRIAGES

There is controversy over whether sex therapy should be attempted in marriages that are clearly troubled. Counselors should be cautious if a couple appear to be on the verge of divorce. They may consider sex therapy as proof of having made the ultimate effort, and its failure the justification for getting out of the marriage.[5]

Occasionally the motivation is not to save the marriage, but to "fix the spouse, so she or he can have a shot at a new marriage" or some such variation. Since descriptions of the sexual functioning of the other spouse are notoriously subjective, be sure to evaluate each spouse's perspective. By hearing from each individually and then both together, we can get a better idea of what actually happens at home.

Both marriage counseling and sex therapy contribute to improving a marriage. Increased sexual satisfaction leads to increased marital happiness, and improved communication results in better sexual communication. Sometimes individual therapy is necessary before couple work can begin. At other times sex therapy provides the couple with an opportunity to develop a comfort level from which other problems can be approached. Do not flatly refuse to bring sexual counseling into a distressed marriage; simply be aware of the pitfalls.

DISORDERS OF SEXUAL DESIRE

Sexual desire is related to both biological and motivational factors.[6] Generally a person's biological drive is activated during adolescence by some unknown process in the brain that causes an increased desire for sexual behavior. Both the male's and the female's biologically induced desire has a base dependence on testosterone, of which the critical level for activation varies according to the individual.

Characteristically there is a reduction of drive in men from thirty on, and a peak in interest for women in the thirties with a decline occurring in the forties. But this biological state does not necessarily affect sexual activity or pleasure. Many other factors are at work on the motivational side of desire that moderate the effects of biology.

Within this typical pattern, a person's sex drive tends to have a consistency over one's lifetime that is probably related as much to extrinsic motivational factors as to intrinsic biological ones. Willingness to express one's sexuality is induced both from the basic drive and from the conscious decision to allow oneself to be responsive. Nonverbal, verbal, tactile, and interpersonal behaviors combine with what the person hears, sees, and reads to order a reaction when an approved attractive man or woman appears on the scene.

The sex therapy that pastors and counselors typically provide deals with the will of the person in question. Kaplan's triphasic model is helpful in understanding specifically what the problem is and focusing on the possible intervention. A few definitions will help to clarify. Desire, excitement, and orgasm are related but separate. Kaplan states it this way: there is a "common generator," but each has its own "circuitry."[7] Problems may occur with all three, any two or just one.

Low desire, for instance, may be the result of discouraging experiences with keeping an erection, or it may be due to an inner conflict that affects one's feeling about being sexual. In the first case, intervention would be focused on maintaining erection, whereas the second would require an examination first of why sex has become fearful, then a look at any secondary dysfunctions. *Lack of desire* can be *global*—which means there is no desire in any situation; or it can be *situational*—a man may masturbate or perform with a prostitute, but not with his wife, for example. Another category is *hypoactive* sexual desire, meaning no desire. *Inhibited* sexual desire refers to a condition in which an individual is sometimes able to function but derives no pleasure. *Genuine low sex drive* is found in people who enjoy sex after they have it, but who otherwise do not think about it or seek it out.

It is commonly but mistakenly assumed that the spouse with the greater desire for sex is healthier, when the discrepancy should be viewed merely as a difference. People have varying levels of naturally occurring sexual interest, or "horn-iness." It is not uncommon for a person who is regarded as having a low desire in one marriage to be considered as having a high desire in a second marriage.

A difference in desired frequency of sex is not a low-drive problem. The difference is not resolved by taking each person's desired frequency and dividing by two! That results in *two* people not getting what they want. Instead a couple should be encouraged to communicate and explore comfortable means by which the one who wants more frequent sex can be satisfied. Approval of self-pleasuring or techniques that do not demand the sexual response of the less interested partner may be one solution. New ways of defining "sex" also enables the partner who views sex as requiring a lot of energy to feel comfortable with less elaborate plans and more casual encounters.

Extreme cases of low desire may indicate a phobic or aversive avoidance of sex. People who experience such strong reactions to the possibility of sexual intimacy may totally "shut down" their ability to feel (anesthetic avoidance) or may experience other panic reactions. Treatment may require medi-cation and long and tedious desensitization procedures.

In all cases of blocked sexual desire, negative thoughts are instituted early in the arousal process. It is normal to shut down sexual responses when a person ends up in the wrong sexual situation. Few respond sexually when they are hard at work, in the company of a child or grandparent, or when raped. This selectivity is normal and protective. But such blocking is pathological when the situation is appropriate and the person continues to call the mechanism into play.

Careful evaluation is required to ensure that one does not work on a dysfunction when the real problem is lack of desire (guaranteed failure), or treat lack of desire when the couple naturally have a low frequency that is satisfying to them. Sex therapist Joseph LoPiccolo at Texas A & M uses the following guidelines after checking out all other extenuating circum-stances: if a couple are under forty-five and have sex less than once every two weeks or over forty-five and have sex less than once a month, they are accepted for treatment.

CAUSES OF LOW DESIRE

It can be generalized that ". . . patients suffering from blocked desire have, as a group, deeper and more intense sexual anxieties and/or greater hostility towards their partners and/or more tenacious defenses than those patients whose sexual dysfunctions are associated with erection and orgasm difficulties."[8]

Ironically, the same involuntary turn-off mechanism that works so efficiently to suppress sexual desire in wrong settings is the workhorse of low-desire problems. Individuals learn to put themselves in negative states by implementing "turn-offs" that succeed in making them angry, fearful, disgusted, or distracted.

Persons with low desire may focus on something negative, physically or emotionally, in the partner:

"I can't stand her big thighs."

"He just uses me."

"She spends too much money."

Nonerotic things like work, children, the washing, and money worries are used as distractions. Sometimes people direct the turn-offs at themselves:

"I'm no good."

"My breasts are too small."

"I'm sure I'll never last long enough to please her."

"I'm too tired."

Such thoughts are self-generated and are selected negatives that successfully preclude arousal.

The thoughts themselves are not the whole problem. Often there is a multiple etiology. For many people the thoughts are simply the mechanisms used to keep them away from behavior that engenders fear and anxiety. The fear and anxiety may be linked to religious inhibitions that prove conflicting, but there are other possibilities.[9]

Ambitious, hard-driving people (Christians?) who focus on their work or "mission" sometimes have difficulty allowing themselves to spend time on anything else. Pleasurable activities appear to them to conflict with their work ethic. Perhaps pleasure itself has never been rewarded. Obsessive-compulsive patterns are common among persons who have a hard time feeling good about having fun.

Fear of success causes people to sabotage sexual arousal. Perhaps Mom let it be known there could be only one attractive lady in the house, or Dad made it clear he was the only winner around. Sex with an appropriate, "successful" partner is inevitably undermined in line with the unexamined script of their youth that states success is to elude them. The impairment ranges from total shutdown to performance-but-only-with-the-wrong-person.

There is a similar kind of person who sets up failure when everything is going well:

"You can't have everything."

"I'm not entitled to pleasure."

Success-phobic individuals fail to view sex as something to accept and enjoy; they see it instead as a competitive statement.

Specific phobias and aversions to parts of the body or the sex act in general are found most often in cases of adult survivors of rape or incest. They often require intensive and long-term therapeutic work. Ordinary sexual counseling is usually not the answer to problems brought on by rape and incest experiences.

Sexual deviations make sex "safe" for certain people. The fetish, cross-dressing, or other paraphernalia help displace the anxiety felt about sexual intercourse itself to the acting-out behavior. Without the crutch, the man—it usually is a man—does not believe he can function, or function well. Couples in which this may be a factor may present with a complaint related to low desire. Either the history or the failure to progress may reveal the male's insecurity. Desensitization, reassurance, and understanding can be helpful in breaking a pattern, depending on the degree of importance it holds for an individual. (Chapters 10 and 11 provide further information on this subject.)

Some other causes of low desire may be obvious to the observer but not to the participant: fear of pregnancy, depression, body image, and aging concerns. A rather larger population (including many Christians) fears loss of control once sex urges are acknowledged. Also, problems within a relationship obviously can result in low desire. A partner who has gained two hundred pounds since the wedding or smokes heavily or has poor hygiene can be a turn-off to the spouse. Since it is very difficult to convert a "turn-off" into a "turn-on," the most successful intervention involves working with the annoyance and assisting the offending spouse in making some realistic changes.

Low sexual desire may be the result of having a partner with poor sexual skills. A woman may complain of sex being too rapid, the man not being sensitive to her needs or concentrating simply on having an orgasm. Because husbands and wives care, there is fear of hurting the loved one by telling the truth, or shame at not being able to overlook such "minor" grievances. The body does not lie or shade the truth; it simply refuses to function.

Marital difficulties, especially those that are loaded with anger, significantly affect desire. Anger can vary in intensity; it may be superficial and temporary, or accumulated from childhood. It is not always easy to identify and label. Anger leaves no room for arousal.

However, the most common among the relationship-related causes of low desire have already been alluded to. They are at the heart of male-female differences: fear of closeness, of being vulnerable, of loss, and of trust. These intimacy fears overwhelm as a couple experience the unity and significance of the sex act. Their optimal levels of closeness are invaded, causing one or both to retreat from anything (like touch) that might lead to sex. If the partner who desires sex pulls back from his or her demands, sex will be initiated again later, but the cycle repeats itself.

One should not overlook the possibility that either the man or the woman may use sex as a passive-aggressive solution to a perceived power imbalance. For example, if a spouse feels he or she has little to say in the decisions affecting the marriage, minimal influence over the partner, and negligible control over the household or finances, withholding sex or diminishing one's responsiveness can change the role from "victim" to "victimizer" with minimal overt effort.

TREATMENT OF LOW SEX DESIRE

People who are truly comfortable and conflict-free with their sexuality will arrange life to include sex. Such people will not call into action negative turn-offs, but will choose to recognize and appreciate positively the spouse, an opportunity for sensuousness, and the relationship. They will arrange for Grandmother occasionally to take the children for an uninterrupted evening or weekend. They will avoid arguments and make settings appropriate for sex to occur. The expectation is that it will be invigorating and result in greater closeness.

Because so few people find themselves behaving consistently in such a sex-positive way, it is easy to see why low sex desire is the primary presenting problem in sex therapy. Appropriate treatment involves intervention on four fronts: affectual awareness, insight, cognitive change, and drive induction.[10] The fact that there are four fronts makes the process of intervention somewhat complicated.

Affectual awareness is simply a person's perception of his or her feelings about sex. Couples and individuals are notoriously ignorant about why they do not feel sexual. There is minimal emotional awareness even among the highly sophisticated and well-educated. When they are asked, "How do you feel when you are touched or when you are simply approached?" they may reply, "coerced" or "resentful"or "pushed." But though they may perceive these feelings, they usually lack insight as to their source and meaning for their actual sexual experience.

Insight is sought for a clue to the source of the problem:

"Where did you learn that?"
"Where do you think that comes from?"
"What do you get out of maintaining the problem?"
"What would change if you are able to function well sexually?"

Questions like these make it possible for a counselor to surface a potential insight that could set a course for dealing with the problem. When there is resistance to accepting a new view of a long-held belief, it is sometimes helpful to try a reverse role play. Let the person convince you why he or she should give up a belief or attitude while you attempt to persuade the person to keep it.

Counselors may need to confront clients if they perceive them acting in a self-destructive way:

> "It appears that 90 percent of you wants to change, but the 10 percent that doesn't seems to be working overtime. Why do you think that is?"

> "Why are you doing this to yourself?"

And if it is appropriate:

> "Why are you willing to risk losing your relationship over this?"

None of these questions should be asked without having taken a good history and having established good rapport.

Cognitive change involves what the person or couple want to do with the insight that has been gained. Cognitions have been found to have a major effect on behavior. Many teenage girls harboring romantic notions of marriage are hurt when their inexperienced husbands underestimate the positive value of a night out together or of an unanticipated compliment. She assumes, "He really doesn't love me." Her behavior toward him reflects her disappointment, which in turn makes him even less likely to do something special for her.

Those ideas require intervention. One way to deal with distorted ideas and destructive assumptions is with positive ideas and true assumptions. Have the clients write out on a three-by-five card affirmations relevant to their situations. With these cognitive changes in written form, they have something to consult when anxiety levels rise:

> "God wants me to have a rich and fulfilling sexual relationship with my husband."

> "I will no longer allow the relationship between Mom and Dad to affect my relationship."

> "I don't have to be afraid of my husband."

Larry Crabb, a biblical counselor who has done much work on the integration of the Bible and psychology, asks his clients at this point to overcome their old belief system by taking a "leap of faith" and acting in a way that acknowledges that they have become a "new person" in Christ by putting off the old. At this same point, prayer can also be effective in "renewing" minds and supporting a view of sexuality and problem-solving that reflects God's perspective.

Drive induction, in contrast to the first three interventions, is mostly behavioral in nature. Often sexual anxiety can be rapidly reduced with techniques that enable people to experience arousal in a setting that eliminates as much threat as possible. If the desire problem is mild, the focus will be centered here and the homework will provide the opportunity to deal with anxiety as it surfaces. The deeper the problem, the more probing of unconscious issues must first be done. Attending to arousal decreases attention to resistance.

Drive must be reintroduced. If people are involved in a project, they may forget to eat. By contrast, the flashing of a sundae on TV or the chiming of a clock is an external cue that may cause them to focus attention on the stomach and realize the hunger. People who have turned off their desires frequently are no longer in touch with external cues of arousal. So they must be encouraged once again to become aware of what is sexually stimulating to them and to make note of it. Suggestions are made to reorient the person away from a shutdown of sexual feelings in the appropriate setting and with the husband or wife to an opening up of sexual feelings.

A woman might be encouraged to read a romance novel or watch a romantic movie. There are several books on women's fantasies that might help her become aware of her own sexual feelings. Men are encouraged similarly. One must choose carefully the books to be read and the types of sexual thoughts and pictures that are to be encouraged. With that caution, effective release from inhibited behavior can take place.

SENSATE FOCUS

Masters and Johnson's sensate focus exercises form the basis of many sexual counseling programs and are crucial to the treatment of low desire. They work by prescribing and controlling the sensual interaction between the husband and wife to deal with their avoidance of sex or their high-anxiety pattern in approaching sex. Having been encouraged to put aside a special time, to make it a priority, and to eliminate performance anxiety, they become free to relax and concentrate on pleasurable sensations. New ways of being together are learned that are encouraged and reinforced by the therapist. Thus it is the pleasure derived from communication through touch and verbalization of their feelings that reinforces their new relationship and aids in the breakdown of old patterns.

Besides desensitization and alleviation of performance fears, the exercises are designed to make the couple aware of the specific elements of sexual functioning that are unique to them. They may enjoy lotions or natural body odors, having dimmed lights or a few candles to create a romantic mood. They may like to have music or some other environmental factor as a possible enhancement to their lovemaking.

Despite the intimate setting, there may still be a shutdown of feeling. The emotions and resistance that rise to consciousness can then be taken back to the therapist as well as discussed between the couple. Sensate focus helps a couple increase their ability to communicate about sex.

Step 1 of sensate focus may have to start with exercises designed to get the couple comfortable with each other's nude bodies. Taking a shower together or lying back to back may be all that can be tolerated at first. Throughout therapy, all sessions are to last only as long as they are fun, relaxing, and not tiring. Each is to explore the genitals of the other to learn the anatomy. When the couple are comfortable, they proceed to take turns stimulating one another. There is to be no intercourse or genital touching during this stage.

The goals are many:

1. The couple can learn to touch within a context that is free from anxiety;
2. Their awareness of pleasure to be found in touch can be reawakened;

3. They can develop assurance that their partner is a trustworthy person with whom they can share sexual desires, fears, and concerns;
4. They can learn that giving pleasure is pleasurable;
5. They can discover that their pleasure is unique to them and they must take responsibility for communication about their sexual desires;
6. They can learn that sexual sharing should be attempted only when the body is relaxed or capable of becoming relaxed, or when one is willing to be sexual.

Step 2 of sensate focus exercises is the addition of touching behaviors that involve erotic areas previously kept out-of-bounds. This step is not begun until repetition of step 1 has alleviated most of the anxiety and feelings of silliness. Bringing the partner to orgasm is not the goal in step 2 and is forbidden.

Each partner is to communicate exactly what feels erotic and comfortable. Developing an honest relationship in which it is acceptable to say no is a freeing experience. Unless people can say no, they cannot give an honest and unqualified yes. Each partner can learn from the other how a no can be made to hurt less. Between completing step 2 and beginning step 3, if both partners are capable of orgasm, they are asked to masturbate in the presence of their partner. For those who prefer it, the passive partner's hand can rest on the active one's hand, reducing the feeling of having or being a "spectator" and increasing the sense of sharing. Although this is almost always difficult, it is one of the most valuable steps of therapy. It releases each partner to be able to share such intimate behavior with a trustworthy spouse. Each spouse learns more accurately the partner's response pattern, and a greater bond develops between the couple.

Step 3 is a continuation of pleasurable activities that may result in orgasm, or at least the slow reintroduction of intromission with no specific expectations. Attention is directed to the feelings of "containment." As comfort and excitement levels increase, thrusting can be increased and orgasm allowed as the couple so desire.

If, as often happens, there are secondary dysfunctions to

the low desire, such as premature ejaculation or anorgasm, steps 1 and 2 are practiced concurrently or after individual work on the dysfunction. For example, before masturbation is shared, a previously anorgasmic woman would have to have worked through a program in which she experiences orgasm on her own. Details of treatment for individual dysfunction will be presented in chapters 9 and 10.

The fact that sensate focus is incorporated into every reputable sex therapy program speaks highly of the effectiveness of an *in vivo*, performance-free environment in which sexual relating can be restructured. When sensate focus is not used, the possibilities of positive changes occurring in a couple's sexual life are slim. Talking, sharing, educating, and gaining insight into causes and attitudes are an important dimension of effective therapy. But a structured program of sexual relating is often the only effective follow-through in bringing about a significant change. Without a program like sensate focus in the therapy plan, it will likely yield limited results.

CONCLUSION

Sexual desire disorders have emerged as the primary sexual problem of the eighties. During times of stress or illness, low desire or lack of desire will be a factor with which many people must contend, at least temporarily. For those whose relationships are permanently colored by a desire disorder, the multitude of causes makes improvement not impossible, but definitely a challenge.

In treating desire disorders, the combination of techniques of increased affectional awareness, insight, cognitive changes, and drive induction has been found to result in significant improvements. Through such techniques people are helped accurately to perceive their arousal. Where necessary, they learn to facilitate erotic feelings. They are encouraged to identify and act on the cues that define what is sexual in their relationship and in their personal universe. Change comes by an awareness that they can be all that God intends them to be sexually. Further research and clarification of the interaction of causes may yield even more insight into the many dynamic factors that help bring about positive changes.

Although this chapter has focused much attention on techniques for helping couples with sexual problems, the fundamental challenge is not one of technique. The lack of understanding between men and women calls for a concerted effort among counselors to encourage the development of an atmosphere in which the clients can come to know and appreciate each other. Quite simply, the man must hear and understand the woman, and the woman must hear and understand the man. Then it may be possible for them to become one flesh.

Chapter Nine

HER SEARCH FOR THE PROMISE
Special Concerns of the Female

I have a cartoon of a bride and groom preparing for their first night together. The bride is lying across the bed with a bottle of chloroform in one hand and a cloth in the other. The caption says, "Go ahead, I'm yours, do whatever you want with me."

The cartoon reflects an attitude that has held considerable sway: sex is something the female is to endure, but certainly not enjoy. Times have changed, you say? Perhaps. The modern bride might say she has the right to enjoy sex. But there is still ambivalence when it comes to putting sexual responsiveness and assertiveness into practice. The suggestion that "women are not interested in sex," or at least "good women" are not, lingers. In fact, after the newness of the honeymoon wears off, after the first baby is born, after the ordeal of an eighteen-hour day of job, housekeeping, and doctor's appointments, many women are simply not interested in sex.

In many cultures, women grow up learning to please men by knowing when to take the initiative sexually, by being creative, and by expressing their personal responsiveness. But Western culture, as we have noted, has at times discouraged women from perceiving themselves as sexual and has not encouraged the notion they are to enjoy sex until recently.

Women who are sexually expressive and aggressive are often hindered from expressing themselves as they would like and sometimes view themselves as freaks—a perception that may be reflected by both men and other women. Some men find sexually aggressive women threatening. Women who do not have a strong conviction that sex is good and that they are to participate assertively and enjoy it easily accept a pattern of sexual passivity, if not indifference.

It is not easy to give up truisms that have been broadcast over a lifetime. It is true that in general, women are less sexually aggressive than men. Research supports this belief. The Bible recognizes that men and women have different sexual natures. But Scripture nowhere even hints that women are not to be interested in sex, nor does it suggest that differences between men and women can be used as an excuse for the woman to be sexually passive or unresponsive.

The Song of Songs advises that the husband and wife approach one another in the way that is most pleasing and meaningful to the other. The man is to consider the women's need for romance, the woman the man's delight in the raw energy of the physical. This may not feel natural at first, but it becomes so with effort and experience. Scripture suggests that mutuality is an essential element in sexual relations. Neither owns his or her own body; sex is not to be withheld (1 Cor. 7); mutual initiation, stimulation, and active participation in intercourse (Song of Songs) are all warranted by Scripture.

ARE FEMALES SEXUALLY PASSIVE?

The fact that a woman's sexual response is different from a man's should not automatically imply that women are by nature more passive. Women who see all their roles in life to be passive and dependent will likely view themselves as sexually passive also. A woman may presume that if her role is to submit to a man, it follows that her orgasm should be his responsibility. The more powerless or dependent she feels, the less possible it is for her to respond without the right male using the perfect technique he is naturally supposed to have acquired.

The capacity for orgasm is not merely a physical condition. It also has a very significant psychological component. Highly orgasmic women are not usually passive; they are able to initiate sex and encourage their partners to do what is necessary for them to respond. Less orgasmic women are less likely to initiate sex or even talk about their needs. In a misguided effort to please the partner, they rarely make the very requests that would ensure their sexual pleasure.[1] In such cases it is not the female body that makes the difference; it is the mind in combination with social upbringing and learning that makes sexual responsiveness so challenging.

A woman has just as much capacity for sexual pleasure and expressiveness as a man. With manual manipulation she can experience orgasm as quickly and easily as he does.[2] Her potential for orgasm is greater. Barring anatomical differences, both male and female orgasms depend on the same processes of vasocongestion and myotonia. The amount of engorgement, considerable in both, is simply less obvious in the female.

The genitals of males and females are similar in their embryonic origin. Hormones account for the differentiation and specialization. Cells that develop into the glans on the male penis become the clitoris in the female. Those cells constitute the most sensitive genital area of each sex. The scrotum has the same cellular structure as the female's outer lips, and the inner lips are analogous to the shaft of the penis.

Several years ago much was being written about the "infinite capacity" of the female for sexual stimulation and response.[3] Speculation abounded on what the world would be like should the female unleash her erotic potential! It was even suggested that men, feeling threatened, have deliberately conspired to convince women that they are sexually passive by nature. But in fact, men who are confident in themselves generally prefer responsive, assertive partners.[4] In marriages where females are assertive, there is less reticence to discuss sexual functioning, greater clarity on the necessity and requirements of foreplay, and less sexual anxiety for both.[5]

Females have also been labeled passive because they are considered the "receiving" partner in sexual intercourse. But coitus is better understood if it is looked upon as a sharing of organs. The grasping, tenting, and muscular throbbing of the vagina is not passive! It both responds and initiates, and by so doing it contributes to the pleasure of the man and the woman.

THE PRIMARY SEX PROBLEM IN WOMEN

Difficulty with orgasmic response is the most common female dysfunction. As with desire problems, the cause is often due to an interaction of factors. In contrast to desire problems, most cases are comparatively easy to resolve. Situationally orgasmic problems—those in which a woman experiences orgasms in some situations but not others—have the lowest cure rate.

It is easier to rule out the factors that do not bear on female orgasmic response than those that do. There is no clear link, for example, between lack of orgasm and general mental health. A person who is quite mentally ill may still respond; a person who is psychologically sound may not.[6] Response is not dependent on the presence or absence of the so-called feminine qualities: friendliness, emotionalism, impulsiveness, conventionality, religiosity, or timidity.

The factors that do appear to have a positive effect on a woman's response pattern are fewer in number. Higher education and social class are consistently linked with greater responsiveness. An ability to trust in the relationship in which the woman finds herself is an underlying theme in many studies.[7]

Trust appears to be linked to the type of relationship a girl had with her father. Less orgasmic women often had emotionally or physically absent fathers who appeared to have little interest or concern about them or what they did. A girl may have loved her father, but she could not be dependent on him. A woman's perception of her father as protective and affirming correlates with her ability to have orgasm with intercourse.[8]

Many studies indicate the father's critical role in a girl's evolving sexual identity.[9] His active and caring relationship with her engenders her ability to relate to a man sexually and to be responsive. (We can only speculate as to what will be the case with future generations who are currently growing up in one-parent households.) Just as active and caring involvement of the father engenders trust, so also is trust destroyed by fathers who sexually abuse their daughters.

WHAT IS AN ORGASM?

The lingering myth of the vaginal orgasm continues to cause difficulties. I know of situations where inability to have a vaginal orgasm has been used as "proof" of a woman's inability to accept her wifely role, giving the husband one more justification for leaving the marriage.

The fact is, orgasm is a reflex. A woman's orgasm has a single physiological trigger regardless of the method of stimulation. It is not strange that a woman might feel that the vagina is the source or a source of stimulation toward orgasm. It makes sense because of the geography and topography of the woman's genitals. But the clitoris is the trigger that initiates a set of reactions. The claim that a woman's psychological state and her ability to surrender or not surrender to her husband determines whether she experiences orgasm vaginally is dubious and possibly misleading.

Some of the confusion about vaginal orgasms stems from the differences among women in the sensitivity of the vagina. Women can become more aware of potentially sensitive areas through training. Fithian and Hartman[10] encourage women to feel the vaginal walls for excitable areas as one of their self-exploration exercises. Alan and Donna Brauer in their book *ESO* train people to locate reactive areas in order to heighten the orgasmic response and to experience an "extended sexual orgasm."[11]

Perry and Whipple, the authors of *The "G" Spot*, speak specifically of a nodule that is found on the anterior wall of the vagina. Systematic attempts to prove that such a spot exists for all women have been futile.[12] LoPiccolo[13] has concluded that reactive areas may exist, but their locations vary among women along with women's awareness of them, the ease with which they may be stimulated, and the subjective labeling the sensation is given. Because there is no single, authoritative "map" of a woman's reactive areas, it is ill-advised to suggest that a particular woman will experience this or that by stimulating such a mystery spot.

So far, the so-called ejaculate that is sometimes reported with stimulation of the "G" spot has yet to be proved to be anything but leakage of urine squeezed out by the contractions of the orgasmic platform. Since urine is sterile, there is no health hazard involved.

The great variation in patterns of female orgasm is often underestimated and unappreciated. A number of women consider themselves abnormal because their responses do not seem to conform to the typical model of female orgasm. Many women are orgasmic and do not know it because what they experience does not conform to the glorified movie or romantic novel description.

Women who expect to be orgasmic immediately upon marriage may be surprised and frustrated by the fact that an exciting orgasm does not materialize overnight. Because they have learned to suppress their sexual feelings while single, the sensations of sexual stimulation do not automatically bring the desired result. The orgasmic reaction requires time in which the woman begins to overcome inhibitions, develops an awareness of her own sexual mechanisms through sexual experience, and becomes skillful. Practice helps. Most women realize increased orgasmic response the longer they are married.

TREATMENT OF ORGASMIC DYSFUNCTION

A thorough history is necessary to rule out the possibility that low-desire problems may be the primary difficulty in orgasmic dysfunction. Similarly, a history will help identify women who have orgasms but are not recognizing them as such. Whether a woman suffers from primary-global problems (never having experienced orgasm under any circumstances) or secondary orgasmic dysfunction (orgasmic in the past but currently unable to respond), the treatment is the same: an integrative, systematic therapy is applied to desensitize, reeducate, and provide experiential reinforcement of new behavior.

Such a program is usually highly successful. A woman may work through the program alone or with aid from a therapist. One program I have found to be well-accepted and easy to follow is outlined in the book *Becoming Orgasmic: A Sexual Growth Program for Women*, by Julia Heiman, Leslie LoPiccolo, and Joseph LoPiccolo. After seven to ten weeks, 90 percent of the women following the program achieve orgasm in some way, 80 percent with their partner, and 40 percent solely with intercourse and no manual stimulation.[14]

Besides enabling women to become sexually responsive, the program has several other goals. The participants are helped to understand and be more aware of their attitudes toward sex. They learn that they possess sexual feelings capable of being expressed when the proper setting is at hand. Many are made aware for the first time that they can be enticed to be hungry for sex just as they can be enticed to eat when delicious and appetizing food is placed in front of them.

A good marriage and a good sexual relationship will not usually materialize for those people who assume that it comes by way of the mystical forces of magic and romance. The fact is that sexual expressiveness, like other good things in life, must be consciously worked on. One's sincerity and commitment to the marriage in general do not ensure achieving the goal.

THE PROGRAM

The program begins with an evaluation of early influences on the woman's attitude toward sex through directed questions. For example:

"In what ways did your religious upbringing influence your attitudes towards sex?"

"Were your parents verbally or physically affectionate with one another?"

"At what age did you start to date?"

"Did you have any unpleasant experiences of physical intimacy with strangers or a family member or friend?"[15]

That first stage of developing psychological self-awareness is followed by a stage of physical self-awareness in which the woman explores her own body by observing and by touching. This is an important stage, for many women have never really looked carefully or objectively at their bodies, and fewer still have actually located the clitoris and the vaginal and urethral openings or have observed the uniqueness of their labia minora and majora.

Because most women find this exercise threatening, relaxation methods are introduced[16] and women are reminded to pay attention to environmental and internal factors that contribute to their comfort level. Learning to relax is essential to all aspects of the program.

Once a woman can objectively view her body without anxiety, she is asked to explore it for the pleasurable sensations it can produce. If negative feelings and blocks arise, they are dealt with. As the sessions continue, touching becomes increasingly focused on the areas of the body that she finds highly arousing. The woman is taught to focus on her feelings and pleasurable experience and in her exercises to avoid the role of spectator so as not to block the body sensations.

As the self-exploration exercises move her closer to orgasm, she is asked to role-play an exaggerated orgasm. Women who feel they are on the verge of having an orgasm often find role-playing to be extremely freeing, enabling them to "let go" and experience full orgasmic pleasure. The role-playing can actually pave the way for an orgasmic response.

SOME IMPORTANT POINTS

From the very beginning of the program, training for Kegel exercises is suggested.[17] Kegel exercises are used to increase control and heighten the feeling of the muscles surrounding the genitals of both men and women. Though some therapists feel that strengthening the orgasmic platform is *the* secret to female orgasm, most agree only that it is at least helpful. Isolating and controlling appropriate muscles and squeezing down in intercourse does intensify the sensation of pleasure.

The Department of Psychiatry and Psychology at Texas A & M has modified the use of the treatment described in *Becoming Orgasmic* by insisting that husbands get the same homework assignment as wives. Both are to work through the sexual history and the exercises that increase the comfort and pleasure levels. There are sound reasons for this recommendation. There is a tendency to place blame for orgasmic dysfunction solely on the woman. Husbands have been known to shift all responsibility for improvement onto the wife. But sexual problems are relationship problems. So when the husband participates, he becomes part of the process of improvement. His willingness to explore his body gives his wife permission to learn to enjoy her body, for he is doing the same exercises and experiencing similar fears, inhibitions, and difficulties.

The husband's attitude has a tremendous impact therapeutically. The impact can be either positive or negative. Usually his message is "I'm the expert, you're the problem." He may resist or resort to excuses such as "I know how to masturbate." The counselor can counter with "Good, you will have no problem following the program. Your participation will give your wife the permission and encouragement she needs to do the exercises."

If the husband says, "I can't do that!" he should be told, "Good, if it's difficult for you, you can be sympathetic with how much work it is for her." Sometimes a counselor has to confront a couple with something like this: "I don't understand. You say you both want sexual fulfillment in your marriage and this program will help. Why won't you follow through with it?"

For some Christians, a major stumbling block to such a program may be the necessity of exploring the body and masturbating. Individuals and couples must be given an opportunity to discuss their reservations about participating in what may appear to them to be wrong or improper. It is the case that women who masturbate have the same relationship with their husbands as those who do not.[18] But they also tend to think about sex somewhat more than women who do not masturbate. Since the vast majority of married women do not give sex a priority in their thought-life—a necessary ingredient to responsiveness and willingness to be sexual—the heightened sexual awareness of such women does not appear to be a threat either to their husbands or to society at large.

A woman who decides to spend some time, energy, and thought to develop her sexual responsiveness need not fear that she is acting against her Lord's wishes. It is His idea that sex be pleasurable. For most women it is through experience and conscious development that pleasurable responses can be achieved. The clitoris has no function in the female body except as an organ of sexual pleasure; this fact obviously suggests that God intended sex to be enjoyable for women as well as for men. The self-focus of therapeutic programs should be for the enhancement of the marriage; their purpose is not to create solitary pleasure for its own sake. Consequently the most important factor in helping the couple or the individual comply with the exercise is the approval and the encouragement of the pastor or counselor. (Masturbation is discussed in greater detail in chapter 11.)

Getting the sexual response cycle functioning is analogous to a person's learning to stand on her head or ride a bike. One tries and fails many times before catching the balance point, which then is never lost. Finding the "balance point" of sexual response enables a wife to share increased pleasure with her husband. A person does not talk herself into learning to stand on her head or ride a bike anymore than she can talk herself into being orgasmic. The response is learned experientially.

Some therapeutic programs suggest using fantasy or erotic materials in anorgasmic treatment. These suggestions must be handled with great discernment. Although 90 percent of men and women fantasize at least occasionally when they make love, those who fantasize excessively—and who might be encouraged to do so by some therapeutic programs—are more likely to be passive in sex and, not surprisingly, are more likely to be women. Perhaps such people are more passive because they cannot maintain two relationships—the real and the imagined. The more they become involved in the reality of the actual experience, the less the fantasy is used.[19]

A QUESTION OF GOALS

Maintaining a good sexual relationship is a struggle. Married believers are to offer themselves to each other in a manner that results in their sexual expression bringing mutual pleasure, increased closeness, and a bonding and unity that can be found in no other relationship. Whether a sexual act is appropriate depends on whether it achieves these goals. When a sexual relationship is not working, each person must ask himself or herself what he or she will do to realize improvement. Each must seek God's counsel in what should be learned from the difficulty; it may be patience, a stretching beyond perceived limitations, true unconditional love, or the accurate message of God's promise of pleasure.

Orgasm is not seen by all women as the epitome of sexual satisfaction—a fact incomprehensible to most younger men. Women can and do find pleasure and contentment in sexual relationships without orgasmic response. Even readily orgasmic women do not feel a need to be orgasmic within each sexual encounter. This is so because a woman tends to view "sexual success" in terms of the totality of the experience—did it result in increased feelings of unity, closeness, and pleasure?—instead of mere physical accomplishment.

Women often feel the pressure to be "normal" and experience orgasm regularly, especially with intercourse. The irony is that an orgasm produced merely by the movement of the penis in intercourse is not normal. Only 30 percent of all women can regularly have orgasm with coitus and no other means of stimulation.[20] In most encounters, additional stimulation must be part of the foreplay and actual orgasmic moment if orgasm is to occur.

Both men and women worry about a woman's ability to respond. Pressure on the female to have an orgasm may come from an insecure male who doubts his masculinity. A responsive female may also vicariously provide an outlet for a man's own inhibitions and feelings that he fears a macho man cannot express. Her uninhibited response, which may include tears, enables him to experience secondhand what he dare not allow himself to express. A female will put pressure on herself because of her need to have her femininity reinforced or out of a desire to please her husband.

After the woman is able to experience orgasm, the second half of treatment for orgasmic dysfunction involves transfer of the newly learned responsive behavior into a setting with her partner. Eighty percent of the women who go through the program are able to apply their ability to have an orgasm through self-stimulation to having an orgasm with a partner. (The procedure is described in chapter 8.)

Once a woman has learned to be confident and comfortable in being stimulated, she is ready to discover the coital positions that offer maximum stimulation of the clitoris or that allow for the possibility of simultaneous manual stimulation.

The basic approach to treatment of female orgasmic dysfunction involves a relatively standardized procedure that includes the following steps:

1. A look at past and present influences that may affect the ability to respond sexually
2. Self-exploration, which begins with observing oneself nude in a mirror, moves on to locating and naming of the female genitalia, and concludes with the woman comfortably looking at and touching her entire body
3. Relaxation procedures, taught to ensure a woman's ability to maintain a relaxed body within a sexual situation
4. Self-stimulation exercises, which help the woman learn specifically what she must do to achieve orgasm
5. The second part of treatment, which begins when the woman feels confident enough to share her ability to have an orgasm by having her partner present
6. Sensate focus exercises, through which the partners learn to stimulate one another in intercourse, manually, or through other means they are comfortable with in order to help the woman achieve orgasm

For difficult cases, various methods can be applied. For some it may be repeating the material in the book and the program of exercises—in whole or in part. For others—a woman who can have an orgasm only by squeezing her thighs, for instance—achieving success may require the use of a psychological technique known as systematic desensitization. This technique progresses in increments. First she simply rests a finger on the clitoris while stimulating herself in her usual way by squeezing her thighs. When she can be orgasmic with this new element, finger movement about the clitoris is added. Later the husband is brought into the room as she gets close to orgasm. If she is able to continue with him present, he lies down beside her the next time. So it goes: a disciplined and time-consuming desensitization.

Because it is mechanistic and sequential, desensitization requires much effort and patience. Often the couple decide to be content with whatever method enables the woman to respond and to no longer worry about orgasm within the confines of intercourse. This is generally a wise decision.

Sex is not a success simply because it results in orgasm. Nor does it succeed because both partners are simultaneously orgasmic. Coordinating two bodies to peak simultaneously can be distracting and tedious work. The sexual experience should be pleasure, not duty. The ten seconds or so of intense feeling in orgasm should never overshadow or dominate the totality of the experience—the sharing and intimacy that is truly "sex."

Causes of orgasmic dysfunction are varied. Inexperience, an unskilled lover, upbringing, or any of the factors mentioned in conjunction with desire problems can have their effect. With treatment the vast majority of inorgasmic women will experience orgasm. But a woman's response will always be more easily distracted than a man's. She must understand this. A baby's cry, a flash of tomorrow's obligations, or a misplaced hand can easily divert her attention. Staying focused becomes a major contributing factor in her ability to respond. Focusing is an art that requires a commitment and conscious effort.

PAINFUL INTERCOURSE

Painful intercourse can have either an organic or a psychogenic origin. A physical cause can be found in about 60 percent of the cases.[21] Examples are mentioned in chapter 6. Careful questioning can help one distinguish between the two types of causes. Complaints of hurting "down there" accompanied by declarations of never having liked sex are clues to a psychological origin. So is the inability of the person to imagine herself sexually successful. One needs to obtain specific information about how, when, and where the pain occurs, along with any personal evaluations a person may make, such as "Sex was good until after the baby." If there is any indication that the causes are not psychological, then a physical examination by a competent gynecologist is warranted.

VAGINISMUS

Vaginismus can be diagnosed only with a physician's help. True vaginismus is the reflexive and involuntary clamping down of the muscles surrounding the vaginal opening. The result is painful intromission and intercourse or, most often, a complete inability to accept the penis into the vagina.

Most cases present as unconsummated marriages. While one would assume that a couple finding themselves in this situation will immediately seek help, the average span of time that passes before help is sought is six years. By that time most couples work out alternative methods of sexual intimacy. It is common for such women to be orgasmic.

Husband and wife are treated together. There is usually some evidence of a couple's collusion in maintaining the status quo. Husbands may unconsciously fear the aggressiveness of sex and be overconcerned about injuring the wife or causing pain. They are often sexually inexperienced, so it is common for husbands to need help developing their skills as lovers.

It is essential that both understand that the woman does not consciously will the muscular clamping down. Kegel exercises are introduced to demonstrate that control of the pubococcygeous muscle is possible. Relaxation exercises are designed to put her at ease with her body. The opening chapters of *Becoming Orgasmic* can be adapted successfully to help women who suffer from vaginismus.

Once a comfort level with the body is achieved, dilators[22] are progressively introduced to stretch the introitus physically. If the couple view a film that demonstrates the use of the dilators, they will usually find the therapy less threatening.[23] As the woman succeeds in placing each gradually larger dilator into her vagina, her confidence increases in her ability to accept a penis.

When the woman's comfort level allows, the husband is introduced to the dilators and trust is developed as he helps in their insertion. Once success has been achieved with the largest dilator, the woman is instructed to attempt intromission from a female-astride position. This provides the assurance she needs that she is in control. The penis is different from the dilators, requiring much patience and encouragement. When containment is accomplished, the next session introduces slow thrusting. The woman is asked to be especially aware of her state of mind and relaxation level whenever she attempts intercourse. Sexual sharing is to take place with the maximum number of positive environmental and psychological factors.

Twenty-five percent of vaginismus cases are readily and easily treated; the rest are moderate to difficult. The most resistant are those caused by incest or rape. It is quite common to find instances of trauma of some sort in the history of women with vaginismus. It is not unusual to find cases in which insensitive physicians have inadvertently traumatized them as young children or have made remarks suggesting their genitals were ugly or unsatisfactory in some way.

At the heart of the problem is often anxiety and fear: fear of pain, a sense of vulnerability, or fear of the inability to function satisfactorily. A woman with vaginismus commonly has been raised in a home with a rigid, restrictive attitude toward sex. Her motivation to change is often external, such as the desire for pregnancy. The most crucial factor in treatment is her accepting the fact that her condition is involuntary. Usually this can be demonstrated in a doctor's office, although the ability to undergo a pelvic exam does not exclude the diagnosis of vaginismus since a pelvic exam may be perceived to be different from intercourse.

Chapter Ten

HIS SEARCH FOR THE PROMISE
Special Concerns of the Male

Men and women express their emotions differently. It is unfair and inaccurate to categorize men as unemotional. After the death of a loved one or a divorce, a man will generally experience a longer period of grief, more physical illnesses, more severe emotional distress, higher mortality rates, increased suicide attempts, and more antisocial and aggressive behavior. Men have emotions, and their emotions are real if not always expressed directly.

Men rely on women for emotional support. Woman was made to be a man's "helper." When a husband depends on his wife emotionally, he is acting in accordance with God's design for their relationship. To suggest that a man is weak unless he is independent of her, and masculine only if he controls and suppresses his emotions, is clearly unbiblical. Increasingly men are listing love and family above work in importance. Studies on marriage find that married men are more content with life and healthier than their single counterparts, married women, or single women. Divorced men remarry quickly because they want their needs for love, romance, and intimacy met. If sex was all a man wanted, there would be no need for him to marry.

A man often chooses to express his feelings in a different

way than a woman. His friendships may have a side-by-side character rather than face-to-face. A man might encourage a friend by inviting him to a ball game, whereas a woman might choose to talk directly about the matter. Both methods can be effective and appropriate. But the man's approach is often indirect and subtle.

A man's sexual functioning is affected by his emotional needs. If he is unable, out of fear of shattering the masculine image, to share his fears, to express his needs, and to articulate his expectations, he may suffer from various kinds of sexual difficulties. Sometimes a man finds himself pursuing sex because he cannot ask or does not know how to ask for his real needs to be met. It should not surprise him, therefore, when sex is not fulfilling.

MEN AND PERFORMANCE

Men grow up expecting their worth to be equated with their performance. A woman seldom faces the lifelong struggle to prove herself that so characterizes a man's existence. Every year on the job must be better than the year before, his tennis game must make steady progress, and each time he makes love, his penis must function on demand. If failure occurs in any area, his self-image plummets; past achievement provides no safety net.

A man expects to get results. His life of action is supposed to be sufficient testimony to his caring. He did not tell his wife he loved her last year, but he bought her a new car and took her to San Francisco. His reluctance to talk to her is an attempt to stay away from having to act on emotional situations he does not have a ready answer for or is confused about. It is difficult for him to understand that her expectation is not necessarily that he provide a solution, but merely that he offer an understanding ear.

If a person believes that the only thing worthwhile is something for which he or she must work, the fun of life can be missed. The effect of this belief on sex is to relegate it to a place of unimportance, reduce it to a practical means of relieving tension, or approach it as work. Approaching sex as work is hardly gratifying, because work demands performance and performance insists on reaching a goal. Striving for a goal causes anxiety. Anxiety and sexual response do not mix. Sex is not an achievement; it is a way of relating and having fun.

A major component in the treatment of all male dysfunctions is encouragement of the man to live through the worst scenario of failure he can imagine. If he can accept the image of himself suffering with the problem and still living through it and feeling okay, he can begin to reduce the anxiety he may experience in another (real) setting and begin to reduce his performance fears.

People are rarely cognizant of the ideologies they live with. Few men understand how deeply rooted their performance orientation is. If a man can confront and deal with his performance mentality, the result will be an improvement in his sexual functioning.

MEN AND SEXUAL MYTHS

The appropriate sexual equipment enables an individual to function well. But men often take that truth and draw some faulty conclusions. Some men have been known to cite inadequate vaginas as the source of their problems; nine out of ten such complaints have no validity. Others suspect that their problems are due to the small size of their penises. Female pleasure, the fantasy myth tells them, depends on its fantastic proportions. Erotic literature is replete with stories of the massive penis which, by its mere insertion, causes the female to go into ecstasy. Many men grow up actually believing the stories they hear!

The myth is contradicted by many facts that are often ignored. The most sensitive parts of a woman's genitalia are either external or one to two inches into the vagina. Furthermore, with erection, smaller penises get proportionately bigger than larger ones; most erect penises are in the same size range. The idea that sexual satisfaction is derived from something huge being placed in the vagina is not found among females, but commonly believed by men. The vagina is simply a collapsed tube that in almost all cases accommodates the size of the penis as necessary.

Another common myth is that only through stimulation by a fully erect penis can a woman be sexually content. In fact, pleasurable sex can occur for a woman even in the absence of an erection in the same way that she is not always dependent on having an orgasm. But in the fantasy model of sex, foreplay and touch are devalued when compared with intercourse and mutual orgasm.

Let me remind you that an important premise of this book is that sex has meaning beyond the mere physical and performance aspects of intercourse. Most Christians agree that sex is not simply bodily contact. But that belief in itself hardly begins to eliminate the questions. For example, why does sex continue to be defined—even by well-meaning theologians—in its narrowest and most reduced sense? Why is sex perceived as the performance of dancing genitals instead of as the oneness and unity that occurs when a man and a woman each have sensitively met the needs of the other person? A perfect performance can be an unloving act if it does not assuage loneliness, create bonding, and promote intimacy.

Because performance is not the criterion for loving sexual relationships, the attempts to define what is proper and improper in relation to marital sexual functioning often miss the point. Limits are determined by the motivation of the heart and by mutual agreement:

Are my desires loving?

Are my partner's needs and preferences considered?

Is there a sense of oneness by which God is glorified?

Defining sex as a way of loving rather than a way of performing may be especially helpful to the man who otherwise finds himself trying to meet expectations and standards that put him under tremendous pressure. It is freeing for him to know he can ask to be held, to be stroked, or simply to caress the body of his wife. He must develop an attitude that understands sex to be more than the ability to have an erect penis within a moist vagina.

THE GREATEST MYTH OF ALL

The expectation that men know all about sex is accepted by both men and women. It contributes to the passive role played by many females and the pressure to perform felt by many males. The origin of the myth relates perhaps to the pattern of the man's being head of his household and possibly to the greater freedom he has had historically to be exposed to new and different experiences. Because women have traditionally been "protected" from knowledge about sex, it has been assumed that men have had access to this knowledge.

Apparently few people have questioned the myth that men know it all. Where is the evidence that men have access to sound knowledge about their own sexuality and the female's? They have no formal training. Nor do they have any significant informal training. They do not get their "expertise" from their dads, because almost all sex education shared in the home is from Mom. The only source left is their peers. Need we wonder any longer why things often do not go well in the bedroom?

As well-read or experienced as a man might be, he cannot be an authority on another person's sexuality or know in advance all that fits a specific relationship. That is why communication is so vital for healthy sexual functioning. But often a man hesitates to admit he does not know what to do— and the woman, not wishing to damage his ego, declines to spell out what is needed. Some women draw significant conclusions from such situations: "If he really loved me, he would know how to please me." It is unrealistic for people to expect that another's skill or lack of skill is a true indication of their esteem and love. Men are not sexually psychic. There is no way husbands and wives can know the sexual needs of their partners without their communicating them.

After couples have known one another for a while, they do become aware of their own and the other's preferences. If I know the type of food my husband prefers, I can make an educated guess as to what he might want any given day. But I have no way of knowing unless he tells me that today he has an absolute craving for pecan pie. Each person is the world's authority on his or her own appetite.

THE MOST COMMON MALE DYSFUNCTION

Premature ejaculation is often called the "young man's disease." It is not uncommon to have a premature ejaculator come in for therapy with an anorgasmic wife. Frequently coitus does not last long enough for her to reach the levels of arousal that are necessary for orgasm.

"Premature ejaculation" can be a problematic term. What is the "normal" amount of time that one should expect to pass before ejaculation occurs? Masters and Johnson attempt to resolve the problem by defining premature ejaculation as the inability to satisfy the female at least 50 percent of the time. But that definition ignores the fact that one woman may need thirty minutes and another may need only five. The fact is, "premature ejaculation" is a relative term describing a condition of the couple and not simply a condition of the man.

THE TREATMENT FOR PREMATURE EJACULATION

For men who want to become more flexible and have greater control over the length of time spent in intercourse, the treatment procedure is highly effective. Usually within a month, and generally within seven to ten sessions, there can be major changes. Fifteen to twenty-five sessions may be required for severe problems.

The etiology of premature ejaculation is unknown. There are theories that support its being a learned behavior. Young men sometimes have their first experiences of sex under less than ideal circumstances and hurry to finish, or they visit a prostitute whose job it is to make them ejaculate quickly. However, there are many men with these experiences who do not develop the problem.

Some men lack awareness of their own point of inevitable ejaculation and fail to control. Yet other premature ejaculators monitor themselves extremely well. Psychological factors such as the suppression of anger are rarely significant. This is supported by the high rate of success through physical retraining. Almost all men will find improvement if they stick with the retraining program.

The only correlation that seems to be consistently linked to the ability to control ejaculation is frequency and duration. As the man gets older and as he finds himself in a stable and long-term relationship, the less problem he has. Just raising the frequency does not provide a cure; frequency has to be raised consistently over time.

The focus of most treatment is the "squeeze technique." There are numerous descriptions of the technique, but all essentially consist of the man being brought to an aroused state, which is then interrupted by a squeeze along the coronal ridge or at the base of the penis. It is helpful for a man who is comfortable with masturbation to experiment first. This enables him to gain confidence that the procedure does work before introducing the female to the technique. If the couple prefer, they may begin the program together. If their frequency for sex is once a week, they are to practice three times a week. If their coital frequency is three times a week, they are to practice five times. This relates to the correlation of increasing frequency consistently over time.

A couple may need to experiment with the parameters. If stimulation brings the man too close to ejaculation before applying the squeeze, they must stop sooner. A fair arousal is all that is necessary. One man may find the coronal squeeze too arousing and use instead the squeeze at the base of the penis. Still another may find a pause is sufficient to reduce arousal. Some prefer lubrication, others a dry hand.

The procedure of stimulation and squeeze should be repeated four or five times a session if possible. The man should not use methods of distraction or sabotage his arousal in any way. Control is learned with full appreciation of the sensations of the body. Once the couple can achieve five minutes of stimulation with only one pause, they are ready to move on to penile containment.

With the female astride, the woman gently guides the penis into the vagina. She is not to thrust, and both are to become aware of the sensation of containment. There must be careful preparation for this step to succeed. The counselor can reduce anxiety over the outcome by saying, "I don't know what will happen when you try this. If it doesn't work, keep a good record to share with me next time and remember to have fun!" The "squeeze" can still be applied by the woman reaching around and grasping the penile base. When they are comfortable, she can begin slow thrusting.

Treatment for premature ejaculation is like going to the gym to build muscles. Physical retraining will get results. Allowing the problem to persist can lead to avoidance of sex or to secondary problems with intercourse that are not experienced with masturbation.

Occasionally the woman resists helping her spouse. Usually it is because she resents not receiving pleasure for herself. Most women understand that passing up their immediate gratification is to their long-term advantage. If a wife feels she is being deprived, however, the counselor can recommend that after the husband's practice sessions, they can finish with intercourse.

To summarize, the basic treatment for premature ejaculation goes as follows:

1. Focus first on conscious interruption of the arousal process by pausing or by squeezing the base or coronal ridge of the penis;
2. Strive to practice the arousal–pause/squeeze sequence four or five times a session;
3. When control reaches the point where the male can be stimulated for five minutes with one pause, penile containment with no movement can be attempted with the female astride and using the squeeze as needed;
4. When control is established with containment, the female can begin slow thrusting.

TREATMENT OF ERECTILE DYSFUNCTION

Labeling can be critical to the way a person views himself. References to "erectile failure" and the habit of calling men who have problems getting erections "impotent," or those who can not ejaculate "incompetent" or "retarded" ejaculators, does nothing therapeutic. It is less threatening if we refer instead to problems of erectile dysfunction and inhibited ejaculation.

Having an erection on demand is assumed by many men to be the essence of male sexuality. But with no muscle available to contract, the penis can only respond as a result of the parasympathetic nervous system causing arteries to dilate. And the parasympathetic nervous system cannot be willed into operation. It reacts when a man's conditions for sex are met. For most men that means an atmosphere of love, warmth, and tenderness.

An accurate diagnosis of erectile problems can be difficult, but a good history will reveal clues. Men can suffer from desire disorder problems as much as women can. (See chapter 8 on the treatment and diagnosis of low desire.) Time should also be spent considering medical causes; men in their fifties commonly complain of erectile dysfunction.

The possibility of interacting factors contributing to erectile dysfunction is also high. For some men the major problem may be psychological, but a poor physical condition can make them vulnerable to problems a healthier man can avoid. Conversely, a man who has a positive attitude about his maleness and who loves and trusts the woman he is with is often able to avoid sexual problems that arise from physical causes. (Chapter 6 lists offending medications and diseases.) If a man sometimes achieves erections with intercourse and usually with masturbation or petting or while asleep, there is probably a psychological factor at work.

FEAR OF PERFORMANCE

Behind the majority of cases of psychologically oriented erectile dysfunction is fear of performance. Performance anxieties result when a person believes he must never fail, must always meet the needs of his partner, and will be a failure if he does not. They can also result from considerations such as loss of interest in the partner, hostility, and anger.

The attitude of the partner is extremely important. Erectile dysfunction can be caused by a women if she is perceived as putting too much pressure on the man or if, by her disinterest, she fails to provide the stimulation or encouragement needed for his arousal. On the other hand, a woman can help immensely by loving and understanding involvement in treatment.

A woman's failure to communicate sexual preferences will leave the man in the dark or working with false assumptions. He may be feeling that he is instinctively supposed to know what to do in any and all sexual situations. Sometimes he guesses right and is reinforced, but more frequently he guesses wrong and the experience turns out badly. Consequently he becomes fearful of trying again or begins to avoid situations that might lead to sex.

Many men conclude that they are losing their ability to perform when all they are actually experiencing is the normal process of aging. Declining frequency of sexual activity can cause erections to become less efficient. If the wife's interest in sex is waning, her lack of enthusiasm leaves the aging male sexually vulnerable because so much of his self-esteem is tied to his sexual performance.

The situation becomes more complex for the husband if his wife also lacks understanding of the natural changes of aging. A woman may suspect that her husband's failure to produce an immediate erection is undeniable proof of his lack of desire for her. She may conclude that she is no longer attractive to him or that he is having an affair.

Healthy people establish conditions for sex. Mature sexual functioning involves making discriminating choices. That people cannot and should not function in certain situations says much about the "natural wisdom" of the body. The myth that suggests men are always ready, willing, and able to have sex often results in their seeking therapy. They are unaware that the problem is rooted in false expectations and that what they really need is to reevaluate their situation.

Therapists, counselors, and teachers need to confront and dispel these and other myths to alleviate anxiety. By attacking the false thinking—"I must perform . . . I'm a failure . . . I must be in charge"—and supplanting it with new, healthy affirmations and biblical understanding, counselors can deal effectively with many of the problems that are channeled into the therapeutic process.

A CHANGE IN BEHAVIOR

The behavioral aspect of the treatment of erectile dysfunction begins with a ban on intercourse until the couple have worked through the sensate focus exercises described in chapter 8. Relaxation techniques are taught, and the man is told to be aware of his own unique conditions for sensuousness. He is never to attempt an exercise when he is angry, upset, or unable to relax. Increasingly intimate homework is assigned, usually on a weekly basis.

When husband and wife have established new and relaxing patterns of being together, the ban on intercourse is lifted. Quite frequently the ban is ignored as a natural turn of events. This is acceptable as long as it occurs far enough into therapy that it is not being used to sabotage improvement.

An important adjunct to therapy is the help given to establish communication about sex and other marital concerns. Two recent studies report a high degree of success in the treatment of erectile dysfunction by effectively improving sexual communication techniques with minimal therapeutic intervention. Directed exercises helped to facilitate discussion.[1] Such findings are extremely significant for the busy pastor. Directed reading and use of communication worksheets and techniques can change people's lives and, perhaps, save marriages. The minimal effort and time required to develop a program of reading and exercises using appropriate materials are clearly worth it.

In conclusion, treatment of erectile dysfunction has the following three components:

1. The possibility of a medical cause must be considered and ruled out;
2. Cognitively, the counselor must help the client counteract myths and other beliefs that contribute to fear of performance. General marriage counseling, especially techniques geared to improving communication, is equally helpful;
3. The behavioral grid requires a ban on intercourse while the couple discover new ways of being together, through sensate focus exercises, that do not result in anxiety.

TREATMENT OF INHIBITED EJACULATION

As with erectile difficulties, be sensitive to the possibility of a medical cause for inhibited ejaculation. Diabetes is a possible reason. Inhibited ejaculation is often the very first symptom of multiple sclerosis. It is sometimes a side effect of drugs, alcohol, all major tranquilizers (melleril is the worst), some minor tranquilizers, hypertensive medication, and ganglionic blockers.

Less common is the Post Concussion Syndrome, which results in inability to ejaculate after receiving a blow on the head. No one understands yet why this sometimes happens, but it is documented in medical journals.

Less regular ejaculation is a normal phenomenon of aging and should not in any major way affect a man's satisfaction with his sex life. Older men, especially those who are quite sexually active, frequently experience a feeling of satiation but no ejaculate. An older man who remarries or becomes more sexually active—after a period of illness, for example—may experience irregular ejaculation.

The major psychological component of inhibited ejaculation is fear. When my husband was stationed in the Philippines, a young airmen presented with inability to ejaculate. The problem began when he and his Filipino bride decided to have a child. A few questions revealed the source of the difficulty: as a respectful young man raised in Alabama, he was terrified of his parents' reaction to a brown-skinned grandchild. Treatment consisted of one phone call to his parents, who, by their positive acceptance, relieved him of his anxieties.

Here again is an example of the wisdom of the body. When mouth declares one message and the body another, the body is always the wiser of the two. If the body does not work, it is always reasonable to examine the situation. Too many men ignore such messages, preferring to believe the myth that men are always ready, willing, and able. A number of secular psychologists agree with them, collecting fees for therapy designed to release the clients from their "hang-ups."

A few men have an aversion to the vagina. Perhaps they are influenced by advertisers that spend two million dollars a year in an effort to convince people the vagina is dirty so they can sell their products to make it clean. And our society has generally been brought up on teaching that genitals are inherently dirty and present a genuine threat to human health. Cognitive therapy is necessary to correct the misinformation, but desensitization is equally important. A step-by-step procedure slowly enables the man to look at the vagina, touch it, and finally have intercourse. He can become functional even if he never develops a high comfort level.

Intervention requires a great deal of patience and encouragement. Slowly getting the man used to lubrication on his hands is followed by his acceptance of its similarity to vaginal lubrication. Pleasurable sexual activities would be encouraged but linked to the vagina by looking, then touching, and so on.

On rare occasions a man convinces himself that his failure to ejaculate means the marriage is not consummated and he can get out of it. Sometimes he may no longer be attracted to his wife or harbors fears of loss of identity or of commitment.

In some situations men will try to force ejaculation by thrusting harder. They forget about the body's need to respond naturally to good feelings, so the penis eventually becomes numb. They should instead slow down, allowing the mind to register all the good sensations.

Using orgasm triggers can be helpful to men who suffer with inhibited ejaculation. Orgasm triggers occur spontaneously when the body is functioning normally. Men are directed to concentrate on them to heighten arousal rather than on trying to ejaculate. Holding one's breath, throwing the head back, bearing down of the pelvis, Kegel exercises, and clinching the buttock muscles all add to natural orgasmic response.

SURGICAL SOLUTIONS

New procedures are being developed to correct obstructed blood flow to the perineal and penis. Diagnosis is difficult and expensive at this time. Surgery can be done to close arteriovenous corporal cavernosal shunts, preventing leakage of blood and loss of pressure. Revascularization to increase or decrease blood flow into the penis is a new technique used by some urologists. There are no guaranteed results as yet, but within the next few years improved surgical techniques will make this a possibility for a greater number of men.

Insertion of a penile prosthesis, for all intents and purposes, kills the natural ability to produce an erection. Therefore careful consideration must be given before such a final and drastic step is taken. The decision should never be made without a sleep lab exam and a thorough check of hormonal and blood-flow factors. Home devices that purport to measure night erections are not reliable. Large university settings generally have the means to do the type of workup required.

Penile implants have been available since the seventies. The first and most common was a solid rod prosthesis. Relatively inexpensive, this allows intromission and can be installed under local anesthetic. There are few complications, although there are some disadvantages. Occasionally there is insufficient rigidity for easy intromission, since these erections usually amount to about 80 percent of the natural erection of a young man. The solid rod can fracture during intercourse, and some find the prosthesis uncomfortable and difficult to conceal.[2]

Inflatable and hydraulic prostheses are later developments that involve transferring fluids from an implanted reservoir to the penis. Surgically they are not as easy to put in place. However, when solid rod prostheses were replaced by inflatable devices in twenty-two patients, nineteen said they preferred the inflatable type.[3]

Pharmacological solutions, such as papaverine, for erectile difficulties are in the experimental stage. Men can be trained to inject the drug directly into the penis when intercourse is desired. Injection of the penis with vasodilators works, but can cause priapism, damage the corpora, and result in other complications. The most successful use of papaverine is in diagnosis. Such injections can be used in conjunction with venous arteriograms to permit a view of penile vascularity.

PART FOUR

SPECIAL CONCERNS IN CHRISTIAN SEXUAL COUNSELING

The Christian faith is redemptive. It has the power, or draws on the power, of God's Spirit, so that corruption and decay can be replaced by wholeness and newness of being. The moral standards of Christianity help to point the way to that wholeness. The only way we can begin the pilgrimage toward that wholeness is first to admit our responsibility in the corruption.

It is not enough for Christians who counsel people with sexual problems to find the immediate source of a problem and offer a simple solution. We must also offer that which has the power to make people whole again: the redemptive love of Jesus Christ. Christian counselors are the only ones who have the possibility of directing people toward wholeness because that possibility lies in forgiveness of sins, new minds, new hearts, and new commitments—all of which come from Jesus Christ. The message and the power we have need no apology nor should they be adulterated in any way. They simply need to be offered in love with compassionate understanding.

This final part explores methods of intervention that will allow the pastor or counselor to help marrieds, singles, or about-to-be-marrieds. These chapters consider some of the larger goals of sexual counseling that Christians want to fulfill. The final chapter is my attempt to help the reader decide when he or she should refer a client to another type of helper.

Chapter Eleven

THORNS AMONG THE FLOWERS
Special Concerns of the Christian

Whatever you do, work at it with all your heart, as working
for the Lord, not for men (Col. 3:23).

A number of years ago I found myself evaluating from a
new vantage point the way I had been running my marriage
and family counseling practice. I had only recently become a
Christian and, although my counseling was not known as a
Christian counseling service, I began to notice differences in the
way I was conducting myself. I was working with the assurance
that I had a Helper to guide and encourage me. It felt good to
share the responsibility of such intimate intervention in people's lives. It was a relief when I could encourage the client to
seek the wisdom of the Master Counselor.

But I soon became aware that doing my best "as working
for the Lord" was raising a number of serious questions. What
was the goal of my counseling to be? Was I to patch and mend,
taking just enough pressure off the couple or individual to
accomplish a satisfactory adaptation to the situation? Was I
there to help ensure that couples would have marvelous sex
lives? Was I to focus on relationships only? How was I to help
the single with sexual concerns?

I discovered that I was not alone in my quandary. Such
questions are seriously debated in organizations such as the

Christian Association for Psychological Studies (CAPS) and in professional journals for clergy and Christian counselors. As we might expect, vast differences of opinion are extant. It seems, however, that when the rhetoric is cleared away, a very basic truth is left: *The goal of Christian counseling (including sexual counseling) must be to help people come as close as possible to living their lives in line with God's design.*

God's design for sexuality is that men and women understand and accept themselves fully as either masculine or feminine. And if they are married, Christians are meant to have a mutually satisfying and exclusive genital sexual relationship with their spouses.

Achieving such a goal involves three components:

1. Helping people place Christ at the center of their lives. Too often Christians believe God made them to be happy, get married, have children, or be successful. Instead they were made to ". . . seek first his kingdom" (Matt. 6:33). Anything beyond that is a bonus!
2. Helping them develop a rich relationship with God. Relationships do not exist without each person having a personal knowledge of the other. Getting to know God requires educating oneself through knowledge of the Scripture and establishing an openness to His grace. As the relationship grows, a desire is born to conform to the image of Christ. Healthy conforming is the result of the inner self's responding to the love and devotion of God, not to outside pressures. When everything is done as if "working for the Lord," our sexuality cannot be excluded!
3. Helping them accept the abundant inheritance that is theirs for the taking. Living in a society that is oriented toward getting makes it difficult for many to accept the gift of life. While the world focuses on what is lacking, the Christian must be discovering the abundance to be found in Christ.

God's plan of redemption works, whatever the cause of sin. The first step, He reminds us, is confession—accepting responsibility for the problem. "My sexual functioning does not measure up to God's standards."

The second step is a plan of action that acknowledges the

intervention of the Holy Spirit in overcoming even the most monumental and discouraging problems. An individual's responsibility is bringing the hidden hurts from their dark place deep within up to where God's healing light can shine on them.

The Christian counselor or pastor is an important guide in both these processes. The helper and the client work together to explore and modify any beliefs, attitudes, feelings, or behaviors that prohibit the expression of sexuality in the way God intended.

A PLACE OF ACCEPTANCE

Dr. William Masters is infamous for one of his teaching lines in his Human Sexuality Workshops: "If a client says, 'I have sex with a dog,' you are to ask, 'What kind?'" Being shocked at the sexual proclivities that certain clients may reveal in therapy does nothing to help the process of exploration and healing; neither does a convicting or judgmental attitude.

Change is most likely to occur in an atmosphere of acceptance. A counselor who overtly reacts to something said by the client can close the door to any real healing. Much discussion is needed to discover reasons for attitudes and behavior. It takes time and requires sensitivity. For example, people often engage in sex for nonsexual reasons. A sensitive and nonjudgmental counselor can help a client discover such things.

A counselor must never lose sight of the complexity of people and their sometimes strange behaviors. Symptoms are only one part of the puzzle that makes up the whole person. Treating a malfunctioning penis or an unresponsive clitoris is often a job only half done. An individual seeking help is a whole person. He or she has relationships, responsibilities, expectations, and a spiritual life along with a problem. Sex must be understood to have meaning for each person within the particular framework of his or her life.

An accepting attitude on the part of a counselor does not imply that his or her own standards and values are to remain hidden. Eugene Kennedy writes, "Counselors do not help anybody in any situation, sexual or otherwise, by uncertainty, passivity, or vagueness about the symbol system by which they lead their own lives."[1]

WHAT MODEL OF INTERVENTION DO WE USE?

Jesus met people at their point of need. Starting where they were, He then moved them to where they needed to be. Sometimes He supplied comfort, at other times He confronted. He listened, humbled Himself, ruled, made judgments, gave answers, and nourished. His teaching style was diverse and included using stories, dialogue, exposition of Scripture, and lecture.

Whatever role Jesus used, it was proper for the situation at hand. He acted authentically. His bearing displayed authority even when He was doing the most menial tasks. His manner indicated respect and positive regard for the person even if He had to confront him or her in the process. The most important thing for us to imitate is His motivation—love.

SEX FOR NONSEXUAL REASONS

It is often difficult for Christians to grasp the fact that people engage in sexual intercourse for reasons other than simple sexual desire. Many Christians suppose that illicit sex in particular is motivated by a love of pleasure and unbridled lust. Unquestionably some people are merely responding to such inclinations. More often than not, however, through sex an individual is acting in response to a conflict or need in some other part of life.

People who follow this path often become quite disappointed because they are expecting sex to do something of which it is not capable. They may then determine that they have the wrong partner and set out on a quest to find the "right" one. Or they may conclude that something is wrong with them sexually, perhaps escalating the problem into a sexual dysfunction.

The most common nonsexual motivation for sex is the seeking of self-esteem. Ironically, almost anything else a person might do to feel better would have a greater chance of success.

Getting the attention of another does make one feel better, but as soon as that attention wanes or is withdrawn, the person is back where he or she started. When we equate sexual activity with confirmation of our personal worth and acceptability, we begin to make a series of decisions that undermine our worthiness, not to mention our fragile *sense* of worth.

Seeking self-esteem through "successful" sexual experiences ignores the fact that the body is not a machine. It will not function in any and all circumstances. When things go well, the person is likely to take credit and his or her esteem is enhanced; when things go poorly, the partner can be blamed (and a new one sought) or a person might decide that he or she is a poor lover and self-esteem will surely plummet.

Many people seek to use sex to keep from being alone and feeling lonely. Such persons so dread the prospect of being alone that they miss the truth that sex with just anybody soon becomes sex with nobody. Others, perhaps more insecure, fear that saying no will preclude their being liked or cared for. Sexually active young girls, especially those with poor father relationships, often find themselves in sexual relationships in which they find no pleasure. I have never met a sexually active teenaged girl whose sole motivation for being sexual was the physical pleasure she experienced.

The need to express power, get revenge, or punish can motivate sexual activity. Within marriage, sex may be used as a weapon by either husbands or wives. A woman may withhold orgasm because of her lack of trust in the relationship. Or she may do so to make her mate feel powerless: "You may make the most money and lord it over people at work and tell me how to dress, but you can't make me have an orgasm if I don't want to!" A man might express his rage and hostility by demanding that his partner participate in demeaning and degrading acts, all in the name of love.

If a counselor reacts with moralistic outrage before learning whether such motivations are at work, he or she may cut off the opportunity to discover the reasons for the behavior. Unless causes of behavior are dealt with, the solutions to many sexual problems may be only temporary at best. A major task of the competent counselor is to help people sort out their nonsexual desires of sex and to reinforce and teach those behaviors that conform to God's plan for His people.

THE THORNY ISSUES

There are a number of sexual issues and problems that generate special concern for the Christian. Some, like masturbation, fantasy, pornography, voyeurism, and homosexuality, are not necessarily considered problematic within many segments of our society. We need to examine such concerns from the perspective of Christian values.

Obsessive Behaviors

I begin with obsessive behaviors because the possibility exists that each individual behavior that will be scrutinized has the potential of developing into an obsessive concern. Not all obsessions are sexual in nature. A person can be obsessed by almost anything that demands attention, time, and perhaps money. The price of the obsession is high: one's freedom.

Nick, for example, became obsessed with the idea of breaking out of what he considered his "goodie-two-shoes" image. A highly placed executive with a veteran's hospital, he had lived his life doing what he felt he was supposed to do. At age forty his obsession to experience what he thought had passed him by resulted in an affair that left his marriage in shambles. Counseling helped both him and his wife determine to maintain their marriage.

Things improved, but Nick's reluctance to drop certain sexual rituals he had begun with the affair (use of marijuana and pornography) increasingly diminished his wife's desire for sex. By the time they returned to counseling it was clear that these "enhancers" were a necessary part of Nick's arousal—he was no longer free to have spontaneous relations with his wife.

The human body monitors and reacts to input with a limited number of possible responses. The arousal felt when one is narrowly missed by a car involves the same bodily processes that are triggered by the erotic touch of a partner. Experience enables a person to label one "fear" and the other "sexual arousal." The pounding of the heart, the heightened alertness, and in many cases for the male, the erection that accompanies the high arousal state are amazingly similar. It is easy to see how the fear associated with "forbidden" fruit can be interpreted as desire.

Obsessive behaviors are often fed by certain popular beliefs. As Earl D. Wilson points out, society works to persuade us "the grass is greener on the other side" and "more is better."[2] Many people assume that forbidden territory offers more pleasure than could ever be experienced at home. It is assumed that anything that is out of bounds will certainly be more fulfilling. Ironically, research suggests that the opposite is true: people experience the most free and most responsive sexual functioning within marriage.

Having been reared on instant food, instant relief, and instant entertainment, many people conclude that delayed gratification is both difficult and unnecessary and that denial is impossible. Not acting on a sexual desire appears to be too much trouble and possibly unhealthy. The person decides to satisfy the aroused feeling, not realizing other options exist.

These assumptions and patterns result in people labeling themselves (womanizer, chronic adulterer, hopelessly-in-love, homosexual) and passively accepting their fate! They seldom evaluate themselves spiritually because the labels appear to be the final reality. Nor do they seek help to overcome what seems humanly impossible to accomplish. In the act of submitting to an obsession, Christians must realize that a most serious sin is committed. Something other than God is acknowledged as being in control. But they must not be deluded into thinking that obsessions are beyond God's power to break.

How does a pastor or counselor help someone escape from the prison of compulsive behaviors? Begin by being as realistic about the problem as possible. Sinful behavior can be "fun" and offer at least temporary rewards and distractions.

Since Adam and Eve, humankind has been subject to temptation. Temptation is not sin; giving in to it can be. Succumbing is a decision of the will. Sin knocks first and waits for the door to be opened.

People with obsessive behaviors usually have opened

doors leading to the serious situation in which they find themselves. Many little yeses paved the way for a big yes. Recognizing the process that established the obsessive behaviors offers hope that a person can extricate himself or herself from a compromising or sinful situation by reversing the process. The doors can be closed and the yeses can become nos.

The Intervention

When it has been established that a person is truly "hooked" on negative behavior, steps can be taken to break the cycle of reinforcement. Even when the behavior is not an obsession, the same procedures can be helpful in changing habit patterns. Begin by mapping out a logical course of action that gives the person hope of overcoming the problem.[3] Prepare him or her for possibly failing at times, and expect to supply plenty of encouragement, patience, and rewards. Help set up personal progress rewards that can be given as improvement occurs.

Rewards serve several purposes. To be sure, they help motivate. More important, they indicate and confirm the progress that is being made. Breaking an obsession can seem a monumental task, just as staying sober for the rest of life must seem to an alcoholic. That is why a person needs to be attending to one day—one step—at a time.

Although positive rewards are very effective with children, adults sometimes respond best to positive *and* negative consequences. I heard of a situation in which a man wrote out three checks for contributions to three organizations he loathed. If he did not make certain changes by certain deadlines, the checks were to be put in the mail by his pastor. Less drastic procedures can be equally effective: rewashing dishes, cleaning toilet bowls, or a ban on favorite TV shows, books, or magazines.

The steps to overcoming obsessive behavior are generally recognized in Scripture.

Sin can be anything that masters or enslaves us. " 'Everything is permissible for me'—but not everything is beneficial. 'Everything is permissible for me'—but I will not be mastered by anything" (1 Cor. 6:12).

Progress begins when the behavior is acknowledged as

sin. "O LORD, have mercy on me; heal me, for I have sinned against you" (Ps. 41:4).

Admission is followed by confession. "Then I acknowledged my sin to you and did not cover up my iniquity. I said, 'I will confess my transgressions to the LORD'—and you forgave the guilt of my sin" (Ps. 32:5).

Accept the idea that healing, for some people, is a process that does not necessarily run smoothly. "I do not understand what I do. For what I want to do I do not do, but what I hate I do" (Rom. 7:15).

Behavior will change as the the Spirit provides order, direction, and hope. Maximize the possibility of success by doing the following:

1. Encourage accountability between counselor and client or between client and a sensitive and trustworthy person in the fellowship. "Carry each other's burdens, and in this way you will fulfill the law of Christ" (Gal. 6:2).
2. Deal with the sense of guilt that a client may have in light of the sacrifice of Christ for forgiveness of sins. "We have been made holy through the sacrifice of the body of Jesus Christ once for all" (Heb. 10:10).
3. Teach that when temptation comes, a person should not waste time debating, pondering or, justifying. "Flee from sexual immorality" (1 Cor. 6:18).
4. Teach thought-stopping techniques, i.e., the substitution of positive, healthy thoughts for negative, recurring ones.[4] Such substitute thoughts must be planned ahead of time, before the situation arises in which they are needed. Encourage the use of thought stopping *every time* it is needed, not haphazardly! "Do not be overcome by evil, but overcome evil with good" (Rom. 12:21).
5. Make sure the clients surround themselves with positive Christian fellowship and activities that keep them busy and productive. "Do not give the devil a foothold" (Eph. 4:27).
6. Encourage study of the Word and setting aside time each day for study and contemplation. "Put on the full armor of God so that you can take your stand against the devil's schemes" (Eph. 6:11).

7. Do not allow the focus to be on the sin, but on the Lord. "Let us throw off everything that hinders and the sin that so easily entangles, and let us run with perseverance the race marked out for us. Let us fix our eyes on Jesus, the author and perfector of our faith" (Heb. 12:1–2).

8. Call on the Lord through prayer. Have the focus be a change in the individual, not necessarily the circumstances. "And we know that in all things God works for the good of those who love him, who have been called according to his purpose" (Rom. 8:28).

Masturbation

From Old Testament times to the present there has been no sexual practice more controversial or one about which people have been more constantly warned than masturbation. This, despite the fact that the practice is not specifically alluded to in Scripture. Ambivalence is reflected even in the supposed origin of the word itself. While everyone agrees on *manus* as the Latin word for "hand," the remainder of the word is reported as stemming either from *stuprare*, "to defile," or from *turbatio*, "agitation or disturbance."

When Thomas Aquinas declared sexual sins either natural or unnatural, masturbation was defined as unnatural and a "mortal sin" because pregnancy could not result. But prostitution was merely "venial" or minor in nature because the possibility of pregnancy existed.[5] This was not a new thought; early Jewish tradition speaks of the crime of "Onanism" as a grave offense. But the story of Onan in Genesis 38:6–10 speaks of *coitus interruptus* and the breaking of the law of the levirate (specified in Deut. 25:5–6). Yet it became the biblical prooftext misused to demonstrate God's wrath against masturbation.

As long as the church held sway over the populace, masturbation continued to be secretly enjoyed while publicly condemned. As the church lost its influence, the clamor against the practice shifted to the secular community, especially behavioral scientists who saw its power as detrimental to society at large. Connections were drawn between masturbation and mental illness, weakness, poor eyesight, and criminal behavior.[6] I saw a police book published in the 1950s in which the history of each criminal included his reported masturbatory pattern as undisputed proof of his deviant lifestyle.

Because such claims have no validity, most opposition today centers on the self-centeredness of the practice and the potential misuse of God's plan of sexuality for His people. Nevertheless, as late as 1975 Pope Paul declared masturbation "an intrinsically and seriously disordered act."[7] After such a history, one wonders how anyone could feel anything but ambivalent!

We must seek to discern God's will as clearly as possible, but care must be taken not to speak authoritatively where God has not spoken. I have seen people invest forty-eight hours of self-wallowing condemnation and guilt as a result of four minutes of self-indulgent pleasure! This demonstrates our typical lack of a sense of proportion. By comparison, how much time, attention, guilt, and despair do the same people invest in response to gluttonous eating, malicious remarks made to a friend, or envy over the abundance of a neighbor?

There is no question that self-stimulation is a solitary pleasure. But there are others. Losing oneself in good music, in the steady drum of shower water on the back, in the beauty of a sunset—these are singular experiences most people have had. Is solitary pleasure a sin in itself? Or is solitary pleasure a sin only if it is derived from masturbation?

Paul's statement that "everything is permissible but not everything is good" helps us to clarify the issue. There must be a realistic examination of the heart. Is someone enslaved to the act? Is it their new god? Does it hinder building a healthy relationship with a partner? Is it the loving thing to do? Has the person been led to better emotional health and a greater sense of well-being, or increased worry and guilt?

At least one-fourth of the people who masturbate feel motivated to do so when suffering from loneliness, when tense about nonsexual problems, when sleepless, or when feeling rejected.[8] Others may use it for physical relief when their desire is greater than that of their spouse, when there is illness, or when celebrating with the Lord the sheer joy of being blessed with a body that has the capacity to feel so good.

We have gone through a time when masturbation could not be conceived as anything but sin. Are we now to insist on it for everyone? By no means! Paul tells us in Romans, "One man's faith allows him to eat everything, but another man, whose faith is weak, eats only vegetables. The man who eats everything must not look down on him who does not, and the man who does not eat everything must not condemn the man who does, for God has accepted him. . . . Therefore let us stop passing judgment on one another. Instead make up your mind not to put any stumbling block or obstacle in your brother's way." (14:2–3, 13).

The greatest evidence of the Lord's creativity has to be the vast differences we see among people. These dissimilarities extend to our physical needs and appetites. Although masturbation can now rightly be viewed as a personal matter for which our attitude and motivation will be held accountable, there are some people for whom it should be a forbidden practice.

Masturbation is bad for anyone who interprets Scripture as precluding it. Anyone who acts against his conscience sins. It is bad if it keeps someone from solving major personal problems. It is dangerous when used as a weapon against a mate or as a protest against the opposite sex. It is wrong when it is used to avoid responsible sexual intimacy with one's mate.

The Intervention

The first question that comes to my mind when people seek help for excessive masturbation is what "excessive" means to them. The vast majority of people masturbate at times, even in marriage.[9] "Excessive" to some means occasional behavior; for others, daily. It is necessary for people to describe the regularity or irregularity of their masturbation to determine its role and significance.

Someone seeking counsel must be helped realistically to explore the problem in light of the fact that Scripture does not condemn masturbation. How seriously is he or she trying to live an obedient life? Is masturbation singled out as *the criterion* for being either faithful or unfaithful to Christ? What is the person's attitude toward the obligation to love one another, to praise and worship God, to be of service to the body of believers? Is there thankfulness for a body that feels and responds? Does he or she "consider it all joy . . . whenever you face trials of many kinds, because you know that the testing of your faith develops perseverance. Perseverance must finish its work so that you may be mature and complete, not lacking anything" (James 1:2–4)?

The second concern is to discover the motivation for the behavior. Treating masturbation when the problem is anxiety over something else is doomed to failure and discouragement. However, guilt over a habit pattern that takes too much time and attention or conflicts with one's understanding of the Bible is amenable to successful treatment.

I will never forget a college student I once taught whose mother observed seminal fluid on his pajamas. He was immediately taken to the priest to confess. His "sin" was having a functioning body going through a purely natural, normal, and involuntary process of nocturnal emission. The experience was so traumatizing, the young man vowed it would never happen again. He began to masturbate habitually, four to five times a day, to prevent a recurrence.

Encourage forgiveness of self and the lifting up of the problem to the Lord. Since overcoming a habit pattern that can be so reinforcing is difficult, remind the person of the Lord's ongoing forgiveness. If worry about the problem, poor sex education, or other factors have resulted in true obsessive masturbatory behavior, follow the guidelines for overcoming obsessions.

Fantasy

It is appropriate to consider fantasy right after a discourse on masturbation. Fantasy frequently accompanies self-pleasure. Although most people fantasize a loved one, it is a source of concern for those who take Jesus' admonition in Matthew 5:28 seriously.

Everyone fantasizes.[10] Most dreams and accomplishments are the result of hours of rehearsal within our mind. Poets, writers, and others of a creative nature are able to envision their works before they ever appear on paper or canvas. There are few major events of the day that are not thought over with an eye toward figuring out a solution, imagining our successful handling of an event, or all too often, seeing ourselves failing to master a situation.

Despite the so-called sexual revolution, the most popular sexual fantasies revolve around typical male and female scenarios. The primary male fantasy—sex with more than one woman—symbolically associates his sexuality with activity, power, and performance. The most popular fantasy for females involves submission. This allows the woman to participate without guilt and responsibility. Her self-image of passivity and submission remain intact. There appear to be no differences in the amount of fantasizing between the two sexes.[11]

Fantasies rightfully extend into our sexual lives. Shulamith and Solomon spent time thinking erotic thoughts about each other. The Song of Songs seems to take it for granted. The analogy of a teakettle is helpful in understanding the importance of fantasy in sexual functioning. A teakettle placed on simmer all day quickly reaches a boiling point when one returns home at night and hikes the temperature; a teakettle left on the shelf all day requires considerable heat and time before it boils. Without thinking positively of our loved one, without putting a little energy into imagining a satisfying and pleasurable time together, we should not be surprised when a boiling point is not reached. It takes more than the psychic and physical energy that can be mustered at the end of a busy day to be responsive.

Fantasies are harmful when they reinforce a fear of failure or escalate emotions for someone other than the appropriate partner. They are detrimental when they provide an escape from the reality of everyday living. I have a similar feeling about the romance novels prevalent today, even in the Christian market; they are potentially harmful when they offer an escape from a relationship and avert the need to fix what is wrong. Soap operas provide the same kind of escapism.

A 1984 study lends credence to my concern. Readers of erotic romance novels are often motivated by a need to escape, in contrast with readers of other material who read for self-knowledge. Although erotic novel readers reportedly had sex more often, their focus tended to be on the fantasy. The report concluded that erotic novels are a form of soft-core pornography that provides sexual stimulation in a way that women find acceptable.[12]

Almost everyone at times has rather bizarre sexual fantasies. Like dreams they mask their meaning. Fantasies about homosexuality may represent fears about dependence, submission, or humiliation. Also, sado-masochistic and masochistic thoughts may involve concerns over relationships of power or being close. Thoughts of rape may reveal a fear about sex or the desire to be swept away in passion. People need to know that exploring the meaning and significance of such imaginings is a healthy and correct thing to do.

The Intervention

The motivation for fantasy and the balance it plays in one's life determine whether it is problematic or not. Ironically, rather than needing to be discouraged, women often need to be encouraged to fantasize more about their sexual relationships with their spouses. When fantasies are negative—rehearsals that set them up for failure or are preoccupied with unsuitable people or behaviors—the steps used for overcoming an obsession are helpful. Thought stopping coupled with filling the mind with the Word of God can be effective.

Lust

Lusting is not admiring God's handiwork in the form of a beautiful woman or handsome man. Nor is it the normal and natural reaction of the body responding to erotic situations. Erotic feelings are not in themselves sinful and destructive.

Lusting is losing perspective. It is desiring something so much that a plan is set in motion that nurtures the desire or promotes acting on it. When a person lusts, the possibility of a relationship is denied, for like the junkie, the only thing that matters is gratification of the desire, the sooner the better. Lusting is by no means confined to the sexual.

To Ted it seemed everything had taken on erotic meaning. He could no longer sit and have coffee with his neighbor without sexual overtones. He was shocked when his daughter's teenaged girlfriends aroused him, but the more he prayed and determined to control his lustful thoughts, the more out of control they became.

By the time he appeared for counseling, Ted was maintaining control by isolating himself psychologically. To outsiders he appeared cold and disinterested. To his family he was withdrawn and distant. Because he was a naturally expansive and outgoing person, this distancing made his life unbearable.

Ted's problem began when he failed to understand that his body naturally and frequently reacts when exposed to certain stimuli. (A stimulus is not always what one would judge erotic.) The body's first reaction is a reflex resulting in blood flowing into the genital region and, in females, weeping of the vaginal walls. This is beyond conscious control. It is only after one is aware of the feelings of arousal that a decision can be made as to whether the reaction is appropriate.

Ted, a committed Christian, had not learned that the erotic feeling was not the real problem, but rather his reaction to it. His concern, ironically, caused him to focus and nurture his response instead of marshaling the physiological forces to stimulate the sympathetic nervous system to contract the genital arteries and cut off the pleasurable messages to the brain. Ted's problem began when the conscious or unconscious decision was made to nurture the arousal instead of extinguishing it.

Lustful feelings can be controlled. Jesus traveled with women, a most unusual practice for the day. If there was any impropriety, the Pharisees would have been the first to point it out. On a more mundane level, physicians are exposed to potentially lustful situations daily and resist them with ease.

The Intervention

It is true that lustful thoughts do not involve another person in the same way that adultery and fornication do. But there is good reason why Christians are to focus on what is good, honorable, and true (Phil. 4:8). Thoughts are the precursors to action, a fact that Jesus impressed on his disciples. Change results first from a "renewing of the mind" as

198

the choice is made to "flee immorality" by controlling one's thoughts.

When a person lusts, he or she has given in to uncontrolled passion. Mastering lust requires acknowledging this and making a conscious decision to handle the situation appropriately. Just thinking of the consequences of lustful behavior is a deterrent for many, followed by the substitution of a new thought, perhaps of a joyous experience with the family, or some neutral situation. Thought-stopping techniques work best when used immediately and consistently. (More discussion of thought stopping can be found in endnote 4 for this chapter.)

Only limited healing occurs if people depend on cognitions, thought substitutions, and willpower to free themselves from negative behavior. It is through the Lord's grace of allowing us access to God's supernatural "full armor" that victory can be confidently claimed.

Pornography

A definition of pornography compatible with the Bible might read as follows: "Any material depicting sexual activity which, by design and emphasis, encourages and promotes the desire in the observer to engage in illicit sexual activity."[13] This definition takes into account both the intent of the producer and the effect the material has on the reader or the observer. Pornography cannot simply be equated with nudity or eroticism. Naked bodies are not in themselves pornographic. Nor is lovemaking, a discussion of lovemaking, or even a depiction of lovemaking per se pornographic. The central moral issue in pornography is illicit sexual desire and illicit sexual activity. From this perspective it is clear that much of what we see in advertising, in television programming, and in many magazines is pornographic because of its intent.

There is great controversy among "experts" over the value of pornography. It may be that some people find it an outlet for sexual tendencies that are best not acted out. If so, it is a mere stopgap measure better served by good sex education and a correct understanding of the meaning and purpose of sex. For those who can take it or leave it, remember Paul's admonition in Romans 14:13 not to be a stumbling block for a brother who has a greater problem handling something than we do.

Pornography places an overwhelming emphasis on the physical aspects of sex and separates sex from love and the personal relationship. Power over another—almost always male over female—is a common theme. Even the slick, soft-core pornography can be destructive in that it sets up mythical standards of appearance and performance that no ordinary person can match. It places sex in a realm where there is no responsibility, commitment, mutuality, and self-discipline so necessary for healthy and fulfilling sexual functioning. The blatant display of pornographic material to which our young people are exposed gives them a view of distorted sexuality before they have a chance to be soundly grounded in a realistic and Christian view of love and sex.

Some Christians use mildly pornographic material occasionally to add spice to their love-life. With consideration of the cautions cited, it is likely that little harm is done. What brings couples to therapy—usually the wife—is concern over the habitual use of pornography in lovemaking and the escalation of its nature. The couple's focus shifts from the joy and pleasure of a shared experience to technique, scenarios, books, videos, or paraphernalia. Frequently the man is convinced he cannot function without its use.

The Intervention

The counselor can help by providing a place where both parties can vent their feelings. The focus of the sex act must be returned to the relationship. Sensate focus exercises are helpful in beginning a new sexual relationship that proves exciting and fulfilling because of the communication and commitment of both partners to make the act creative, fun, and meaningful. The couple require suggestions, encouragement, and sensitive understanding of their unique needs from the counselor.

Education regarding the dangers and dehumanizing effects of pornography must become a responsibility of the Christian community. The most blatant violations can be handled through the courts. Change will come about as people begin to grasp the full implications of the use and influence of pornography in society—that material intended to encourage our thoughts and actions to illicit sexual activities is not to be taken lightly.

Variant and Deviant Behaviors

Our sexual lives are to be characterized by mutuality (Phil. 2:1–4; Eph. 5:21). Although everything is permissible (1 Cor. 10:23), Christians are not to be obsessed or enslaved by anything (1 Cor. 6:12). The point is that a spouse's needs must be met by mutual consent. This means the more inhibited partner must stretch and the more adventuresome one be especially sensitive to the concerns of the spouse. The Song of Songs makes it clear that married people are to take delight in one another.

Sex is a form of play. Self-consciousness can be forgotten as the pleasurable feelings immerse one in the business at hand. Honesty, joyfulness, and delight in the raw energy of the physical expression of love sweep mundane career and domestic cares away. Created with imagination and inventiveness, our nature longs for variations of sexual expression.

Well-meaning Christian authorities teach that to express sexuality in any way other than through conventional sexual intercourse is wrong. This conflicts with God's depiction of the sexual relationship in the Song of Songs. Nor does it make sense. To imply that the mouth, the tongue, or the hands were not made for sexual purposes denies creativity and the fact that people use body parts for a multitude of purposes. Jesus made it clear that it is not what goes into a man that matters, but what comes out. If this truth is extended to sexual matters, it seems to suggest that sin is more a matter of internal heart and soul condition than of body parts and their use.

There are, however, certain sexual behaviors that are specifically spoken against in Scripture. For the record, masturbation and oral sex are not among them. Bestiality (Exod. 22:19), incest (Deut. 22:30), prostitution (Eph. 5:5), and homosexuality and lesbianism (Rom. 1:26–27) are mentioned in several places and are not to be indulged in by Christians. Anal sex is referred to only in a homosexual context.

201

What about behavior not specifically mentioned? Sex that is deviant is often characterized by a lack of discrimination in choice of partner, circumstance, or motivation. The choice of activity is selected with little concern or regard for the partner. Frequently the sexual act is an expression of guilt, hate, or other hostility toward the sexual partner, someone else, or self. The intent is not release of sexual tension but reduction of nonsexual tensions. Deviant sex takes on a much more compulsive nature than sex as an expression of love and care.

Normal sex is the culmination of sexual tension building up and a desire for intimacy with one's partner. Sex is meant to enhance the sense of well-being. It augments feelings of wholeness. It is loving. It is in keeping with God's image in us.

Deviant behavior like "swinging" (the flagrant and often open exchange of partners) has a narcissistic focus. It is self-indulgent. It is easier than maintaining a long-term relationship. People who indulge often need the excitement of risk to be able to perform.

Masochism, the desire to be punished, and sadism, the desire to inflict pain, are clear examples of misdirected sexual aim. They are expressions of feelings of hostility against oneself or others, not expressions of sexual love. With the exception of mild pinching and scratching that might normally occur with loving intercourse, violence should have no part in sexual expression; it is alien to the meaning and function of sex. Much of pornography, however, perpetuates the myth that violence and sex are related.

Fetishism is the misdirected association of sexual excitement with an object. Many people find that candlelight, clothing, and music add dimension to their sexual enjoyment. The problem comes when the object replaces a relationship with a real person or when sexual performance is limited by the need of having a ritual, object, or particular item present.

Fetishism lies at the root of my concern for vibrators. Occasional use should not be judged a problem. Incorporating a vibrator to aid in relaxation or for variety should cause no problem if both partners agree and its use adds to the unity, pleasure, and overall satisfaction of a loving sexual act. But there are some women who cannot be orgasmic without them.

Transvestism, the desire to cross-dress, is found chiefly among men. The origin almost always lies in early life experiences. Clothing is used as a stimulus, but in the majority of cases does not indicate a desire to be the opposite sex. Most transvestites are married and, if they have understanding spouses, remain faithful and committed to their relationships. The extent of the behavior can vary greatly. Improvement from psychological counseling alone has proven quite ineffective.

Transvestites are not helped by encouragement to continue even mild deviant practices. Treatment must involve procedures that reinforce traditional marital behavior. Good marital therapy is always advised and is usually helpful.[14]

The Intervention

Nowhere do we see the need for correct, biblical understanding of our sexual conduct more than within the lives of people suffering from deviant sexual practices. It is not too much sexual information that has caused their difficulty, but the fact that their upbringing failed to present them with a picture of healthy sexuality and an opportunity to ask questions or gather information that would ensure functioning within God's guidelines.

Once such behavior is learned and reinforced it takes great patience, time, commitment, and expense to engender change. We can be thankful that there is a Power greater than ourselves to turn to, for human efforts alone prove woefully lacking. The General Conference Mennonite report quoted earlier states,

> For Christians to blend compassion and integrity, wisdom and skill, to offer a redemptive and liberating lifestyle to exhibitionists, transvestites, and others, demand that Christian professionals dealing with human sexuality serve God with heart and mind. Since God's redeeming work in Christ can transform deviants into disciples, we must proclaim the Bible and support therapies that will bring persons to wholeness and health.[15]

Homosexuality

It is not germane here to debate the cause of homosexuality; at this point no one can say definitively why a person has such an orientation. It is our concern as Christian counselors, however, to be ready to deal with the reality that there are Christians who are homosexuals.

Intervention is complicated by the fact that labeling someone a homosexual is not as simple as it first appears. Is a homosexual someone who feels an emotional pull toward the same sex but has never acted on the feeling? Is a person a homosexual who has participated in sexual activity when isolated with the same sex, but is heterosexual in all other situations? Is a homosexual someone who has had two same-sex experiences and five heterosexual encounters?

While all people are alike in having either comfort or discomfort with their sexuality and in their need to be loved and to love, the greatest difference between "straights" and "gays" is the gender choice of the partner. How locked into that selection a person is may be determined by chemical factors, or it may be the result of living in a fallen world in which distortions take place. Homosexuality appears, for many, to be experienced on a continuum rather than as an either/or situation.

This raises two important points. First, if homosexual behavior is greatly influenced by learning and choice, the church must intentionally present the biblical view of marriage and sex in as open and healthy a way as possible. Second, if such behavior, at least in some cases, is indeed amenable to change, the church must be prepared to offer the support for that to happen.

There are at least three possible postures that the church might take toward homosexuals: denial of membership and fellowship, offering an advocacy and support system for individuals who desire to change, or acceptance of monogamous relationships of homosexual couples.

The first option bears little relationship to Jesus' ministry. "I come to heal the sick; the well have no need of my ministry" (see Matt. 9:12). The second provides a positive and loving alternative for restoring "one who is lost." The alternative of accepting homosexual couples whose relationships in all other ways reflect heterosexual commitment is by far the most difficult.

The Intervention

What, then, is to be done when an individual or couple appear in the church office to deal with homosexual concerns? To dismiss the situation is to deny the redeeming power of Christ to make new lives and to ignore that every person is made in the image of God. Forcing the situation back into the closet plays right into Satan's hands. Sin loves the darkness; it avoids the healing power of light whenever possible.

For persons who appear open to change, psychologists George Rekers[16] and Elizabeth Moberly,[17] among others, place parental influences as most significant in developing children with normal sex orientation. The factors said to be most influential mirror the biblical ideal of family authority and balance. Developing a heterosexual orientation means a person must first accept his or her own identity within the family framework as a male or female. Identification with the same-sex parent is part of the process.

If this developmental process has been distorted, progress toward one's true sex identity comes through spending time reestablishing identification with same-sex persons, but not as sexual partners. A loving, accepting fellowship along with a specific support group can assist one in breaking away from habit patterns that keep him or her entrapped and filling the gap left by inadequate family systems. Hostility, hurts, and other inner wounds can be healed as the person is helped to pray concerning the situations and people that have contributed to a lifestyle in rebellion against God's design.

To encourage a heterosexual marriage is not to offer a solution. Instead, such counsel merely multiplies the extent of the hurt as spouses and children become involved. Single homosexuals have no greater difficulty living a celibate lifestyle than single heterosexuals. Such a choice is the biblical mandate for all unmarrieds. Remaining sexually uninvolved in a world that encourages the opposite, especially within the homosexual milieu, requires an understanding and sensitive support system.

While asking someone to remain celibate with little hope of marriage is asking for much, it is not asking the impossible.

Thousands of people live with disabilities and problems that exclude many activities and commitments. They manage. God understands both the temptation and the hurt:

> For this reason he had to be made like his brothers in every way, in order that he might become a merciful and faithful high priest in service to God, and that he might make atonement for the sins of the people. Because he himself suffered when he was tempted, he is able to help those who are being tempted. . . . For we do not have a high priest who is unable to sympathize with our weaknesses, but we have one who has been tempted in every way, just as we are—yet was without sin (Heb. 2:17–18; 4:15).

Adultery

For the first time in his life my son is "heavy in like" with his new girlfriend. I know this time is different because he willingly spends money on her! I will not say he is infatuated, for it is obvious that more than "eros" is at work. But I do not use the word *love* because I know he is not ready to commit to or is capable of true, *agape* love. He is not yet willing to act in a loving way when he does not feel loving, or to put her needs consistently above his own.

The word *love* is so loosely used, as the ♥ bumper stickers attest, that few give thought to what it really means. The Bible defines three kinds of love: *eros*, erotic love; *philia*, brotherly love; and *agape*, love that transcends our self-centered desires and concerns. Human beings may fall into infatuation or into *eros* but we never fall into *agape*. *Agape* love is a choice. An inability to discern one kind of love from another contributes to some adulterous situations.

Our cultural preoccupation is with romantic, erotic love. If it is lacking, a license—albeit an unwritten one—is given to find it. The cost is no matter. The operating assumption is that the spouse is supposed to provide fulfillment of all our needs. If the husband or wife cannot do this, the expectation is that he or she can look elsewhere: most people will understand. "There is nothing more awful than not having my needs met, no one is expected to endure that! Besides, my self-esteem has improved

100 percent, I'm a more sensitive person since the affair, and my marriage has actually improved!"

People can build one case after another to justify their seeking "love" outside the marriage vows. And that of course, is one of the major issues a counselor must deal with. Proverbs 14:12 speaks to that: "There is a way that seems right to a man, but in the end it leads to death." Adultery is never really the loving thing to do. God's plan for marriage is clearly one of monogamy and lifelong commitment. No matter how reasonable, rewarding, or "blessed" an outside relationship may seem, it is still sin in the eyes of the Lord.

Besides breaking the marriage covenant and thereby rupturing one's covenant with the Lord, adultery affects an individual's ability to trust and to consider himself or herself as a person of integrity. No matter who has strayed, rejection and failure are felt by *both* parties. Often the pain of rejection and failure is greater than the pain of the physical betrayal.

For those seeking affirmation of their sexual functioning in adultery, the odds are against them. Fifty-three percent of women involved in affairs report regular orgasm with their husband, whereas only 39 percent of the same women experience orgasm with a lover.[18] The newness and excitement of stolen moments tend to wear off quickly.

People approach an affair with different agendas. The "cool" person may try to perform and receive appreciation but remain aloof from passion and commitment, while the other may be wanting to be totally vulnerable and open with his or her passion. Needless to say, the unequal involvement will create great personal pain. Pain and brokenness are the inevitable result of most adulterous relationships.

The Intervention

While recognizing and being sensitive to all the extenuating circumstances and pressures that lead a person into an affair, pastors and counselors must nevertheless reaffirm the purpose of Christian counseling by helping people put Christ, instead of themselves, at the center of their existence. Adultery is a focus on oneself and one's needs and desires. It is an attempt to make one's personal world better. Unfaithful spouses will usually recognize the breach they have created, although they may feel justified for having done so.

Both husband and wife must be helped to accept responsibility for the areas in which they are culpable. This might involve considerable time and unraveling, which sometimes cannot begin until the anger, rage, and hurt are expressed. I often see the wounded party vacillate between wanting the marriage to end and being willing to do anything to maintain it. It is important that those wishing to stay together be allowed and encouraged to present the mixed feelings that need to be expressed. If they are fearful that honesty will cause the spouse to leave, resentment and unresolved issues will surface as soon as they become more secure that the spouse will stay.

Counseling involves helping each party to accept his or her sphere of responsibility and to begin forgiving. Most people— especially the spouses who have remained faithful—have a difficult time with this. Although they may accept culpability in some matters, they protest that forgiveness is beyond them. With this the counselor readily agrees: they are right. Forgiveness is not possible under human power. Vulnerability and brokenness remind humans of their need for God.

The Great High Priest (Heb. 2:17–18; 4:15) can intervene for these people. He understands and has taken their punishment. Daily penance is not needed, because the sins are forgotten "as far as the east is from the west" (Ps. 103:12). Continuing to wallow in guilt and setting up the expectation that their lives are ruined miss the point. Having received God's forgiveness, these people's next step must be *to experience* forgiveness for themselves and from their spouses.

Praying for the suprahuman power needed to forgive can be accompanied by some very urgently needed intervention such as reestablishing pleasant contact between the spouses.

What did they used to enjoy?

What were the elements that made the activity special? (Was it the activity itself, or the sharing, being alone, or something else?)

How might those elements be reintroduced into the relationship?

Looking for points of commonality reestablishes communication. But specific work on how to talk and hear each other is essential.

Sexual communication is also begun again. Insight offered through education and good history taking, along with the opportunity to share within the safety net of an objective party, opens up sex as a legitimate topic of conversation and concern. I am often asked which is more important: having a good sexual relationship, or having a good nongenital relationship? The reality is that the two go together. Marriage was never defined as one or the other. They are both on the same circle.

Successful intervention can begin at any point on the circle, depending on the clients' comfort level. (This excludes those cases where couples are convinced they can identify their problem, but it is clear they cannot.) Reestablishing a touching relationship may have to begin with sitting together on the same couch! Comfortable touch must be established before genital intimacy can be attempted. Suggestions for reestablishing physical intimacy can be found in the discussion on sensate focus in chapter 8.

Often resolving an adulterous situation means a lover must be given up. Even with a recommitment to the marriage and a sincere desire to be uninvolved, there is a sense of loss in the adulterer. The uninvolved spouse must be helped to see that although physical contact can be severed immediately, emotional "divorce" takes time. It will not be accomplished unless the person is allowed to grieve. Denial, bargaining, anger, and depression are worked through before final acceptance is reached. Acceptance does not imply the person becomes happy about the situation, but that he or she is able to move on.

The depression of grief has two components. The first relates to the feelings of emptiness that were being pacified by the lover. Getting in touch with those issues is the beginning of sound marital therapy as unmet needs and unrealistic expectations that contributed to the dilemma are examined. The second aspect of the depression has more of an existential nature. It is the reconciling by the person of who he or she is as revealed by his or her actions. Inner healing takes place as the individual realigns his or her life and priorities.

Whether or not a spouse is told of an affair depends on a number of factors, the first being the motivation for wanting to share something so hurtful. One can appreciate a desire for honesty, but love takes priority over honesty. The loving thing to do is to take the course of action that results in the greatest good. Often the motive is a selfish desire to unload a guilty burden, to hurt, or to advertise a message that can and should be shared another way.

Symbolically reaffirming vows, burning a list of hurts, and burying a list of disappointments are not just silly gestures. Actions reaffirm and reinforce the choice to love again. Feelings will follow. Just as "faith by itself, if it is not accompanied by action, is dead" (James 2:17), so love by itself, if it is not accompanied by action, is dead.

Choosing marriage means giving up the freedom to do exactly what one wants. But as Lewis Smedes points out, this can be viewed positively, for "fidelity is an affirmation."[19] It is a "calling" sealed with sexual faithfulness. The commitment makes it more than *eros*.

It is ironic that true freedom is experienced within the "bonds" of marriage. Nowhere else is found the safety net of trust and permanence that allows a person to be himself or herself.

Adulterous relationships are broken relationships, not destroyed ones. Gradually, with good counsel, sincere desire, understanding, and commitment to marriage as it was intended to be, a new, honest relationship begins to replace the old, inadequate version. The pastor or counselor is essential in providing the correction, teaching, and encouragement that reinforce the strides that are being made.

Chapter Twelve

LOVE AND RELATIONSHIPS WITHOUT SEX

Special Concerns of the Christian Single

Joel is eighteen years old. He announced to his youth leader his plan to marry. "She doesn't know yet, but after all, in five-and-a-half months I'll be in college, and I'm ready."

Cindy is a very bright college coed who has mapped out a career that excludes marriage for the next ten years.

John is a twenty-eight-year-old pilot for Mission Aviation. He is a zealous Christian and looks forward to the day he will be sent to the most remote area the Lord can find for him.

Marjorie is an eighty-three-year-old widow who does not want remarriage, but she is lonely and needs companionship.

Jolene's life will not be complete until she finds a man to love her. Her first marriage ended in divorce; she is thirty-five and scared.

If you have been feeling guilty because your church has no singles program, perhaps the problem is not insensitivity, but the awesome task of meeting the needs of such a diverse group. About the only thing Joel, Cindy, John, Marjorie, and Jolene have in common is their singleness. I am not saying that churches are excused from trying to meet the needs of what is typically one-third of their membership. The difficulty of the task is no excuse for ignoring the concerns of a growing segment of our society.

There is dissimilarity among singles in their personal acceptance of their single state. Some have what appears to be the gift of singleness that Paul speaks of. They are not without problems, but are content that, at least for this season of life, they are exactly where God wants them. A vast majority, however, feel their life is on hold and are waiting for the day *the* person walks in and life can be lived to the fullest. Others struggle with ambivalent emotions that one day finds them restless for a mate and the next appreciating the freedom of being answerable only to themselves and God.

Yet, despite their many differences, these people do have something besides singleness in common. All men and women are sexual persons. Reflecting God's image, they are sensuous, feeling individuals who were made to desire intimate relationships and be nurtured by the caring touch of a member of the opposite sex as much as their married brothers and sisters.

Humankind mirrors the divine model. God is a unity of Father, Son, and Holy Spirit. Mankind is a unity of man and woman. Adam was designed to need a complement; he was incomplete without Eve, she without him. Wholeness resulted from the man and woman's interdependence and relationship. Genesis does not suggest that wholeness is found simply in fatherhood, motherhood, or family. Only after Adam and Eve were in a relationship were things declared "very good."

For marrieds and singles, the complementary relationship is to extend beyond genital sexuality. Each sex brings nuances of difference and dimension having the potential to enrich the individual, the man-woman relationship, and society as a whole. Men and women think differently, have dissimilar perspectives of children, and have distinct problem-solving approaches. Such differences are usually perceived to be sources of conflict and disagreement rather than complementary gifts for supporting life.

CONFUSION OF RELATIONSHIP AND SEX

Many people today—and down through the centuries—have confused the need for relationships with the opposite sex and the need or desire for a genital sexual relationship. People assume that one cannot be found without the other. So in a desperate attempt to fill the God-given need for intimacy, individuals find themselves quickly escalating their physical involvement, only to experience greater aloneness afterward.

The reason for this is not difficult to discern. Casual sex is like candy: it seems good while one is eating it, but it is nutritionally unhealthful. Eventually it causes tooth decay, weight gain, bad feelings toward oneself, and susceptibility to diseases or conditions that undermine good health. Rarely does the person relate the effects to the original source of the problem: the candy. Scarcely does the person seeking intimacy through sex relate the emptiness, complications, and health problems back to their source: the sex with no commitment.

In the past, a person worried whether or not he or she would allow a relationship to lead to a sexual encounter. Today a person frets over how well he or she performed. "Was it fulfilling?" "Did it have meaning?" The question of meaning is, ironically, a valid question: sex cannot deliver what it was not meant to deliver.

For many today, sharing one's soul has become more difficult than sharing one's body. The result of this reluctance is that sex becomes a way to avoid the very thing it is purportedly seeking—a unifying closeness. If a couple jump into bed immediately, they do not have to talk. Good sex can cause frightening feelings to well up for those who fear commitment and closeness. Confusing messages result: "If you really loved me . . ." followed by "It's obvious we can't control our emotions, so we'd better not see each other again."

Such games result in painful injuries far more hurtful than the pain that drove them to be played in the first place! Not having a relationship can be hurtful. But the real destruction is in the broken relationships. All things considered, the pain of being alone can motivate people to make healthy choices and not be driven by impulses.

A PURPOSE IN CELIBACY

People without God seek fulfillment through work, recreation, the latest guru, or very commonly, sex. God does not ask singles to remain celibate simply to give them a challenge in life. Celibacy is a form of identity, a way of being a disciple and learning discipleship. The Bible presents celibacy as a way to honor God and accomplish a greater good than mere self-fulfillment.

Pastors and counselors can help singles view their state as one of purpose and meaning. Their calling is to be "holy," for their God is holy. Through a study of the many callings in the Christian life and and awareness of their particular gifts and abilities, singles can be helped to discern the plan and purpose of their lives. While this is equally important for marrieds, it is especially significant for singles who may assume that without a mate there is no significance or purpose in life. The church can do far more than it usually does by publicly affirming and encouraging the single's commitment to a life-plan that is pleasing to the Lord.

Many people who have tried to control their weight have had the experience of going on a diet and feeling so deprived that, as soon as the magic number was reached, they rewarded themselves with enough food to put the pounds they had lost right back in place. As long as a single person has an attitude of deprivation about the lack of sexual release, he or she will find an almost irrepressible preoccupation to have the desire filled. But if he or she perceives the unmarried state to be a calling rather than a deprivation, the sexual feelings can be approached as annoyances that can be handled effectively in a variety of ways. In other words, when a Christian single decides to say no, there is a valid reason. Singles must have a purpose in living life as they do.

Celibacy can be chosen for the wrong reason. Singleness without genital sexuality should never be selected just because a person fears marriage or remarriage. Distrusting the opposite sex is no more credible a reason than is the inability to commit to a relationship.

People who choose virginity are no less complete than those who do not. Studies indicate they have the same number of friends as nonvirgins. They feel capable and no less satisfied with life. There is no truth to the suggestion that they are under more stress. In fact, virgins tend to be more successful than nonvirgins in relation to educational and occupational attainment. On the whole they are well adjusted.[1]

Marriage and singleness are both honored states. According to Paul, the challenge is to "learn to be content in any and every situation" (Phil. 4:11). He recognizes that one "learns" to be content, a process in which intervention, support, and reinforcement of meaning can be impressed upon by a caring pastor, counselor, or teacher. Contentment is related to trusting that the Lord has the person exactly where He wants him or her to be, at least for the time being.

DEALING WITH SEXUAL NEEDS

A single person who tries to come to terms with a sexual drive that seems to be in overdrive might question God's wisdom in declaring mankind and the sexual nature "very good." Perhaps singleness could be endured if a little on-off switch had been included within each person so that the sexual drive could be activated on the wedding day. God could have done that! He chose instead to have men and women relate to each other as creatures who have a natural sexual attraction for the other sex. He understands that sexuality involves far more than acting out sexual desire.

Sexuality includes both the psychological expression of masculinity and femininity and the ability to respond physically to erotic stimuli. The way a man relates to a woman or another man is highly dependent on his masculinity; his personality is his most prominent expression of his sexuality. The same is true for a woman. Humans are who they are because their sexual nature is incorporated into the very core of their being.

Rather than ignoring or denying their sexuality, God wants singles to accept His gift of male or female sexuality and of the sensations that go with it. This strikes fear in many hearts. If singles acknowledge their sexuality, will they not act on their sexual feelings? Will not lust and hedonism take over and destroy them?

Apparently God has expectations for his people that they do not have for themselves. God made them sexual and provided no convenient on-off button. But He did incorporate into His plan the means to deal with sexual concerns rightly. The solution is not so simple as a switch, but the mechanism for control is within each person.

Millions of singles, including Christians, choose simply to act on their erotic feelings. It is the easy thing to do. But because it is common does not make it right. Others play games, avoiding intercourse but participating in everything else. They ignore Jesus' anger with the Pharisees for the hypocrisy of looking clean on the outside while hearts and minds were "unclean."

Jesus teaches that the decision to sin comes from within the heart. Sinning cannot be blamed on some sort of perverse testing by God or the influence of anyone or anything else. "For from within, out of men's hearts, come evil thoughts, sexual immorality. . . . All these evils come from inside and make a man 'unclean' " (Mark 7:21–22). Ultimately each person must answer for his or her choices. The final decision is an internal one, and that is the one that must be lived with.

This is not to deny that the pressures to misuse sex are great. The media incessantly suggest how and what the plan for sex is. People are told they face irreparable psychic damage if they do not fully express themselves sexually. More subtle is the message that their psyches might make it, but everyone else will find them "out of step." People who practice self-discipline or believe in something outside themselves are looked on as strange indeed. More than ever, Christian leaders need actively and lovingly to present, teach, and take a stand for reality: God's plan for the sexuality He made.

If singles accept and respond to the false promises that are offered, it will not be without consequence. There will be physical pleasure, for sex was made to feel good, but other repercussions can be difficult to bear. There are now twenty-seven varieties of sexually transmitted diseases, pregnancy can occur, marriages break up, and children can observe lifestyles that negate the need for commitment and trust.

The consequences are more than the social and physical diseases that might be accentuated. After participating in the promise that sex holds the answer, feelings of being used, unworthy, and empty are left to compete with guilt feelings that gnaw at peace of mind. Worse still for the Christian is the sense of alienation from God, for sin separates. Ultimately a kind of paranoia sets in:

"Who can I trust?"

"How many others were there?"

"How do I compare?"

"Could we be faithful to each other if we were married?"

What Christian singles often need, in light of all this, is simple confirmation of what they know to be true: sexual desire cannot be allowed to rule them. They must be assured, but not with simplistic clichés, that self-control is a spiritual gift and that God's power can be a reality in the lives of people who expect it. The positive feelings that come from self-control can strengthen those people who are committed to God-honoring Christian discipleship.

Singles are accustomed to evaluating their mistakes and failures and often seek counseling after one or more failures have occurred. The process should be reversed. Pastors and counselors must help singles realistically anticipate the problems and then offer methods and support needed to help them live righteously. Then less time would have to be spent picking up the pieces of wrong or poor sexual choices.

The church should not shrink from teaching that self-discipline is healthful. Only a disciplined person can love God in the way He commands. Who is there to make the connection that a self-disciplined person keeps commitments and that marriage is based on commitment? Who is there to celebrate a person's strong value system and obedience to other than one's own ego needs? It is the church, especially her pastors and counselors. There are few others who will take the responsibility. Is the comfort level achieved by avoiding sexual issues worth the consequences?

WHERE IS THE HEART?

Whenever Christians take a stand on sexuality, it is important that legalism not be the basis on which teaching is offered and judgments are made. If it is, there is nothing to guide a person except an arbitrary line that is moved about from one authority to another. The question is not "How far can I go?" It is, instead, "God wants me to be pure, so how do I maintain purity?"

That question brings us back to understanding the profundity of love and still more questions.

"Is my behavior the loving thing to do?"

"Are my partner and I equal decision makers?" (Remember 1 Thessalonians 4:6.)

"Am I doing this to find out who I am?"

"Is the situation based in reality, or have I set up false expectations?"

"Am I using sex as an anesthetic to take care of pain that needs to be dealt with in other ways?"

Part of God's plan for sexual control involves the person knowing himself or herself well.

Acknowledging God's gift of sex is involved in self-acceptance. For sex to have meaning, one must be committed to God's purpose and plan for it. The fullest pleasure of sex is found when it is used for the purpose for which it was designed. It is meant as an outward expression of deep spiritual and emotional unity in permanent relationships. As with anything not used the way it was designed, damage results that thwarts its original intention.

People consciously and unconsciously handle sexual desire in a variety of ways. While some, as we have seen, consider it to be an aggravation, others sublimate (not suppress) their desires. This approach fits beautifully with the biblical vision of the single life's being lived with a purpose outside oneself. Energy is expended in living the life God would have that person live. Thoughts and activities are directed toward accomplishing the goal.

Because of the great diversity among God's creatures and the various effects of learning experiences, there is great variation in how well sublimation works. Counselors and pastors can help individuals identify triggers that reinforce erotic feelings. Remembering songs, reliving special days of a past relationship, or reading romantic novels or erotic maga-zines all serve to make sublimation difficult.

There is great danger in underestimating how hard it is for some people to control their erotic desires. A counselor who finds it easy may not be able to sympathize with the person who finds it the supreme challenge. The counselor can fall into the trap of a "holier than thou" attitude that is both sinful and very detrimental to the helping process. If I do not like or only moderately crave ice cream, it is no big deal to turn it down. If I love it and turn it down, I have made a sacrifice.

Turning down opportunities for sex will feel like a sacrifice if it is not viewed, instead, as a commitment willingly chosen for a greater good. The element of choice indicates a decision from the heart. Some people attempt to control their sexual desires by pretending they do not have them. This is not only unbiblical, but also dangerous and a setup for failure. The repression of erotic feelings is not honest. It cripples the person's ability to deal openly with and conquer erotic con-cerns. Worse, it compromises a person's ability to have the responsive type of sexual relationship that should characterize a Christian marriage.

POSITIVE RELATIONSHIPS

Friendships and the fellowship they offer go a long way toward helping singles deal with their sexual feelings. The need for relationships with the opposite sex is healthy and normal. In every man-woman friendship that has any degree of intimacy, the issue of sexuality must be dealt with. Often this is an unconscious process. If people refuse to recognize the need to face their feelings and attractions honestly, difficulties develop that could have been avoided if they had met the situation head-on. Thinking it through and, if necessary, sharing with the other person provides a natural safety valve. Letting feelings escalate can be far more dangerous.

Friendships between singles get difficult when the hidden agenda is marriage. If they are always measuring each individ-ual they meet against their personal criteria for a mate, the outcome is usually a missed opportunity. Singles are to pursue love, not marriage—just as all Christians are to have as their goal "loving one another" instead of self-serving desires.[2]

A ten-year study comparing sexual attitudes and behavior between 1972 and 1982 revealed that a double standard for behavior still exists for men and women. Increased tolerance toward premarital sex does not mean people automatically indulge in such behavior. The trend is toward more traditional sociosexual values. Following tradition, females who participate in premarital sex have a higher level of emotional involvement and commitment than the majority of males.[3]

When people accept the goal of a relationship to be to get to know someone and accept the person because he or she is also a new creature in Christ, the orientation of the relationship must change from the self-centered "What's in this for me?" to learning to offer something of oneself to build up the other. One implication of this mandate is the responsibility to follow through on difficult relationships. It is very revealing when a person decides to cool off a relationship simply because he or she decides that the other is "not the one for me." It may be determined that not seeing the other person is the loving thing to do. But in most situations, *philia* and *eros* can grow into a form of *agape* that enriches the life of each individual, and they can share a deep, loving friendship.

A counselor who can see beyond *eros* has the potential to teach and help men and women learn to relate in positive and life-growing ways. This is becoming increasingly important, because 48 percent of adults in the United States are single today, and the proportion is likely to get even larger. An article in *U.S. News and World Report* points out that between 1970 and 1982 the number of people in the United States who live alone increased by 78 percent.

I WANT TO GET MARRIED

In Matthew 6:33–34 Jesus speaks prophetically to the single person, as He does to all His disciples: "But seek first his kingdom and his righteousness. . . . Do not worry about tomorrow, for tomorrow will worry about itself." No one is promised marriage; rather, people are promised love, fulfillment, and meaning if the Lord is the center of their lives.

I have a divorced friend whose recent beau announced his intention not to date her anymore. They had a good time together and seemed to be compatible in a number of ways, but he had decided it was time to seek marriage. She did not meet his criteria for a wife. He printed cards with his future wife's qualifications on the back, along with the offer of a reward for anyone who helped him find her. He meant business; he was going to marry!

The confusion and distortions that single people have of themselves are accentuated by messages they receive from people who are married. Both the secular and especially the Christian world offer marriage as the "end-all-and-be-all" for happiness. Romance that leads to marriage is the ultimate experience of life, so they say. This assumption merely adds more distortions and prejudices. Often singles are underused or limited in their church responsibilities because they belong to a class of people viewed as immature and selfish. By not having had the "ultimate experience of life," they may be considered as not yet having reached full adulthood.

To seek marriage as a way to find one's identity so as to *really* begin living is doomed to fail. Yet even among divorced people there is a great rush to make marriage the solution. Some seek to assuage the sexual insecurities they feel by prematurely involving themselves with someone who assures them they are a functioning male or female. Time is required to become ready for remarriage. The healthful fear that prevents one from not trusting in a new relationship is a good gauge for judging when remarriage is even a possibility. Married people's tendency to want to see others "happy" and their personal discomfort with the "extra" person contribute to hasty commitments. A helper's first priority should be to encourage the single to take whatever time is needed for healing to occur.

It is important for people seeking marriage to receive encouragement from those who have gone through similar experiences. Group support sponsored by the church has been invaluable to many hurting people. It is often through such groups that involvement with others can begin again.

Whether in a group setting or individually, singles find that a great deal of anxiety is alleviated when they are helped through open discussion and teaching to reach a firm decision and commitment as to what their sexual conduct will be. This is a major readjustment and decision for many who have been accustomed to regular sexual release. People rarely discuss their sexual behavior commitments except in an atmosphere that is either condemning on the one hand or libertarian on the other. How many times in your role as counselor have you openly and honestly helped someone wrestle with this issue?

I spoke at a large meeting of Christian singles comprised mostly of people who had been married at some time. Only one person in that large group had had the experience of speaking with a pastor openly about the sexual readjustment after a marriage ends. Many of those attending complained that they had not been able to get pastors to speak about sexuality to their singles groups within their respective churches.

The reluctance of church leaders to speak openly stems from their fear of not having an easy answer. But it is not the pat answer that provides healing and illumination. It is the opportunity to talk and receive empathy and support that is vital and necessary for healing. Many who might help hesitate because of ambivalent feelings that they may find themselves in the same situation and not have the answers.

Most singles who are struggling with their sexuality receive counsel after having floundered and found themselves in situations they cannot live with, either morally or emotionally. Counselors will inevitably find themselves intervening after the fact when the situation is the most complex and upsetting for all. Compassionate listening, spiritual guidance, and wisdom are needed in such times of crisis. But such gifts need also to be put to work in giving teaching, direction, and support *before* the crises come.

WHILE I'M WAITING . . .

Remember the story of Nehemiah and the Jerusalem wall? Nehemiah was in despair because his spiritual home lay in ruin. He prayed mightily and long that God would enable him to correct this travesty. But along with prayer, Nehemiah planned and dreamed and prepared. When many months later God opened the door for him with the king, Nehemiah was ready to seize the moment. He was allowed to return to his homeland, he was given the materials he needed, and he even had the king's blessing. Most important, because of his patience and preparation, he knew he was ready and that his mission was in line with what God wanted for him.

There is a strong analogy here. A season of singleness is to be spent growing and preparing oneself socially, educationally, culturally, and spiritually. The autonomy of the unmarried to take advantage of classes, reading, and cultural events is not appreciated until marriage radically changes one's agenda to more mundane pursuits. When the time for the marriage comes and the single is prepared, like Nehemiah, the moment can be seized with assurance.

For the Christian single who has become involved sexually, guilt abounds. Even the most "liberated" often find, to their utter surprise, that their rationalizations do not protect them as they expected. "Being in love makes it okay" hardly enables one to cope with real, gut-level feelings. None of us can ever be reminded too often of the sacrifice made by the Lord Jesus on our behalf and what it means to our fallen lives. But equally important is the truth, "For sin shall not be your master, because you are not under law, but under grace" (Rom. 6:14).

Christian counselors are to exhibit the same wholeness and balance that we find in the gospel. The purpose is not condemnation, but support to enable people to live the life of righteousness to which they were called. Mourning, thought stopping, or breaking habit patterns in thinking and lifestyle may be part of the process. Prayer and sensitivity to the leading of the Holy Spirit certainly are. A major responsibility of the counselor is to communicate the assurance that because of the grace of Jesus Christ, no one has to live a life of sin.

HIS GOOD PURPOSE

Anyone who views God's laws as arbitrary and whimsical will have a hard time following them. The promise that

Christians can trust that God wants the best for them is found in Philippians 2:13: "For it is God who works in you to will and to act according to his good purpose."

A fallen people find it difficult to conceptualize a God who considers them the crown of His creation or who loves them individually and desires a relationship. Nevertheless, mankind was made for relationship with God. No other creature has a body and a spirit deriving from the combination of earthy soil and the divine breath of God. Of all the creation, human beings are the only beings who have the capacity to see beyond themselves to the possibilities of the new creation.

Much of this book has been extolling and celebrating the gift of sexuality that God has given His creatures. So it may appear inconsistent to suggest that learning to live without an opportunity for a sexual relationship is also good. But that is a truth that comes from God. The good gift of sex is not an ultimate value to be placed above all other values. And this is what the single person must come to know.

Singles have the choice of either bemoaning their condition or finding meaning in it by viewing it as a gift given for God's good purpose. They can view singleness as either a state of bitterness or a state of blessedness. They can choose either an earthbound purpose and its momentary pleasures or a kingdom-related calling and its incomparable fulfillment. The promise is clear to those who "have made themselves eunuchs for the kingdom of heaven's sake" (Matt. 19:12 KJV).

For this is what the LORD says:

"To the Eunuchs who keep my Sabbaths,
 who choose what pleases me
 and hold fast to my covenant—
to them I will give within my temple and its walls
 a memorial and a name
 better than sons and daughters;
I will give them an everlasting name
 that will not be cut off." (Isa. 56:4–5)

Chapter Thirteen

STARTING OUT RIGHT
Premarital Sexual Counseling

When I was about to be married, the minister told me that he had reduced his premarital talk to one session. That one meeting was confined to a discussion of communication. It had a positive effect on me. And he was correct in making that his emphasis. By adhering to the pastor's admonitions, my husband and I made it through some difficult adjustments with relatives and clashes of our personalities, not to mention the pressures of medical school.

I think my own experience illustrates well that couples who are just embarking on marriage are more open and willing to listen to helpful advice than at almost any other time. Even though our minister was someone we did not know well, we hung on his every word. Had he mentioned anything related to spirituality, sexuality, or finances, we would have been very attentive. We had not established any basic patterns in our marriage. He was one of a very few people who could provide us with a Christian perspective on our marriage—and our whole life, for that matter.

Because marriage is not a private matter, responsible people like pastors, Christian counselors, and teachers must offer those about to be married relevant and insightful teaching regarding the purpose, realities, and hopes for marriage.

Experts in premarital education often recommend using a small-group setting as an efficient way to help couples work toward marriage.[1] A group enables differences to be brought up safely and provides modeling for problem solving. An effective program for most churches might require sharing responsibility with other churches, perhaps for a monthly workshop. This would not exclude individual sessions with the pastor, but would be a wise use of time for general education.

Many issues should be considered in premarital counseling. Stanley Rock, in his book *This Time Together*, correctly recommends that time be spent discussing the impact of one's family background on current patterns of behavior, spiritual life, coping strategies, parenthood decisions, sexual intimacy, financial planning, and special concerns of remarriage. My purpose in this chapter, however, is to consider the matter of sexual intimacy exclusively.

No matter what the format, scope, or purpose of premarital counseling, it is important to have a plan for follow-up on the couple or couples in question. Accountability helps to motivate people to do their best. In sexual matters, a six-month refresher course may offer couples an opportunity to grow and improve before patterns are set irrevocably. After six months or so, but before a year or more of marriage has passed, people often display a high motivation to deal with problems.

BASIC TEACHINGS FOR COUPLES TO BUILD ON

There are some basic issues in sexuality that couples need to deal with to build a lasting and satisfying marriage.

1. God is the creator of sexuality and the author of our sexual relationship. He meant these to be a source of pleasure, unity, and procreation.
2. Both sexes are to participate equally and intensely in the sexual relationship and enjoy their gifts of sensuousness.
3. Sexual relations are to be a regular part of married life.
4. Husband and wife are mandated to "know" one another. That knowledge entails (a) communicating needs, (b) taking responsibility, and (c) becoming vulnerable.

5. The sexual relationship between men and women is based on mutuality, not the exclusive prerogatives of one or the other.
6. The Christian understanding of love has more to do with giving than taking; it "perseveres" (1 Cor. 13:7).
7. Knowledge of the way the Lord made us is appropriate and worthy of a believer's time and study.
8. Christians are not prisoners of sin. They always have the means available to establish fresh and healthful sexual relationships that glorify the Lord.
9. Expressing our sexuality in God-ordained ways keeps us sexually pure.

WORKING WITH THE COUPLE

The attitude displayed by the counselor is the most important factor in communicating God's message on sex. Other (packaged) forms of communication such as books, handouts, tapes, information sheets, and tests can be used to help begin conversations naturally. But they are not the most essential communication.

Whatever approach seems best for you as the counselor or educator is the one you should use. Provide to each person a handout of questions that stimulate thought and discussion about his or her sexual history before the session on sex. This is often helpful in creating a comfort level and getting the couple used to the idea that sex is an appropriate topic for discussion, even with a pastor!

Questions on sex have more than one purpose. They facilitate discussion of sexual matters in an orderly fashion, provide an opportunity for the couple to share their understanding of sexuality, and give practice in talking about sex. Not many people have experienced opportunities to talk and share sexual information or feelings with a member of the opposite sex. But marriage requires that ability. So the couple are instructed to set aside time to discuss the questions between them, making notes of the significant things they learn or need to bring up with the pastor or counselor.

The sample questionnaire that follows identifies matters that are useful in discussions of sexuality.

1. What was said about your birth? Was it positive or negative? Were you the sex your parents wanted?
2. What did you hear as a child about your sexual curiosity? Were the remarks rational? Threatening? Destructive? Positive? Indulgent?
3. Was the subject of sex ignored? If so, how do you feel about that? What did it teach you?
4. What were your sexual organs called? How did you learn the facts of life?
5. Were you taught how to protect yourself sexually? Were you abused sexually? Did your parents or guardians fail to protect you sexually? Did anyone try to arouse you with stories or actions?
6. What is your primary feeling about your body? About your sex organs?
7. What is your greatest fear about marital sexuality?
8. What is the difference between sex and sensuousness? How does God feel about each of them?
9. What purpose does marital sexuality have?
10. What is your perception of the sexual relationship of your father and your mother? How might this affect you?

USING JESUS AS THE EXAMPLE

Our Lord did not merely talk about the need for our being servants to one another. He demonstrated what that meant in the most humble and dramatic way He could—He washed His disciples' feet. I urge you to ask your soon-to-be-married couples to do no less. Along with the questions, assign an exercise in foot washing. Few people are comfortable with the idea of washing another's feet. It is humbling. For some it is repulsive. There is only one thing worse for some people, and that is having one's own feet washed!

Out of such an experience comes practical knowledge of the meaning of servanthood. Couples must begin to develop an awareness of how each feels about giving to and receiving from the other. Ask them to discuss and write down their reactions. They are to take note in particular of whether giving or receiving is more comfortable and fulfilling.

When a couple return to discuss the experience, you can help them explore their respective reactions in light of the potential effect their preferences might have on their marriage—especially on their sexual life. For example, what might the implications be for the partner who is comfortable giving a foot washing but extremely uncomfortable receiving one?

GOD'S PLAN FOR MARITAL SEXUALITY

Ideally, two sessions should be devoted to sexuality. Getting off to a good start sexually helps a couple weather the storm as challenging situations begin to pressure the new family. There needs to be sufficient time to discuss reactions to the questionnaire and the experience of foot washing. It is not necessary to take up every question, but it is important to evaluate the feelings and new awareness that they stimulate. One meeting should be devoted to these issues if possible.

Having experienced the desensitizing effect of the first exercise and having practiced talking openly about sex, a couple can then take on a more specific assignment. There are a number of tapes, videos, and Christian books that can be assigned as homework for the subsequent session. The Song of Songs will do nicely if you prefer to limit the material to the Bible. Encourage discussion and exploration of feelings between the couple as they consider some of the more threatening issues of sex. Instruct them to write down and bring questions and concerns.

LET THE BIBLE DO THE TEACHING

Nine points were given as "Basic Teachings for Couples to Build On." You may want to enlarge the list. Each point should be firmly backed by Scripture.

Christians often forget that God speaks approvingly to His people about sexuality. Non-Christians are usually unaware that the Bible has relevance to sexual life. Use Scripture, therefore, to discuss the significance of the "basic teachings" and help the couple begin to discover the Bible's positive framework for understanding the sexual relationship. Consider providing a handout with passages for them to read and study together.

Scripture teaches that God is the author of our sexuality and sensuousness:

> So God created man in his own image, in the image of God he created him; male and female he created them (Gen. 1:27).

> For this reason a man will leave his father and mother and be united to his wife, and they will become one flesh (Gen. 2:24).

> For you created my inmost being; you knit me together in my mother's womb. I praise you because I am fearfully and wonderfully made (Ps. 139:13–14).

Scripture teaches that sex is to be enjoyed equally by men and women:

> The man and his wife were both naked, and they felt no shame (Gen. 2:25).

> (Solomon:)   Until the day breaks
> and the shadows flee,
> I will go to the mountain of myrrh
> and to the hill of incense.
>
> (Song of Songs 4:6)

> (Shulamith:)   Place me like a seal over your heart,
> like a seal over your arm;
> for love is as strong as death,
> its jealousy unyielding as the grave.
> It burns like blazing fire,
> like a mighty flame.
>
> (Song of Songs 8:6)

Scripture teaches that marriage involves the regular and continual expression of love by way of the body:

> Do not deprive each other except by mutual consent and for a time, so that you may devote yourself to prayer. Then come together again so that Satan will not tempt you because of your lack of self-control (1 Cor. 7:5).

Scripture teaches that for a man and a woman to know one another involves more than the genital sexual relationship; it implies understanding and vulnerability also:

> Be completely humble and gentle; be patient, bearing with one another in love. Make every effort to keep the unity of the Spirit through the bond of peace (Eph. 4:2–3).

Scripture teaches that mutuality is required in a sexual relationship:

> The husband should fulfill his marital duty to his wife, and likewise the wife to her husband. The wife's body does not belong to her alone but also to her husband. In the same way, the husband's body does not belong to him alone but also to his wife (1 Cor. 7:3–4).

Scripture teaches that married love is not simply *eros*, but *eros* and *agape:*

> Love is patient, love is kind. It does not envy, it does not boast, it is not proud. It is not rude, it is not self-seeking, it is not easily angered, it keeps no record of wrongs. Love does not delight in evil but rejoices with the truth. It always protects, always trusts, always hopes, always perseveres (1 Cor. 13:4–6).

Scripture teaches that God expects us to learn to control our bodies:

> . . . that each of you should learn to control his own body in a way that is holy and honorable (1 Thess. 4:4).

Believers do not have to continue in sexual patterns that are immoral or hinder unity:

> You were taught, with regard to your former way of life, to put off your old self, which is being corrupted by its deceitful desires, to be made new in the attitude of your minds; and to put on the new self, created to be like God in true righteousness and holiness (Eph. 4:22–24).

> For we know that our old self was crucified with him so that the body of sin might be done away with, that we should no longer be slaves to sin—because anyone who has died has been freed from sin (Rom. 6:6–7).

Scripture teaches that it is not sexuality, but sexual immorality that is under the judgment of God:

> But among you there must not be even a hint of sexual immorality, or of any kind of impurity, or of greed, because these are improper for God's holy people (Eph. 5:3).

> Marriage should be honored by all, and the marriage bed kept pure, for God will judge the adulterer and all the sexually immoral (Heb. 13:4).

> It is God's will that you should be sanctified: that you should avoid sexual immorality (1 Thess. 4:3).

AFTER THE MARRIAGE AND INTO THE REAL WORLD

It is unfortunate that "preparation for marriage" is usually a few brief discussions that occur long before the realities of many aspects of marriage and sexuality are experienced by the couple. Often there is no opportunity to deal with many of the significant problems that come only with experience.

I would like to suggest a continued intervention that not only keeps counselors in touch with the couples they have counseled and pastors in touch with couples for whom they have performed marriages, but also provides the couple with a trusted, caring, and spiritual resource in whom they can confide. A six-month follow-up will enable them to evaluate the habits that are becoming established in the new union. An objective observer can then suggest any remedial work that needs to be done. Such evaluations are likely to be heard and followed, for the newness of love and the desire to make the marriage successful are powerful forces at that early stage.

At the end of the final session on sexual intimacy, send each couple home with a packet of exercises that are to be performed at intervals of one, three, and six months after the wedding. You may include a bibliography or prepare a handout with instructions. A booklet or handout entitled "Our Sexual Growth Inventory" provides a record of growth in intimacy to be shared at the six-month counseling meeting.

Such a program should ask the couple to go through a modified version of the sensate focus exercises that are designed to deal with sexual dysfunction and to offer enrichment. This can provide an intentional and nonthreatening evaluation of the direction of their sexual relationship. It can also be an encouragement to strive for growth and improvement in that relationship.

A sample handout is provided at the end of this chapter. Other exercises and handouts can be developed to inform (charts and illustrations of male and female genitalia, for instance) and to enhance communication and awareness on sexual issues. You may be assuming that giving a couple the appropriate book to read is a sufficient response to the need. But do not ignore the fact that many people will read a few pages developed specifically for them, yet they may lay aside a book written for no person in particular.

CONCLUSION

One might think that such a program is either too much trouble or too unusual to succeed. But before you dismiss the whole idea or refuse to try such a radical approach to support the development of healthy marriages, here are a few things to consider:

How might your own marriage have been changed if someone had cared enough to make sure you understood God's purpose for sex?

What difference would there have been if you had been freed from the misinformation and ambivalences you have experienced?

Would you ever stop to evaluate whether your sexual relationship glorifies the Lord by being all it is supposed to be unless someone encouraged you to do so?

Did anyone ever suggest to you that your sexual relationship is dynamic and ever-changing, and you must continue to adjust over a lifetime?

Did anyone teach you that keeping your marriage strong sexually is mandated by God?

Did a pastor ever present sex in a way that revealed the joyful, playful, and sensuous nature it is meant to have?

Was someone there to help you understand that as *eros* tends to wane with time, it is *agape* that keeps the marriage going?

Whether couples report back to you is of less consequence than whether their sexual relationship moves toward fulfilling the promise of pleasure that has come from God. Your time will have been well spent if you are able to help couples discover that sex is a legitimate aspect of the Christian walk. In your equipping people for living fully as God's creatures, you are fulfilling the vocation of ministry.

DEVELOPING A HEALTHY SEXUAL RELATIONSHIP:
EXERCISES FOR COUPLES

Take these exercises home and plan to work through them on your one-month, three-month, and six-month anniversaries. These exercises assume that a sexual relationship, like any other relationship, must be worked on and must develop over time if it is to flourish. I want to help you start in the right direction, so we should plan at your six-month anniversary to get together again and discuss your responses to the exercises.

The following ten questions are designed to encourage communication and evaluation in your continuing sexual development. Answer the first five questions by circling the number on the scale that most closely corresponds with your attitude. Answer the last five questions by filling in the blanks. Because you will be answering the same questions on three different occasions, be sure to put the date at the top each time you work on the exercises.

Work on these exercises when you are alone and in a state of relative objectivity. Plan to talk with your partner about the answers when both of you are in a good mood and communicating well.

Line (a) is your personal response.
Line (b) is your guess as to how your spouse will respond.
Line (c) is your expectation of the ideal response.

1	2	3	4	5
extremely unhappy	slightly unhappy	slightly pleased	moderately pleased	extremely pleased

1. After one (three) (six) month(s) of marriage, what is your overall satisfaction with your sex life?

   (a) 1_____ 2_____ 3_____ 4_____ 5_____

   (b) 1_____ 2_____ 3_____ 4_____ 5_____

   (c) 1_____ 2_____ 3_____ 4_____ 5_____

2. How pleased are you with the frequency of intercourse?

   (a) 1_____ 2_____ 3_____ 4_____ 5_____

   (b) 1_____ 2_____ 3_____ 4_____ 5_____

   (c) 1_____ 2_____ 3_____ 4_____ 5_____

3. How pleased are you with the frequency of nonsexual touching?

(a) 1_____ 2_____ 3_____ 4_____ 5_____
(b) 1_____ 2_____ 3_____ 4_____ 5_____
(c) 1_____ 2_____ 3_____ 4_____ 5_____

4. Is the balance of who initiates sex comfortable?
(a) 1_____ 2_____ 3_____ 4_____ 5_____
(b) 1_____ 2_____ 3_____ 4_____ 5_____
(c) 1_____ 2_____ 3_____ 4_____ 5_____

5. Are you pleased with the time of day usually set aside for lovemaking?
(a) 1_____ 2_____ 3_____ 4_____ 5_____
(b) 1_____ 2_____ 3_____ 4_____ 5_____
(c) 1_____ 2_____ 3_____ 4_____ 5_____

6. If only one thing about my sexual life could be changed, it would be _____

_____

7. I let my spouse know I feel sexual by _____

_____

    He or she tells me by _____

_____

8. I feel most loved when my spouse _____

_____

9. The thing I like best about our sexual relationship is _____

_____

10. I admire and respect my spouse because _____

_____

Matters for discussion between you and your spouse:

Are there dissimilarities in the ways you perceive each other?
What is the most surprising thing you have learned in your sexual relationship?
Discuss some things each of you might do to improve the sexual experience of the other.

Share how you feel about having this checkup.

Make a date to do the body exploration and sensate focus exercises within the next week.

SETTING THE LIMITS
Referral to Other Helpers

Often the secret of being a good helper lies in knowing your limitations. Through reading this book many pastors and counselors will be motivated to investigate further and to begin to put into practice some of the skills described. Others will conclude they have no expertise for such intensive therapeutic work. The vast majority of pastors will struggle, as always, to decide which of the 101 hats they wear should be worn at a given time and which should be left on the hatrack.

Is it possible for a pastor to function as a sex therapist? In most situations the answer is no. But as a sex educator and helpful problem solver, yes.

The reason why I want to encourage pastors to assume the latter role is that they are the key to helping turn the church from being a negative force in developing a healthy sexuality among Christian people to a positive force that will benefit not only Christians, but the world at large. One of my basic themes in this book is that the church must develop an attitude that acknowledges the complexity and importance sexuality plays in the life of every man and woman. If the church can recognize and accept this truth, it can become increasingly sensitive to the needs of its members and be better equipped to intervene in this previously forbidden territory.

Christian counselors must also assume an educator's role and not simply respond to problems. Many common problems could be prevented or at least diminished if Christians were better prepared to be fully sexual beings and knew what responsibilities go with that calling. Nevertheless, counselors will continue to have to deal with problems as they arise. For many of them the skills offered in this book can be put to work. But even these counselors will have to determine their limitations.

One device that might help pastors and Christian counselors determine the level of therapeutic intervention they desire in their sexual counseling is called "Annon's model," also known as PLISSIT.[1] This acronym summarizes four possible levels of therapeutic action to be taken: Permission-giving, Limited Information, Specific Suggestions, and Intensive Therapy.

The most moderate form of intervention, *Permission-giving,* may be all that is needed to help a person grasp the truth about his or her sexuality and begin to live it. I have stressed already what an advantageous position a Christian minister or counselor has to influence church members positively. The ways in which authorities in the church speak about sex promote either a sex-negative or a sex-positive atmosphere and determine whether or not members of the church will be able to grow in their sexual relationships.

The next stage of intervention involves sharing *Limited Information* about sexual functioning. Many problems and concerns that people face can be resolved by correct factual information. The pastor owes it to his flock to be a resource they can depend on. This type of intervention is very much in keeping with the calling that pastors and some Christian counselors have to be teachers of the people of God.

Offering *Specific Suggestions* is the level of direct intervention. At this level, specific problems or issues need specific responses. With minimal but adequate training, considerable encouragement, and the positive transference already in effect, most pastors can be more effective with specific suggestions than they imagine. This, of course, is the level on which most counselors usually operate.

In sexual counseling such problems as failure to achieve orgasm among women, premature ejaculation among men, and the need for enrichment among couples have often been treated well by specific suggestions offered by caring, knowledgable people. Considerable effectiveness has been reported for such problems with limited therapeutic involvement. A key to success is correct evaluation of the situation.

Finally, the level from which the majority of pastors and many counselors can be excused is that of *Intensive Therapy*. The amount of time and the expertise required to do effective, in-depth therapy is beyond the scope of most. Those who have an interest and appropriate comfort level should be encouraged to pursue the necessary educational and training requirements to ensure their proficiency. There is no question that competent sex therapists are in short supply and that the number of Christians in the field is nominal at best.

Most people who have worked through this book should have little difficulty discerning the level of intervention needed in relation to the PLISSIT model. Knowing when it is in the best interest of the client and the helper to refer is genuine wisdom. I want to encourage counselors to realize their limitations and respect them. But I also hope that church leaders will not sell themselves short. Granted, the task of providing Christians with help and direction concerning their sexuality is difficult and requires study, awareness, and self-examination. But the benefits for the church are great.

NOTES

Chapter 1

1. Oliver Clement, "Life in the Body," *Ecumenical Review* 33 (April 1981): 128.
2. Francis A. Schaeffer, *A Christian Manifesto* (Westchester, Ill.: Crossway, 1984).
3. Lewis B. Smedes, *Sex for Christians* (Grand Rapids: Wm. B. Eerdmans, 1976), 30.
4. Ibid., 33.
5. Eric Fuchs, *Sexual Desire and Love* (New York: Seabury, 1983), 92.
6. Ibid., 108.
7. Ibid., 156.
8. Ibid., 159.
9. Ibid., 169.

Chapter 2

1. Oliver Clement, "Life in the Body," *Ecumenical Review* 33 (April 1981): 143.
2. Ibid., 144.
3. Eric Fuchs, *Sexual Desire and Love* (New York: Seabury, 1983), 173.
4. J. J. von Allmen, *Pauline Teaching on Marriage* (New York: Morehouse-Barlow, 1963), 37.
5. Fuchs, *Sexual Desire*, 81.
6. G. Lloyd Carr and D. J. Wiseman, *The Song of Solomon*. Tyndale Old Testament Commentaries Series (Downer's Grove, Ill.: InterVarsity, 1983), 21.
7. Joseph C. Dillow, *Solomon on Sex* (Nashville: Thomas Nelson, 1977).
8. Ibid., 86.

Chapter 3

1. I have seen a number of adolescent boys in my practice who fear being homosexual. Some had advances made to them or to a

friend. Some have a relative or a friend who is gay. Others, pressured by guilt and afraid of loss of control, sought to restrain their sexual urges toward women by attempting to "turn off," substituting fantasies of men for women.

Chapter 4

1. Dean Kliewer, "Sexual Growth for the Servant of God," paper presented to the Christian Association for Psychological Studies, Western Division, 1985.

2. Samuel Johnson, William Gladstone, George Gissing, and Mackenzie King were all famous men known as rescuers of fallen women. Their personal histories, however, suggest that their motivations were not always for the good of the women they tried to rescue.

3. Lyn A. DeAmicis et al., "Three-year Follow-up of Couples Evaluated for Sexual Dysfunction," *Journal of Sex and Marital Therapy*, (1984).

4. Michael A. Campion, "Christian Sexbooks: Countering Some Sincere Simplicity," *Christianity Today* 25 (12 June 1981): 28–31.

Chapter 5

1. Harold K. Schneider, "Romantic Love Among the Turu," in *Readings in Human Sexuality: Contemporary Perspectives, 1976–1977* (New York: Harper and Row, 1976), 48–51.

2. John C. Messenger, "Sex and Repression in an Irish Folk Community," in *Readings in Human Sexuality*, 78–81.

3. Judith Bardwick, "Psychology and the Sexual Body," in *Human Sexuality* (Belmont, Calif.: Wadsworth, n.d.), 210. Her full discussion of female orgasm includes pages 204–217.

4. Herant A. Katchadourian and Donald T. Lunde, *Fundamentals of Human Sexuality* (New York: Holt, Rinehart, and Winston, 1975), 301.

5. Ibid., 203–4.

6. Ibid., 203.

7. Eric Fuchs, *Sexual Desire and Love* (New York: Seabury, 1983).

Chapter 6

1. A.T. Beck, *Depression: Clinical, Experimental, and Theoretical Aspects* (New York: Harper and Row, 1967).

2. Carol Darling and Mary Hicks, "Parental Influence on Adolescent Sexuality," *Journal of Youth and Adolescence* 11 (June 1982): 231–45.

3. W. J. Gadpaille, M.D., "Innate Masculine/Feminine Traits: Their Contributions to Conflict," *Journal of the American Academy of Psychoanalysis* 11 (1983): 401–424.

4. Clifford and Joyce Penner, *The Gift of Sex* (Waco, Tex.: Word, 1981), 209.

5. Mark Sirkin et al., "Guided Imagery of Female Sexual Assertiveness: Turn On or Turn Off?" *Journal of Sex and Marital Therapy* 11 (Spring 1985).

6. Richard Jessor et al., "Time of First Intercourse: A Prospective Study," *Journal of Personality and Social Psychology* 44 (1983): 615.

7. Ibid., 608–626.

8. Ibid., 615.

9. F. Scott Christopher and Rodney M. Cate, "Factors Involved in Premarital Sexual Decision-Making," *Journal of Sex Research* 20 (1984): 363–76.

10. Jessor et al., "Time of First Intercourse," 615.

11. Ann Landers asked in her column if women would be content to be held close and treated tenderly and to forget about "the act"? She received her second-largest response ever, with 72 percent of nearly 100,000 women saying yes.

12. C. A. Papadopoulos, "Survey of Sexual Activity After Myocardial Infarction," *Cardiovascular Medicine* 3 (1978): 821–26.

13. Jack Owen Jardine, "A Cautious User's Guide to Drugs and Sex," *Playgirl* (August 1979).

Chapter 7

1. Rosalie Chapman, "Criteria for Diagnosing When to Do Sex Therapy in the Primary Relationship," *Psychotherapy: Theory, Research, and Practice* 19 (Fall 1982): 365.

2. William Masters and Virginia Johnson, *Human Sexual Inadequacy* (Boston: Little, Brown, 1970).

3. Joseph LoPiccolo and Jeffrey Steger, "Sexual Interaction Inventory (SII)," *Archives of Sexual Behavior* 3 (1974): 585–95.

4. Marilyn Fithian and William Hartman, *Treatment of Sexual Dysfunction* (Long Beach: Center for Marital and Sexual Studies, 1972).

5. Peter Kilmann and Katherine H. Mills, *All About Sex Therapy* (New York: Plenum, 1983).

6. Richard Foster, *Money, Sex, and Power* (San Francisco: Harper and Row, 1985), 103.

7. Grant Miller et al., "Personality Correlates of College Students Reporting Sexual Dysfunction," *Psychological Reports* 51 (December 1982): 180.

8. Ibid., 165–81.

9. Eugene Kennedy, *Sexual Counseling* (New York: Continuum, 1980), 173–80.

10. Scott Willis, "Adult Manifestations of Childhood Sexual Abuse," paper presented to Christian Association for Psychological Studies Convention, 1985.

11. Ibid.

12. Neil Malamuth and James Check, "Sexual Arousal to Rape Depictions: Individual Differences," *Journal of Abnormal Psychology* 92 (February 1983): 55–67.

13. Kennedy, *Sexual Counseling.*

14. Sandra Leiblum and Lawrence Pervin, "New Formats in Sex Therapy: Group and Weekend Approaches," in *Principles and Practice of Sex Therapy* (New York: Guilford, 1980), 18–21.

15. Lyn A. DeAmicis et al., "Three-year Follow-up of Couples Evaluated for Sexual Dysfunction," *Journal of Sex and Marital Therapy* 10 (1984).

16. G. R. Norton and Derek Jehu, "The Role of Anxiety in Sexual Dysfunctions: A Review," *Archives of Sexual Behavior* 13 (1984): 165–81.

17. Ibid.

18. Bernie Zilbergeld, "Myths of Counseling: Professional Therapy is Overpromoted, Overused, Overvalued," *Leadership* 5 (Winter 1984): 87–91.

19. Ibid.

20. DeAmicis et al., "Three-year Follow-up."

21. Kilmann and Mills, *All About Sex Therapy.*

22. Ibid., 192.

Chapter 8

1. Alvin C. Porteous, *The Search for Christian Credibility: Exploration in Contemporary Belief* (Nashville: Abingdon, 1971).

2. Ibid.

3. Howard L. Barnes et al., "Marital Satisfaction: Positive Regard Versus Effective Communication as Explanatory Variables," *Journal of Social Psychology* 123 (1984): 71–78.

4. Andrew M. Greeley, *Sexual Intimacy* (New York: Seabury, 1973), 86.

5. Stephen B. Levine, "An Essay on the Nature of Sexual Desire," *Journal of Sex and Marital Therapy* 10 (1984): 83–95.

6. Helen Singer Kaplan, *Disorders of Sexual Desire* (New York: Brunner/Mazel, 1979).

7. Ibid., xvii.

8. Joseph LoPiccolo, seminar materials: "Advances in Diagnosis and Treatment of Sexual Problems, 1986."

9. People may truly feel they want to have sex and can miss entirely their unconscious desire not to be sexual.

10. LoPiccolo, seminar materials.

Chapter 9

1. Lonnie Barbach, "Group Treatment of Anorgasmic Women," in *Principles and Practice of Sex Therapy*, ed. Sandra Leiblum and Lawrence Pervin (New York: Guilford, 1980), 110–111; and Seymour Fisher, *The Female Orgasm* (New York: Basic, 1973), 20.

2. Herant A. Katchadourian and Donald T. Lunde, *Fundamentals of Human Sexuality* (New York: Holt, Rinehart, and Winston, 1975), 297.

3. Mary Jane Sherfy, *The Nature and Evolution of Female Sexuality* (New York: Vintage, 1973).

4. J. Patrick Gray, "The Influence of Female Power in Marriage on Sexual Behaviors and Attitudes: A Holocultural Study," *Archives of Sexual Behavior* 13 (1984): 223–31.

5. Ibid.

6. Fisher, *The Female Orgasm*, 278.

7. Ibid.

8. Joseph LoPiccolo, seminar materials: "Advances in Diagnosis and Treatment of Sexual Problems, 1986."

9. Fisher, *The Female Orgasm*, 114; C. A. Darling and M. W. Hicks, "Parental Influences on Adolescent Sexuality," *Journal of Youth and Adolescence* 3 (1982): 231–45; and Linda Daugherty and Jerry Burger, "The Influences of Parents, Church and Peers on the Sexual Attitudes and Behaviors of College Students," *Archives of Sexual Behavior* 13 (1984): 351–59.

10. Marilyn Fithian and William Hartman, *Treatment of Sexual Dysfunction* (Long Beach: Center for Marital and Sexual Studies, 1972).

11. Alan Brauer and Donna Brauer, *ESO* (New York: Warner, 1983).

12. Heli Alzate and Ladi Londona, "Vaginal Erotic Sensitivity," *Journal of Sex and Marital Therapy* 10 (Spring 1984): 49–56; and Daniel Goldberg et al., "The Grafenberg Spot and Female Ejaculation: A

Review of Initial Hypothesis," *Journal of Sex and Marital Therapy* 9 (1983): 27–37.

13. LoPiccolo, seminar materials.

14. Ibid.

15. J. Heiman et al., *Becoming Orgasmic: A Sexual Growth Program for Women* (Englewood Cliffs, N.J.: Prentice-Hall, 1976).

16. Relaxation methods vary. Their purpose is to enable people to learn to relax and to become aware of the difference between a relaxed body and a tense one. The most commonly practiced procedure involves having people take a series of deep breaths, exhaling slowly. They are then asked to close their eyes and focus their minds on their feet. They are consciously to relax their feet, becoming aware of the sensation of heaviness. Awareness is progressively directed in this way throughout the whole body. They are then to become aware of any area of their body that is still tense, contract the muscles of that area, and relax again and/or tense and release the whole body three times. With practice the procedure can be reduced to a trigger word that produces the desired effect. A body cannot be sensitive and responsive to sexual impulses and be filled with tension at the same time.

17. Kegel exercises were suggested a number of years ago by an obstetrician-gynecologist, A. H. Kegel, to help stop the leakage of urine in certain of his patients. Strengthening the pubococcygeus muscle occurs when patients identify the muscle by stopping the flow of urine midstream (lifting the penis in the case of men) and consequently contracting the muscles ten times in a row, six times a day. Within a couple of weeks, muscle tone improves considerably and the person becomes aware of increased sensations in sexual functioning.

18. Fisher, *The Female Orgasm*.

19. Danielle Krafo and Yorum Jaffe, "Sexual Fantasizing in Males and Females," *Annual of Research and Personality* 18 (1984): 460.

20. Shere Hite, *The Hite Report: A Nationwide Study of Female Sexuality* (New York: Macmillan, 1976), 134.

21. LoPiccolo, seminar materials.

22. Dialators can be purchased from E. F. Young and Co., 1350 Old Skokie Road, Highland Park, IL 60035. Telephone: (312) 831-4080.

23. Films for use in sexual therapy can be ordered through Multi-Focus, Inc., 333 West 52nd Street, New York, NY, 10019. Telephone: (212) 586-8612.

Chapter 10

1. Janet Takefman and William Brender, "An Analysis of the Effectiveness of Two Components in the Treatment of Erectile Dysfunction," *Archives of Sexual Behavior* 13 (1984): 321–39.
2. John G. Gregory, "Treatment of Organically Impotent Men," *Medical Aspects of Human Sexuality* 20 (March 1986): 92–98.
3. Ibid., 98.

Chapter 11

1. Eugene Kennedy, *Sexual Counseling* (New York: Continuum, 1980), 4.
2. Earl D. Wilson, *Sexual Sanity* (Downers Grove, Ill.: InterVarsity, 1984).
3. Breaking behavior down into manageable "bits" gives a person hope. Knowing what the procedures for changing behavior will be, what problems might arise, and what they can expect along the path sets in motion a "vision" of a process that is feasible.
4. "Thought stopping" is a mechanical, behavioral device that, used properly, will eliminate negative thoughts and keep thoughts from wandering into unproductive areas. It involves retraining: new, appropriate thoughts are put in place of the old, inappropriate ones. The person is asked to make a list of the most positive and pleasurable scenes he or she can think of (as long as they do not involve a person or activity he or she is trying to dissociate from). The lists may be long or short. As soon as the thought to be extinguished appears, the person is to yell "stop" and pop a rubber band on the wrist or in some way react instantly to break the thought. Then the person replaces the thought with something from the prepared list.

This exercise results in a sense of control. It does take time and commitment. It is helpful for the person to keep a record of the times they must use the technique. It must be used consistently even though at first it may not always be successful. Eventually, with determination the technique effectively refocuses a person's thought life.
5. William E. Phipps, "Masturbation: Vice or Virtue?" *Journal of Religion and Health* 16 (1977): 184.
6. Ibid., 185–86.
7. Ibid., 187.
8. Morton Hunt, "Sexual Behavior in the 1970s: Masturbation," *in Readings in Human Sexuality: Contemporary Perspectives, 1976–1977* (New York: Harper and Row, 1976), 108–110.

9. Herant Katchadourian and Donald Lunde, *Fundamentals of Human Sexuality* (New York: Holt, Rinehart, and Winston, 1975), 267.

10. Danielle Knafo and Yoram Jaffe, "Sexual Fantasizing in Males and Females," *Journal of Research in Personality* 18 (1984): 451–62.

11. Ibid., 451–62.

12. C. D. Coles and M. J. Shamp, "Some Sexual, Personality, and Demographic Characteristics of Women Readers of Erotic Romances," *Archives of Sexual Behavior* 13 (1984): 187.

13. *Human Sexuality in the Christian Life* (Newton, Kans.: General Conference Mennonite Church in U.S., 1985): 138.

14. The latest studies indicate that married transvestites are not helped by being allowed to continue even mildly deviant practices. What typically happens is that once the wife is comfortable with a particular behavior, the transvestite usually escalates his conduct to greater extremes. The correct procedure is to insist on dropping the behavior and reinforcing more traditional marital behavior. A person must be prepared to detect even the very early stage of arousal by deviant factors. Thought-stopping techniques can be helpful so that the arousal by a deviant stimulus is supplanted by thoughts of the wife. More extensive therapy with a person specializing in this type of problem is available and recommended.

15. *Human Sexuality in the Christian Life*, 127.

16. George Rekers, *Shaping Your Child's Sexual Identity* (Grand Rapids: Baker, 1982).

17. Elizabeth Moberly, *Psychogenesis: The Early Development of Gender Confusion* (London: Routledge and Kegan Paul, 1983).

18. Katchadourian and Lunde, *Fundamentals of Human Sexuality*, 315.

19. Lewis Smedes, *Sex for Christians* (Grand Rapids: Wm. B. Eerdmans, 1976), 167.

Chapter 12

1. John E. Donovan, "Time of First Intercourse: A Prospective Study," *Journal of Personality and Social Psychology* 44 (1983): 619.

2. John Fischer, "A Single Person's Identity," Discovery Papers (Palo Alto: Peninsula Bible Church, cat. no. 3154 [5 August 1973]).

3. Lyn Lawrance and Laurna Rubinson, "Sexual Attitudes and Behaviors: Trends for a 10-year Period, 1972–1982," *Journal of Sex Education and Therapy* 10 (Fall-Winter 1984): 22–29.

Chapter 13

1. Stanley A. Rock, *This Time Together* (Grand Rapids: Zondervan, 1978).

2. Adapted from Mary Ann Mayo, *Parents' Guide to Sex Education* (Grand Rapids: Zondervan, 1986), 22–23.

Chapter 14

1. Jack S. Annon, "The Behavioral Treatment of Sexual Problems, Volume 1: Brief Therapy" (Honolulu: Enabling Systems, 1974).

BIBLIOGRAPHY

Adams, Jay E. *Competent to Counsel*. Grand Rapids: Zondervan Publishing House, 1970.

Alcorn, Randy C. *Christians in the Wake of the Sexual Revolution*. Portland, Oreg.: Multnomah Press, 1985.

Alzate, Heli, and Londona, Ladi. "Vaginal Erotic Sensitivity." *Journal of Sex and Marital Therapy* 10 (Spring 1984): 49–56.

Bancroft, John. "Interaction of Psychosocial and Biological Factors in Marital Sexuality—Differences Between Men and Women." *British Journal of Guidance and Counseling* 12 (January 1984): 62–71.

Barbach, Lonnie. *For Each Other: Sharing Sexual Intimacy*. New York: New American Library, 1984.

_____. *For Yourself: The Fulfillment of Female Sexuality*. New York: Anchor Press, 1976.

_____. *Women Discover Orgasm: A Therapist's Guide to a New Treatment Approach*. New York: The Free Press, 1980.

Barbach, Lonnie, and Levine, Linda. *Shared Intimacies*. New York: Bantam Books, 1980.

Beck, A. T. *Depression: Clinical, Experimental, and Theoretical Aspects*. New York: Harper and Row, Publishers, 1967.

Barnes, Howard; Schumm, Walter; Jurich, Anthony; and Bollman, Stephan. "Marital Satisfaction: Positive Regard Versus Effective Communication as Explanatory Variables." *Journal of Social Psychology* 123 (1984): 71–78.

Bell, Alan P., and Weinberg, Martin S. *Homosexualities*. New York: Simon and Schuster, 1978.

Bogle, Darlene. *Long Road to Love*. Grand Rapids: Zondervan Publishing House, 1985.

Borowitz, Eugene B. *Choosing a Sex Ethic*. New York: Schocken Books, 1974.

Brauer, Alan P., and Brauer, Donna J. *E.S.O.* New York: Warner Books, 1983.

Brusatti, Louis T. "A Philosophical Base for the Ministry of Pastoral Counseling." *Journal of Pastoral Counseling* 16 (Fall-Winter 1981): 50–52.

BIBLIOGRAPHY

Bufford, Rodger K., and Johnson, Trudi. "The Church and Community Mental Health: Unrealized Potential." *Journal of Psychology and Theology* 10 (Winter 1982): 355–62.

Bussell, Harold L. *Lord, I Can Resist Anything But Temptation.* Grand Rapids: Zondervan Publishing House, 1985.

Byrne, Brendon J. "Sinning Against One's Own Body: Paul's Understanding of the Sexual Relationship in 1 Corinthians 6:18." *Catholic Biblical Quarterly* 45 (1983): 608–616.

Calderone, Mary S., and Johnson, Eric W. *The Family Book About Sexuality.* New York: Harper and Row, Publishers, 1981.

Callahan, Sidney Cornelia. *Beyond Birth Control.* New York: Sheed and Ward, 1968.

Cameron, Paul. "Homosexual Child Molestation/Teacher-Pupil Sexual Interaction." Lincoln: Institute for the Scientific Investigation of Sexuality (ISIS), n.d.

Campton, Michael A. "Premarital Sexual Counseling: Suggestions for Ministers and Other Counselors." *Journal of Psychology and Christianity* 4 (Winter 1982): 53–60.

Carr, G. Lloyd, and Wiseman, D. J. *The Song of Solomon.* Tyndale Old Testament Commentaries Series. Downers Grove, Ill.: InterVarsity Press, 1984.

Cerling, Geraldine. "Selection of Lay Counselors for a Church Counseling Center." *Journal of Psychology and Christianity* 2 (Fall 1983): 67–72.

Chapman, Rosalie. "Criteria for Diagnosing When to Do Sex Therapy in the Primary Relationship." *Psychotherapy: Theory, Research, and Practice* 19 (Fall 1982): 359–67.

Christopher, Scott, and Cate, Rodney. "Factors Involved in Premarital Sexual Decision-Making." *Journal of Sex Research* 20 (November 1984): 363–76.

Clark, Mary Franzen. *Hiding, Hurting, Healing.* Grand Rapids: Zondervan Publishing House, 1985.

Clement, Oliver. "Life in the Body." *Ecumenical Review* 33 (April 1981): 128–46.

Coles, Claire, and Shamp, Johnna. "Some Sexual, Personality, and Demographic Characteristics of Women Readers of Erotic Romances." *Archives of Sexual Behavior* 13 (1984): 187.

Collins, Gary. *Helping People Grow.* Santa Ana, Calif.: Vision House, 1980.

Comiskey, Andy. "Homosexuality and the Church: Relational Problem, Relational Solution." Paper presented to the Christian Association for Psychological Studies, Western Division, 1985.

Cooper, Robert M. "Sex, Images, Fantasies, and God." *St. Luke Journal* 24 (March 1981): 84–94.

Corsini, Raymond, ed. *Current Psychotherapies*. Itasca, Ill.: F. E. Peacock Publishers, 1973.

Crabb, Lawrence J. *Effective Biblical Counseling*. Grand Rapids: Zondervan Publishing House, 1977.

Darling, C. A., and Hicks, M. W. "Parental Influences on Adolescent Sexuality." *Journal of Youth and Adolescence* 3 (1982): 231–45.

Daugherty, Linda, and Burger, Jerry. "The Influences of Parents, Church and Peers on the Sexual Attitudes and Behaviors of College Students." *Archives of Sexual Behavior* 13 (1984) 351–59.

DeAmicis, Lyn; Goldberg, Daniel; LoPiccolo, Joseph; Friedman, Jerry; and Davis, Larry. "A Three-year Follow-up of Couples Evaluated for Sexual Dysfunction." *Journal of Sex and Marital Therapy* 10 (December 1984).

Dillon, M. C. "Toward a Phenomenology of Love and Sexuality: An Inquiry Into the Limits of the Human Situation as They Condition Loving." *Soundings* 63 (Winter 1980): 341–60.

Dillow, Joseph C. *Solomon on Sex*. Nashville: Thomas Nelson Publishers, 1977.

Edwall, Glenace E., and Roe, Michael D. "The Development of Sexuality: A Perspective on Issues and Values." *Journal of Psychology and Christianity* 4 (Winter 1982): 23–29.

Eyrich, Howard A. *Three To Get Ready: A Christian Premarital Counselor's Manual*. Phillipsburg, N.J.: Presbyterian and Reformed Publishing Company, 1978.

Fabes, Richard, and Strause, Jeremiah. "Youth's Perceptions for Sex Education." *Journal of Sex Education and Therapy* 10 (Fall-Winter 1984): 33–37.

Fields, Nina S. "Satisfaction in Long-term Marriages." *Social Work* 28 (January-February 1983): 37–41.

Fischer, John. "A Single Person's Identity." *Discovery Papers*, no. 3154. Palo Alto, Calif. (5 August 1973).

Fisher, Seymour. *The Female Orgasm*. New York: Basic Books, 1973.

Fithian, Marilyn A., and Hartman, William E. *Treatment of Sexual Dysfunction*. Long Beach: Center for Marital and Sexual Studies, 1972.

Foster, Richard J. *Money, Sex, and Power*. San Francisco: Harper and Row, Publishers, 1985.

Freund, Kurt; Heasman, Gerald; Racansky, I. G.; and Glancy, Graham. "Pedophilia and Heterosexuality vs. Homosexuality." *Journal of Sex and Marital Therapy* 10 (1984): 193–99.

Fuchs, Eric. *Sexual Desire and Love*. New York: The Seabury Press, 1983.

Gibson, Terrill L. "The Grace of Transference: God as Redemptive Process in Pastoral Psychotherapy." *Journal of Pastoral Counseling* 16 (Fall-Winter 1981): 14–24.

Gifford, Robert. "Projected Interpersonal Distance and Orientation Choices: Personality, Sex, and Social Situation." *Social Psychology Quarterly* 45 (1982): 145–52.

Goldberg, Daniel; Whipple, Beverly; Fishkin, Ralph; Waxman, Howard; Fink, Paul; and Weisberg, Martin. "The Grafenberg Spot and Female Ejaculation: A Review of Initial Hypothesis." *Journal of Sex and Marital Therapy* 9 (1983): 27–37.

Granberg-Michaelson, Karin. *In the Land of the Living: Health Care and the Church*. Grand Rapids: Zondervan Publishing House, 1984.

Gray, Patrick. "The Influence of Female Power in Marriage on Sexual Behaviors and Attitudes: A Holocultural Study." *Archives of Sexual Behavior* 13 (1984): 223–31.

Greeley, Andrew M. *Sexual Intimacy*. New York: The Seabury Press, 1973.

Grossberg, Daniel. "Sexual Desire: Abstract and Concrete." *Hebrew Scholarship* 22 (1981): 59–60.

Grunlan, Stephen A. *Marriage and the Family*. Grand Rapids: Zondervan Publishing House, 1984.

Harrison, Beverly W. "Human Sexuality and Mutuality: A Fresh Paradigm." *Journal of Presbyterian History* 61 (Spring 1983): 142–61.

Hart, Archibald D. *Coping with Depression in the Ministry and Other Helping Professions*. Waco, Tex.: Word Books, 1984.

Hartman, Lorne M. "Resistance in Directive Sex Therapy: Recognition and Management." *Journal of Sex and Marital Therapy* 9 (1983): 285–93.

Heiman, J.; LoPiccolo, L.; and LoPiccolo, J. *Becoming Orgasmic: A Sexual Growth Program for Women*. Englewood Cliffs, N.J.: Prentice-Hall, 1976.

Hettlinger, Richard. *Human Sexuality: A Psychosocial Perspective*. Belmont, Calif.: Wadsworth Publishing Company, 1975.

Hite, Shere. *The Hite Report: A Nationwide Study of Female Sexuality*. New York: Macmillan Publishing Co., 1976.

Horner, Tom. *Sex in the Bible*. Rutland, Vt.: Charles E. Tuttle Company, 1974.

Jeffords, Charles R. "The Impact of Sex-Role and Religious Attitudes Upon Forced Marital Intercourse Norms." *Sex Roles* 11 (September 1984): 543–52.

Jessor, Richard; Costa, Frances; Jessor, Lee; and Donovan, John E. "Time of First Intercourse: A Prospective Study." *Journal of Personality and Social Psychology* 44 (1983): 608–626.

Kaplan, Helen Singer. *Disorders of Sexual Desire.* New York: Brunner/Mazel, 1979.

Kassorla, Irene. *Nice Girls Do and Now You Can Too!* Los Angeles: Stratford Press, 1980.

Katchadourian, Herant A., and Lunde, Donald T. *Fundamentals of Human Sexuality.* New York: Holt, Rinehart, and Winston, 1975.

Kennedy, Eugene. *Sexual Counseling.* New York: Continuum Publishing Co., 1980.

Kilmann, Peter R., and Mills, Katherine H. *All About Sex Therapy.* New York: Plenum Press, 1983.

Kliewer, Dean. "Sexual Growth for the Servant of God." Paper presented to the Christian Association for Psychological Studies, Western Division, 1985.

_____. "Spiritual/Emotional/Sexual Growth Among Christians: Problems We Face." Paper in the Fresno Pacific College Chapel Series—Part 1, 1984.

Knafo, Danielle, and Jaffe, Yoram. "Sexual Fantasizing in Males and Females." *Journal of Research in Personality* 18 (December 1984): 451–62.

Koblinsky, Sally A. *Sexuality Education for Parents of Young Children.* Fayetteville, N.Y.: ED-U Press, 1983.

Kronhausen, Phyllis, and Kronhausen, Eberhard. *The Sexually Responsive Woman.* Secaucus, N.J.: Castle Books, 1964.

Ladas, Alice Kahn; Whipple, Beverly; and Perry, John D. *The G Spot.* New York: Dell Publishing Co., 1982.

Lahaye, Tim. *Sex Education Is for the Family.* Grand Rapids: Zondervan Publishing House, 1985.

Leiblum, Sandra R., and Pervin, Lawrence A., eds. *Principles and Practice of Sex Therapy.* New York: Guilford Press, 1980.

Levine, Stephen B. "An Essay on the Nature of Sexual Desire." *Journal of Sex and Marital Therapy* 10 (1984): 83–95.

Levoy, Alexander. "Personality Changes in Sex Therapy." *Journal of the American Academy of Psychoanalysis* 11 (1983): 425–33.

Libman, Eva; Fichten, Catherine; and Brender, William. "Prognostic Factors and Classifications Issues in the Treatment of Secondary Orgasmic Dysfunction." *Personality and Individual Differences* 5 (1984): 1–10.

LoPiccolo, Joseph. "Guidelines for Assessment and Treatment of Sexual Deviance." Paper, 1985.

LoPiccolo, Joseph, and Steger, Jeffery. "The Sexual Interaction Inventory: A New Instrument for Assessment of Sexual Dysfunction." *Archives of Sexual Behavior* 3 (1974): 585–95.

Lovett, C. S. *The Compassionate Side of Divorce.* Old Tappan, N.J.: Fleming H. Revell Company, 1975.

Lukens, Horace C. "Training of Paraprofessional Christian Counselors: A Model Proposed." *Journal of Psychology and Christianity* 2 (Fall 1983): 61–66.

Lyn, Lawrance; Rubinson, Laurna; and O'Rourke, Thomas. "Sexual Attitudes and Behaviors: Trends for a Ten-Year Period, 1972–1982." *Journal of Sex Education and Therapy* 10 (Fall-Winter 1984): 22–29.

McAllister, Edward. "Christian Counseling and Human Needs." *Journal of Psychology and Christianity* 3 (Fall 1983): 50–60.

Mace, David N. *The Christian Response to the Sexual Revolution.* Nashville: Abingdon Press, 1979.

Malamuth, Neil, and Check, James. "Sexual Arousal to Rape Depictions: Individual Differences." *Journal of Abnormal Psychology* 92 (February 1983): 55–67.

Masters, William H., and Johnson, Virginia E. *Human Sexual Inadequacy.* Boston: Little, Brown and Company, 1970.

————. *Human Sexual Response.* Boston: Little, Brown and Company, 1966.

————. *The Pleasure Bond.* Boston: Little, Brown and Company, 1974.

Mayo, Mary Ann. *Parents' Guide to Sex Education.* Grand Rapids: Zondervan Publishing House, 1986.

————. *The Sexual Woman: Understanding the Unique Identity of a Woman.* Eugene, Oreg.: Harvest House, 1987.

Menninger, Karl. *Whatever Became of Sin?* New York: Hawthorn Books, 1973.

Mennonite Church and General Conference Mennonite Church. *Human Sexuality in the Christian Life.* Newton, Kans.: General Conference Mennonite Church, 1985.

Messenger, John C. "Sex and Repression in an Irish Folk Community." In *Readings in Human Sexuality: Contemporary Perspectives, 1976–1977.* New York: Harper and Row, Publishers, 1976.

Miles, Herbert J. *Sexual Understanding Before Marriage.* Grand Rapids: Zondervan Publishing House, 1971.

Miller, Grant; McLoughlin, Caven; and Murphy, Norman. "Personality Correlates of College Students Reporting Sexual Dysfunction." *Psychological Reports* 51 (1982): 1075–82.

Narramore, Bruce, and Counts, Bill. *Freedom From Guilt.* Irvine, Calif.: Harvest House Publishers, 1974.

Norton, G. R., and Jehu, Derek. "The Role of Anxiety in Sexual Dysfunctions: A Review." *Archives of Sexual Behavior* 13 (1984): 165–81.

Penner, Clifford, and Penner, Joyce. *A Gift for All Ages: A Family Handbook on Sexuality.* Waco, Tex.: Word Books, 1986.

—————. *The Gift of Sex.* Waco, Tex.: Word Books, 1981.

Phipps, William E. "Masturbation: Vice or Virtue?" *Journal of Religion and Health* 16 (1977): 183–95.

Renshaw, Dommena. "Sexuality and Depression in Infancy, Childhood, and Adolescence." *Medical Aspects of Human Sexuality* (June 1975): 24.

Richards, Lawrence O. *The Believer's Guidebook.* Grand Rapids: Zondervan Publishing House, 1983.

Richardson, Peter. "Judgment in Sexual Matters in 1 Corinthians 6:1–11." *Novum Testamentum* 25 (January 1983): 37–58.

Rinzema, J. *The Sexual Revolution.* Grand Rapids: Wm. B. Eerdmans Publishing Co., 1974.

Rock, Stanley A. *This Time Together.* Grand Rapids: Zondervan Publishing House, 1978.

Rolfe, David. "Developing Skills and Credibility in Marriage Preparation Ministry." *Pastoral Psychology* 33 (Spring 1985): 161–71.

Rubin, Lillian B. *Intimate Strangers.* New York: Harper and Row, Publishers, 1983.

Sattler, Henry V. *Sex is Alive and Well and Flourishing Among Christians.* Huntington, Ind.: Our Sunday Visitor, 1980.

Scanzoni, Letha, and Mollenkott, Virginia Ramey. *Is the Homosexual My Neighbor?* San Francisco: Harper and Row, Publishers, 1980.

Schaeffer, Francis. *A Christian Manifesto.* Westchester, Ill.: Crossway Books, 1984.

Schneider, Harold K. "Romantic Love Among the Turu." In *Readings in Human Sexuality: Contemporary Perspectives, 1976–1977.* New York: Harper and Row, Publishers, 1976.

Schover, Leslie. *Prime Time.* New York: Holt, Rinehart and Winston, 1984.

Shandler, Michael, and Shandler, Nina. *Ways of Being Together.* New York: Schocken Books, 1980.

Sillars, Alan L.; Pike, Gary R.; Jones, Tricia S.; and Murphy, Mary A. "Communication and Understanding in Marriage." *Human Communication Research* 10 (1984): 317–50.

Simpson, William. "Treating Performance Anxiety in Men: How the Female Partner Can Help." *Journal of Clinical Practice in Sexuality* 1 (1985): 21–31.

Sirkin, Mark, and Mosher, Donald. "Guided Imagery of Female Sexual Assertiveness: Turn On or Turn Off?" *Journal of Sex and Marital Therapy* 11 (Spring 1985).

Slowinski, Julian. "Reflections of Sex Therapy: An Interview With Harold I. Lief and Arnold A. Lazarus." *Journal of Sex Education and Therapy* 10 (Fall-Winter 1984): 13–21.

Small, Dwight Hervey. *Christian, Celebrate Your Sexuality.* Old Tappan, N.J.: Fleming H. Revell Company, 1974.

Smedes, Lewis B. *Sex for Christians.* Grand Rapids: Wm. B. Eerdmans Publishing Co., 1976.

Smith, Harold Ivan. "On Sexuality" (audio tape). Franklin, Tenn.: Franklin House Publishing, 1982.

Spanier, G. B., and Marigolis, R. L. "Marital Separation and Extra Marital Behavior." *Journal of Sex Research* 19 (1983): 23–48.

Stone, Alan. "Sexual Misconduct by Psychiatrists." *American Journal of Psychiatry* 140 (1983): 195–97.

Strong, Bryan; Wilson, Sam; Clarke, Leah Miller; and Johns, Thomas. *Human Sexuality: Essentials.* St. Paul: West Publishing Company, 1978.

Takefman, Janet, and Brender, William. "An Analysis of the Effectiveness of Two Components in the Treatment of Erectile Dysfunction." *Archives of Sexual Behavior* 13 (1984): 321–39.

Ukleja, Michael. "Homosexuality in the New Testament." *Bibliotheca Sacra* (October-December 1983): 350–58.

_____. "Homosexuality and the Old Testament." *Bibliotheca Sacra* (July-September 1983): 259–66.

Von Allmen, J. J. *Pauline Teaching on Marriage.* New York: Morehouse-Barlow Co., 1963.

Wabrek, Alan J. "Taking the Initial Sexual History." *Journal of Clinical Practice in Sexuality* 1 (1985): 15–20.

Watson, J. "Sexual Counseling." *British Journal of Guidance and Counseling* 12 (1984): 52–61.

Wheat, Ed, and Wheat, Gaye. *Intended for Pleasure.* Old Tappan, N.J.: Fleming H. Revell Company, 1981.

White, John. *Eros Defiled.* Downers Grove, Ill.: InterVarsity Press, 1977.

Whitlock, Glenn E. *Preventive Psychology and the Church.* Philadelphia: The Westminster Press, n.d.

Williams, H. Page. *Do Yourself A Favor: Love Your Wife.* Plainfield, N.J.: Logos International, 1973.

Willis, Scott Cobot. "Adult Manifestations of Childhood Sexual Abuse." Paper presented to the Christian Association for Psychological Studies, Western Division, 1985.

Wilson, Earl D. *Sexual Sanity*. Downers Grove, Ill.: InterVarsity Press, 1984.

Young, Janice. "Implications of Male and Female Co-Therapists for a Pastoral Theology of Family Therapy." *Journal of Psychology and Christianity* 2 (Summer 1983): 52–55.

Zilbergeld, Bernie. *Male Sexuality*. New York: Bantam Books, 1980.

_____. "Myths of Counseling: Professional Therapy Is Overpromoted, Overused, Overvalued." *Leadership* 5 (Winter 1984): 87–91.

SUGGESTED READINGS

RECOMMENDED FOR CHRISTIAN COUPLES

Dillow, Joseph C. *Solomon on Sex* (Nashville: Thomas Nelson, 1977).

A helpful study of the Song of Solomon that examines the puzzling Hebrew metaphors and helps the reader appreciate the original intent of this love poem and its message of joyous sexual expression for married life today. Especially good for couples who suffer from problems of inhibition or those who misunderstand God's plan for their married life.

Mayo, Mary Ann. *Parents' Guide to Sex Education* (Grand Rapids: Zondervan, 1986).

An easy-reading book that urges Christian parents to take responsibility for educating their children about sexual matters and stresses the impact of parental attitudes and behavior toward sex on their children.

Penner, Clifford, and Penner, Joyce. *The Gift of Sex* (Waco, Tex.: Word, 1981).

A sex manual written with Christians in mind. Enjoyable reading, accurate and helpful. Useful to most couples for general information and sexual enrichment.

Wheat, Ed, and Wheat, Gaye. *Intended for Pleasure* (Old Tappan, N.J.: Fleming H. Revell, 1981).

A thorough sex manual for Christians. The style is not so light as The Gift of Sex, *but the information is accurate and clearly presented.*

RECOMMENDED FOR PROBLEMS AND SPECIAL CONCERNS

Barbach, Lonnie. *For Yourself: The Fulfillment of Female Sexuality* (New York: Anchor, 1976).

A book primarily for women. Geared toward group work although it can be used individually. Focuses on women who have difficulty being orgasmic.

Heiman, J.; LoPiccolo, L.; and LoPiccolo, J. *Becoming Orgasmic: A Sexual Growth Program for Women* (Englewood Cliffs, N.J.: Prentice-Hall, 1976).

A book for women having problems with being orgasmic. Easy to follow and recommended in conjunction with therapy or for self-help.

Mooney, T. O.; Cole, T. M.; and Chilgren, R. A. *Sexual Options for Paraplegics and Quadriplegics* (Boston: Little, Brown, 1975).

Sexual concerns for people with cord injuries or neurologic diseases.

Schover, Leslie R. *Prime Time* (New York: Holt, Rinehart and Winston, 1984).

An excellent book for those over fifty for general information on sex and practical aspects of aging and sexuality. Particular attention given to the effects disease and medication have on sexual functioning.

Shipes, E.; and Lehi, S. *Sexual Counseling for Ostamates* (Springfield, Ill.: Charles C. Thomas, 1980).

Suggestions and discussion for people with ostomy procedures.

Vaeth, J. M.; Blomberg, R. C.; and Adler, L. *Body Image, Self-Esteem, and Sexuality in Cancer Patients* (New York: S. Harger, 1980).

Discussion of the problems of sexuality of those suffering from various forms of cancer.

Zilbergeld, Bernie. *Male Sexuality* (New York: Bantam Books, 1978).

An excellent book on sexuality for men. General information in the first half. Discussion of problems in the second half. Useful as a self-help book or in conjunction with therapy, and useful for both husband and wife.

APPROACHES TO SEX THERAPY

Kaplan, Helen Singer. *Disorders of Sexual Desire* (New York: Brunner/Mazel, 1979).

Discussion of the most frequently presented sexual problem in the eighties: desire problems.

Katchadourian, Herant A., and Lunde, Donald T. *Fundamentals of Human Sexuality* (New York: Holt, Rinehart, and Winston, 1975).

A college-level, complete overview of human sexuality.

Leiblum, Sandra R., and Pervin, Lawrence A., eds. *Principles and Practice of Sex Therapy* (New York: Guilford, 1980).

A look at sex therapy as it is practiced by a variety of professionals.

LoPiccolo, J., and LoPiccolo, L. *Handbook of Sex Therapy* (New York: Plenum, 1978).

A sound overview of treatment procedures for sex therapy.

Masters, William H., and Johnson, Virginia E. *Human Sexual Inadequacy* (Boston: Little, Brown, 1970).

Good basic information. A helpful section on sexual history-taking for those unfamiliar with the format.

CHRISTIAN PERSPECTIVES

Fuchs, Eric. *Sexual Desire and Love* (New York: Seabury, 1983).

A superb Christian book that traces the origins and history of the Christian ethic of sexuality and marriage. Highly recommended.

Small, Dwight H. *Christian, Celebrate Your Sexuality* (Old Tappan, N.J.: Fleming H. Revell, 1974).

A positive look at sexuality from a Christian perspective. Highly recommended.